In Search of the Buccaneers

ANTHONY GAMBRILL

MACMILLAN
CARIBBEAN

Macmillan Education
Between Towns Road, Oxford, OX4 3PP
A division of Macmillan Publishers Limited
Companies and representatives throughout the world

www.macmillan-caribbean.com

ISBN: 978-0-333-97652-4

Designed by Gary Fielder
Typeset by Carol Hulme
Illustrated by Göte Göransson and Tech Type
Cover design by Gary Fielder

Author's own collection pp. 44, 102, 111, 169,
198, 208, 237; Alamy / Gary Cook p. 225;
Antiquarian Images p. 189; Archivo General de
Indias, Seville p. 194; Art Directors & TRIP pp.
66, 83; Bibliotheque Nationale, Paris p. 26, 31,
234, 240, 242, 244; Bridgeman Art Library p.
46(l) [Admiral Sir William Penn (1621-70) (oil
oncanvas) by Lely, Sir Peter (1618-80) (attr.to) ©
Atwater Kent Museum of Philadelphia/ Courtesy
of Historical Society of Pennsylvania Collection,/
Atwater Kent Museum of Philadelphia], 47
[Portrait of King Charles II (1630-85), c.1675
(oil on canvas) by Lely, Sir Peter (1618-80)
(studio of) Private Collection/ © Philip Mould,
Historical Portraits Ltd, London], 207 [Nell
Gwynne (1650-87), mistress of Charles II by
Lely, Sir Peter (1618-80) (studio of) Private
Collection/ © Philip Mould, Historical Portraits
Ltd, London], 228 [King Philip II (1527-98)
1550 (oil on canvas) by Titian (Tiziano Vecellio)
(c.1488-1576) Prado, Madrid, Spain/ Giraudon];
British Library p. 8(b) [De Americaensche Zee-
Roovers...by Alexander Olivier Exquemelin,
1678, Shelfmark 1061.g.20.(2).], 62 [Shelfmark
719.m.17.(15)], 103 [Shelfmark 10480.d.26],
138 [Shelfmark 291.i.29], 145 [Shelfmark
1061.g.20], 149 [Shelfmark 10025cc.18(1)
8(2)], 173 [Shelfmark G.7179], 176 [Shelfmark
1061.g.20 fol 98], 216 [Shelfmark 457.f.14],
230 [Shelfmark 457.f14]; James Brunker /
Photographersdirect.com p.132 (t); Christie's
Images Ltd p. 142; Corbis p. 126; Oliver Cox
pp. 49, 50; Ian Cumming p. 43; Antonio D'Ella
and Carlos Cano p. 180; Victor Englebert /
Photographersdirect.com p. 224; Mary Evans
Picture Library p.6, 8(t), 53, 85, 87, 219;
Taken from author's own collection copy of
Alexander Exquemelin "Bucaniers of America
or, a true Account of the Moft remarkable
Affaults Committed of late years of The West
Indies By the Bucaniers of Jamaica and Tortuga
Both English and French" London, Printed for
William Crooke at the Green Dragon without
Temple-bar,1684 p. 40, 41, 57, 158; Getty
Images pp. 9, 162, 174; Göte Göransson p. 12,
13, 15, 19, 22, 24; Istock.com p. iii; Lonely
Planet Images pp. 100, 132(b), 205; Taken from
author's own copy of "Memoires de Ravenau de
Lussan sur son voyage a la mer du sud avec les
filibustiers d'Amerique" 1689 p. 112; Magdalen
College, Cambridge p. 192; Jamie Marshall /
Tribaleye Images / Photographersdirect.com p.
67; John Mitchell / Photographersdirect.com
pp. 99(b), 206(b); Musée de la Marine, Paris p.
232; National Archives p. 166 (CO138-1 f.49);
Courtesy of National Library of Jamaica pp. 46(r),
48(t) (MS105 Vol 2), 75, 146 (MS105 Vol3);
© National Maritime Museum, London p. 51
(B1686/219), 72 (BHC2874), 73 (VV449), 81
(BHC2947), 93 (BHC2996), 114 (BHC2901),
119 (BHC3080), 135 (BHC2663), 183
(PAD6886), 191 (BHC2755), 227 (A6821);
National Museum of Wales p. 157; New Port
Museum & Library p. 156; Picture Collection,
New York Public Library p. 141 (Howard
Pyle "Morgan at Porto Bello", 1888); "Triste
Embarquement". © Photothèque des Musées de
la Ville de Paris p 37; "Burial of Admiral Drake at
Nombre de Dios, January 29th 1596" by Thomas
Davidson active (1863–1903) Collection:
Plymouth City Museum & Art Gallery © p. 136;
Kirsten Risnes p. 128; Royal Armouries p. 185;
South American Pictures pp. 131, 154, 155, 168,
181, 206(t); Topfoto pp. 88, 99(t); James Ford
Bell Library, University of Minnesota p. 184;
Claire Waring / Photographersdirect.com p. 221.

Cover image "Fiesta au Rat qui pette" by Gustave
Alaux, Musée de la Marine, Paris / DACS

Picture research by Kevin Brown

Printed and bound in Thailand

2011 2010 2009 2008 2007
10 9 8 7 6 5 4 3 2 1

Contents

~

~

To
Linda,
Ashley and Laura

~

'God, who watches us with eyes of pity, give me victory over these heretical dogs.'

Don Juan Perez de Guzman, President of Panama, as Henry Morgan and his buccaneers approached.

Introduction to

IN SEARCH OF THE BUCCANEERS

~

This book attempts to cover the lifespan and brief history of the buccaneers in the Caribbean by tracing a series of milestone events that took place between 1630 and 1700. Each event is ultimately the reason for a chapter; each chapter follows the personalities who made the event important; and each place in each chapter has its own story to tell about the conflict between the Spanish, Dutch, French and English during the early colonisation of the region.

It begins with the emergence of the boucaniers in Hispaniola and their transition from hunters to seafaring buccaneers as their ranks grew through immigration, exile, desertion and shipwreck.

I have chosen to call Oliver Cromwell's disbanded army in Jamaica 'the other buccaneers' because once the English authorities realised they needed mercenaries to ensure the security of their West Indian colonies, these men responded enthusiastically to the rallying cry of buccaneer 'admirals' like Edward Mansfield and Henry Morgan. They were to become mercenaries who understood that 'no purchase, no pay' was the convention under which they sailed.

The book will also show how the boucaniers of Hispaniola evolved into the buccaneers of the wider Caribbean. This may be confusing as buccaneers have variously been described in history books as freebooters and privateers by the English, zee-rovers by the Dutch, flibustiers by the French and corsarios or piratas by the Spanish.

The buccaneers have been acclaimed for their daring, condemned for their greed, praised for their accomplishments and vilified for their depravity. They have been recognised as early proponents of democracy in the collective management of their affairs and even recognised for recording the geography of the region. Significantly they have provided a unique body of fact and fiction for every form of literary and artistic endeavour for more than 300 years.

This book, however, whilst telling the buccaneers' story seeks to put the people and events of the Caribbean in the seventeenth century in perspective. What role did the buccaneers play in ensuring the security of the fledgling colonies? To what extent did their plunder contribute to the economies of the colonies? Were they just brutal predators or, as Henry Morgan demonstrated at Panama, capable of being moulded into a remarkably successful fighting force?

They were individualistic by nature so why did they adopt and largely adhere to a remarkably disciplined code of conduct? By compiling enough anecdotal information, is it possible to give relevance to 70 years of buccaneering as a legitimate contribution to the birth of the Caribbean frontier; or were the boucaniers-turned-buccaneers just a passing wave of opportunists who benefited from unique circumstances perfect for piratical endeavours? *In Search of the Buccaneers* should be able to make a case that without the buccaneers it is conceivable that the Caribbean today might still be a Spanish sea as it was for over a hundred years after the arrival of Christopher Columbus. This is not a book written for academic historians but for individuals like myself who enjoy history for the sake of learning about our fascinating and often colourful past. Hence there are no footnotes, although a glossary and a bibliography have been included.

One technical note: sometimes there is a disparity in dates as the French and Spanish at the time used the newly-adopted Gregorian calendar which was ten days ahead of the calendar used by the English.

Finally, I should take this opportunity to recognise a number of people whose encouragement and assistance made writing and researching this book possible. In the academic world: Drs David Buisseret, Patrick Bryan and Barry Higman; in the countries I visited: Richard Leonardi (Nicaragua), Zoraida Perez (Cuba), Judith Hernandez Aranda (Mexico), Claudia Vidal, Maria-Teresa Ripoll de Lemaitre, Ambassador Alfonso Munera (Colombia), Juan-Luis Correa, Liriola Pitti (Panama); friends who lent their support: Martha Corbett-Baugh, Göte Göransson, Karsten Windeler, Oliver Clarke, Freddy Zenny, Paul Henry, Donna Webster, Sheryl Chung, Leo Leonard and my tennis partner/research assistant Norman Marshall; unerring translators: Helen Morris and Sharon Thomas; my cheerful and unswerving typist: Dawn Whittle; Alison Hart and Kevin Brown, and Nick Gillard, without whose invaluable advice and encouragement this book would have been abandoned more than once. To all of them and especially my wife, Linda, who was determined that I should prevail, and my daughters, Ashley and Laura, who unflinchingly ate stuffed baby shark and cammarones del rio respectively on our excursions, many, many thanks.

Anthony Gambrill

Chapter 1

THE BUCCANEERS' CARIBBEAN

~

The buccaneer was the unholy offspring of the Caribbean frontier who flourished during an era of history lasting barely 70 years. Between 1630 and 1700 he could be found lurking in sheltered bays in places as diverse as La Tortue off present-day mainland Haiti, the Cuban cays, Port Royal in Jamaica, the Honduran Bay Islands, Colombia's Providencia and the ubiquitous Isle à Vache on Haiti's southern coast where the legendary Henry Morgan and others regularly rendezvoused. From these refuges they were within easy reach of Spain's trade routes and could easily prey on passing vessels or ravage its colonial ports. Yet the Caribbean Sea proved no easy board on which to play the piracy game.

Piracy has been practised ever since men went to sea with the criminal intent of relieving others of their possessions. Not only did piracy in the Caribbean pre-date the emergence of the buccaneers but pirates often became buccaneers in the time of buccaneering and many resorted to piracy after its conclusion. Quite simply, if a ship's captain had been granted a legal commission, or letter of marque, by the French, Dutch, English, Portuguese or even Spanish authorities to seek reprisals against ships and terrestrial property of an enemy of the state that issued the commission, he was technically no longer a pirate but more usually defined as a privateer.

The buccaneer had his origins in Hispaniola where he was first a boucanier. Here on the Caribbean frontier a remarkable breed of men was to emerge, strictly speaking privateers by definition, but whose personalities and behaviour were shaped by the place, time and events in their lives in the Caribbean. The Spanish, for their part, saw every ship not of Spanish origin as a pirate ship and even the Spanish crown was finally to resort to issuing commissions against their enemies in the Caribbean.

1

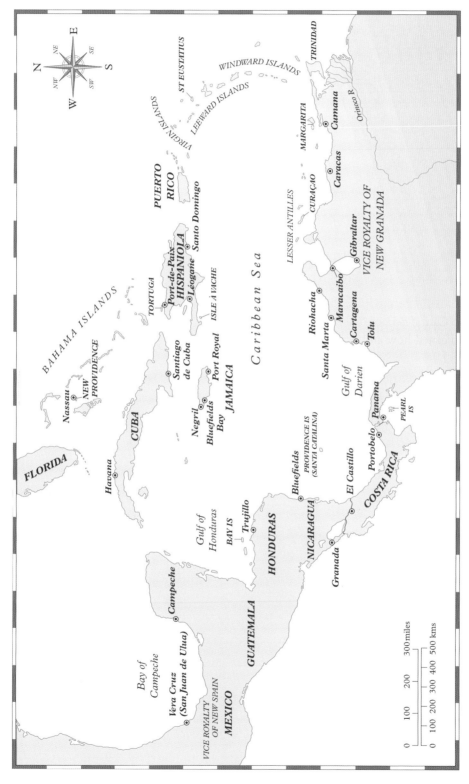

The principal strongholds and targets of the buccaneers in the Caribbean.

There was ample opportunity in the seventeenth century to find an enemy against whom you could seek reprisals. England, France and Holland were frequently in conflict with Spain; the Dutch and the English fought three separate short wars late in the century; Louis XIV's France challenged England and Spain; and Portugal became a bitter opponent of Spain. Not always but quite often their European conflicts reverberated in the Caribbean.

The Caribbean Sea extends from the Florida peninsula, bordered on the Atlantic east by the Greater and Lesser Antilles, south to the Orinoco River in Venezuela and is enclosed on its southern and western side by the coasts of seven South and Central American countries. The tip of the Yucatan peninsula marks the northernmost extremity of the Caribbean Sea. The body of water to the north of the Caribbean that extends to the continental United States round to the Florida peninsula encloses the Gulf of Mexico.

Approximately 2,000 miles from end to end, the Caribbean Sea has provided mariners since Christopher Columbus with a serious nautical challenge. Prevailing winds and powerful sea currents make east–west voyages relatively rapid but return voyages are time-consuming and tedious. Frequent hurricanes that occur between July and October create unwelcome and unpredictable hazards. These conditions in the Caribbean not only caused communications 400 years ago to be difficult but also dictated how and when merchant vessels and treasure ships were best advised to travel to their destinations.

Christopher Columbus, when he arrived in the Bahamas on October 11, 1492, was convinced he was close to achieving his goal of reaching the Orient. Carrying on along the Atlantic coast of Cuba he landed on the shores of an island he called L'Isla Espagnola because it reminded him of Spain. Known now as Hispaniola, it eventually divided into Haiti and the Dominican Republic. Columbus was not to know at the time that it was to become the birthplace of the buccaneers.

For 30 years Spain exclusively dominated the Caribbean, occupying the islands alongside with the Amerindian natives. Santo Domingo on Hispaniola was established as Spain's administrative capital and raising livestock, farming and mining were typical activities on the island as they were in Jamaica and Cuba. However, French pirates began making an appearance in the Caribbean by the 1520s and in November, 1527, a landmark event took place that was to foretell the future for the Spanish.

A substantial three-masted ship flying an English flag and commissioned by King Henry VIII arrived at Santo Domingo harbour requesting safe entrance. This was granted but as the vessel dropped anchor a shot was fired from the fort overlooking the harbour, narrowly missing it. Despite the fact that the Spanish pilots explained that there had been a misunderstanding, the English captain upped anchor and departed before he could trade the goods he was carrying or possibly before he could collect detailed information about the city and its defences. For their part the Spanish authorities should have detained the ship as it was not legally permitted to be there in the first place and had left without being identified. The English landed several days later up the coast and took on provisions, threatening to return with half a dozen ships to attack Santo Domingo, thus fuelling speculation that this incident had been a well-planned reconnaissance mission.

French pirates became increasingly intrusive in the Caribbean, extending their activities from the eastern Atlantic and engaging not only in ship-to-ship attacks but also forcing their way into ports to loot and pillage. By 1537 Cartagena, Nombre de Dios and Havana had been assaulted, Santo Domingo blockaded and Léogane plundered and set on fire. Conflict in the Caribbean between France and Spain finally reached a stage in 1552, when a peace was again aborted, that it could be said for the first time a European war had crossed the Atlantic. Now, privateers with commissions to seek reprisals and royal fleets with political ambitions were sailing under French, Dutch and English flags commanded by legendary figures such as John Hawkins, Sir Francis Drake, Francois le Clerc and Piet Heyn.

Their exploits convinced the Spanish crown that their Caribbean possessions and, increasingly, their shipping needed more adequate protection than had previously been provided. The defences of Santo Domingo, San Juan, Cartagena, Havana and San Juan de Ulua, the island-fort of Vera Cruz, were all at some time during the second half of the sixteenth century strengthened. Efforts to improve naval patrols were periodically introduced but seldom sustained.

In addition, the relentless plundering of Spanish vessels forced the mother country to formalise a convoy system to better ensure the safe delivery of their cargoes. The need was even more emphatic after Spain's advance into Latin America with its wealth of gold, silver and precious stones.

In the heyday of the treasure fleets more than 60 ships often sailed in a single convoy accompanied by the royal navy. The Flota convoy was destined for New Spain, as their growing Mexican empire was known, usually entering the Caribbean Sea by Dominica, taking as long as two months to reach the Mexican port of Vera Cruz. The Galeones convoy left in the late summer, taking a more southerly route for the New Granada region which encompassed the area from Cartagena to the Isthmus of Panama. The Galeones made for Cartagena and then Nombre de Dios to await the Peruvian silver that was shipped along the Pacific coast to Panama and transported overland to the Caribbean. Smaller vessels sailed with the main fleets and carried goods to Hispaniola, Cuba, Jamaica and smaller ports on the mainland.

After a long and difficult return eastward crossing both fleets stopped in Havana on the homeward leg of the round-trip voyage in order to prepare their vessels and take on water and provisions. From Havana, as soon as possible in the next year, they entered the Straits of Florida seeking the Gulf Stream currents which greatly assisted their passages. History records the many disasters that befell the Spaniards as they passed through this region of dangerous shoals and treacherous reefs, unpredictable currents and stormy weather.

On the outward-bound voyage these convoys would carry everyday supplies for the colonies but on the return their cargoes were far more valuable. For example, the Flota which left Havana on July 3, 1581, carried four million pesos worth of bullion, pearls from the island of Margarita, emeralds from Colombia, sugar and ginger from

Santo Domingo and silk from the Spanish colony of the Philippines, which had been shipped across the Pacific, as well as luxury commodities such as cochineal and indigo dye and rare spices. So long as these rich cargoes reached Spain she was wealthy enough to dominate the politics of Europe.

As Spain concentrated her attention on her mineral-rich mainland possessions, the importance of her original Caribbean colonies began to diminish. Although still strategically important, Cuba, Jamaica and Hispaniola were now primarily suppliers of farm products and used as staging grounds for the invasion of the mainland. When Spain's merchant ships began calling less regularly, other Europeans were quick to see opportunity where neglect was creating unfulfilled needs.

In 1494 Spain and Portugal had signed a treaty which recognised Spain's territorial and trading rights in the Caribbean. At the same time this treaty denied any other European nation the right to trade in the region.

However, even before the Dutch, who were to become the most successful Caribbean traders in the early seventeenth century, the French had regularly called on Spanish ports in Spain's island colonies. The entrepreneurs of Rouen in France dealt in hides with which to supply the European leather industry whilst smuggling goods, including their renowned linens, out to the West Indies to sell to Spanish settlers. Before long the Dutch, Portuguese and English were also defying Spain's prohibition on non-Spanish commerce in the Caribbean, trading in slaves and merchandise for hides, sugar and tobacco with these same settlers who wanted cheap goods and had found their own country's supplies unreliable. These smugglers usually sailed on ships that were armed and threats of force were commonplace should local Spanish authorities be hesitant to condone trading.

But it was the Dutch who were to predominate in the Caribbean as they were in much of the world as the seventeenth century began. The Dutch herring industry required salt and this was found close to the mouth of the Orinoco at Araya. This inevitably brought the Dutch into conflict with Spain. Defending the right to trade became an aspect of European policy in the Caribbean that was a pursuit appropriate for buccaneers.

The political complexion of the Caribbean region was inexorably changing. Spain's principal focus was the American mainland with wealth which continued to support the country's gradually declining power. The Leeward and Windward islands of the Lesser Antilles chain were virtually impossible to defend and soon other European nations capitalised on this weakness to establish colonies. England colonised St Kitts in 1624, forming an alliance on the island with the French in the following year to drive out the warlike Caribs. Barbados in 1627, initially an Anglo-Dutch commercial venture, was seen to offer better prospects for growing sugar than tobacco. Antigua and Montserrat were settled by the English in 1632; Curaçao by the Dutch in 1634 and in the same year Guadeloupe and Martinique by the French; the Dutch occupied St Eustatius in 1630. Although the Spanish carried out a number of successful attacks on these new island-colonies, the Spanish territorial monopoly in the Caribbean was coming to an end.

However, it was Oliver Cromwell, the Puritan ruler of England after having beheaded King Charles I, who was the first to permanently annex a Spanish colony and begin a turbulent new era in Caribbean history. England's traditional hostility to Spain made easy a decision to attack her Caribbean possessions in order to share in the wealth of the Americas. Not unexpectedly, the Spanish rejected Cromwell's request that all Englishmen be granted liberty of conscience and freedom to trade in the West Indies as conditional on England's continuing friendship and neutrality. So began Cromwell's 'Western Design'.

Two men who will appear more than a few times in this book had a considerable influence on his decision to launch a military and naval expedition to the Caribbean. The first was Thomas Gage, an Englishman who as a Dominican priest had travelled extensively in the West Indies and Central America, publishing a book in 1648. In an audience with Cromwell he elaborated on Spain's vulnerability in the region. Although his argument was persuasive, he underestimated Spain's defensive capabilities and made no mention of the tropical diseases that would eventually decimate the troops. The second adviser was Thomas Modyford, a planter in Barbados for several years, who was later appointed governor of Jamaica in which post he successfully employed the buccaneers to secure England's tenancy of the island.

Jamaica proved to be in a strategic location as it was ideally situated for monitoring Spain's trade routes and not that far from her colonies on the mainland. Given that Oliver Cromwell's specific instructions were to destroy all Spanish fortifications on land and seize all ships at sea, it was less than two months after the successful invasion of the island in 1655 that Admiral William Penn's vice-admiral, William Goodson, set out to sack Santa Marta. The English were on the offensive and before long the word spread that men of fortune were needed.

Earlier, the northern coast of Hispaniola had become virtually uninhabited and too far from Santo Domingo to warrant effective administration by the Spanish. Many colonists abandoned the island in search of their fortunes on the mainland leaving behind cattle, pigs, horses and even dogs to roam the empty valleys and forests.

As time went by groups of mainly French hunters, who came to be known as boucaniers, began making a livelihood out of killing these animals for their meat, fat and hides which they traded with passing vessels. Their origin remains obscure although originally they were probably sailors who had been shipwrecked, or had deserted or had even been marooned. Some time before 1630 many of them crossed the two-mile wide channel to the small island of Tortuga – La Tortue – in the Atlantic where they believed they would be better able to resist Spanish attempts to expel them.

Oliver Cromwell, the Protestant Lord Protector of England, had no compunction in launching an attack on Catholic Spain's Caribbean colonies.

It was from the island of Tortuga and the town of Port Royal that the English were to build in Jamaica that the buccaneers' enterprises usually began. The buccaneers ultimately included a hodgepodge of adventurers, misfits and social outcasts but their origin lay in Hispaniola as boucaniers, so-called from their custom of curing meat on a boucan, a barbeque-like structure made of sticks supporting strips of meat slow-cooking over a smoky fire. The brotherhood of buccaneers subsequently included the remnants of Venables's army disbanded in Jamaica, French and English renegade indentured servants, fugitives from the law, Huguenot Protestants escaping persecution in Europe, merchant seamen and navy sailors, even escaped slaves.

We shall see later, as they took to the sea in search of Spanish plunder, how they employed to advantage their marksmanship and fearlessness. They voluntarily came together to create 'the Brotherhood of the Coast', a democratic, free enterprise society that was far ahead of its time. The establishment of the English in Jamaica and the formal colonisation of northern Hispaniola by the French led to the employment of the buccaneers as military mercenaries and naval auxiliaries. The English and French authorities for their part offered a safe harbour, a reliable outlet for their spoils and somewhere to spend their 'pay' in debauchery.

History would have known only the scantiest of facts about the exploits of the buccaneers were it not for a unique book written by a man who sailed with them. His name was Alexander O Exquemelin and his book, first published in Dutch in 1678 with an English translation in 1684, is entitled *Bucaniers of America*. In 1666 he was shipped to Tortuga as an engagé, or indentured servant, but three years later joined the buccaneers as a barber-surgeon, or ship's doctor, serving until 1674. His national identity is uncertain but he was probably French and, as a Huguenot Protestant, chose to settle in Holland. His book, which has been translated into several languages and reprinted down the centuries, was an immediate best-seller thanks to his colourful account of life amongst the buccaneers.

The reputation for the romantic mythology surrounding buccaneers and buccaneering must primarily rest with Exquemelin. His recollections, in some instances, proved exaggerated or blatantly false and his opinions are sometimes influenced by personal prejudice. In fact, the English publishers were successfully sued for libel by Henry Morgan for including Exquemelin's claim – calling him a pirate – that Morgan had arrived in the Caribbean as an indentured servant when in all likelihood he accompanied the English invaders as a soldier. It is believed that Exquemelin felt that after Morgan's unprecedented attack on Panama many, including himself, had not received a fair share of the booty. At least a third of Exquemelin's book follows Henry Morgan's campaigns against the Spanish. Similarly, because this book focuses on those places that suffered from the depredations of the buccaneers, Morgan's name inevitably appears with some frequency.

Alexander Exquemelin published Bucaniers of America *in 1678 in Dutch. Editions in other European translations were to follow, making it one of the most popular books of its era.*

The men the reader will meet in this book fall into three categories: buccaneer captains, those who employed them, and those who wrote about them. The captains, or admirals as at least two were known, will obviously dominate the narrative. The acknowledged English 'admirals' of the buccaneers were Edward Mansfield and Henry Morgan who led some of the largest and most successful forays against the Spanish. John Morris, who sailed up the San Juan River to sack Granada, and John Coxen, whose career took many unexpected twists and turns, are two lesser but no less fascinating personalities.

The French buccaneer de Grammont captured Campeche before he joined up with the Dutchmen de Graaf and Van Hoorn for their spectacular attack on Vera Cruz, all sanctioned to harass the Spanish. More renegades were L'Ollonais, Rock Brasiliano, Bartholomew Portuguese, Diego el Mulato, Abraham Blauvelt and Sir Thomas Whetstone amongst many others.

The three men who saw the political advantage of engaging the services of the buccaneers were Sir Thomas Modyford, governor of Jamaica from 1664 to 1671, and two successive governors of French Hispaniola, Bertrand d'Ogeron and Jean-Baptiste DuCasse. Recognising that their mother countries had few resources to defend their West Indian colonies, these men commissioned the buccaneers to undertake ventures, not always with great success, that would weaken the Spanish and provide some degree of security.

Finally, it is to an unusual collection of diarists and writers that this book largely owes its existence. As well as the ubiquitous Exquemelin, the history of the buccaneers owes a debt to men like the English priest, Thomas Gage, Sir William Beeston who kept detailed records before and after he became governor of Jamaica, the buccaneer Ravenau de Lussan whose journal was published in 1688, Lionel Wafer, a buccaneer surgeon who wrote his memoirs and, of course, William Dampier, the buccaneer who eventually sailed around the world.

For every brilliant ship's captain and masterful leader of armed men amongst the buccaneers there were brave and accomplished individuals amongst the Spanish they confronted. Don Juan Guzman, President of the Audencia of Panama, despite being seriously ill, valiantly rallied his reluctant defenders as Henry Morgan approached and, although acquitted of charges of failing to defeat his enemy, probably died of a broken heart thousands of miles from his beloved city.

William Dampier (1652–1715), English buccaneer and diarist wrote Voyage Around the World *and other best-sellers. His recollections of a buccaneer's life amongst the logwood cutters revealed another side of the Caribbean frontiersmen.*

Chapter 2

BOUCANIER TO BUCCANEER

~

Defining a boucanier is a simple task; the origin of boucaniers, a little more difficult. The transition of boucaniers – 'cow killers' – to buccaneers should prove easy to trace, although it did not happen at a single place or at a specific time. There is a documented connection between a boucanier and a buccaneer as readers will recognise from what follows. Boucaniers originated in the northwestern part of Hispaniola that is now Haiti, including the island of La Tortue known to the English as Tortuga.

Northern and western Hispaniola, now Haiti, and the Atlantic island of Tortuga were populated by herds of wild cattle, pigs and other once-domesticated animals.

The Spanish had settled in Hispaniola as a result of Christopher Columbus' arrival but lured by the prospect of great mineral wealth on the mainland, they began emigrating to Mexico and Peru before long. They had originally brought with them the animals of Europe: pigs, horses, cattle, dogs, even sheep. From time to time the Spanish would also leave a few pigs or cattle on an uninhabited island as a source of food for passing vessels or, possibly, shipwrecked sailors. These domestic animals thrived in the tropical climate, nourished by ample food and water until they became abundant. The departure of the colonists from Hispaniola only accelerated the increase in a large population of wild herds.

The problem of a declining population in Hispaniola came to a head in 1605 when a Spanish royal cedula or decree ordered the northern and western regions of the island to be abandoned and settlements there laid to waste. The intention was to deny commercial opportunity to illegal Dutch traders and to concentrate the decreasing number of settlers in the more densely populated and defensible southern side of the island nearer to the capital, Santo Domingo.

The decree was met with hostility. Many of the Spanish settlers refused to leave their haciendas and initially defied the enforced evacuation attempts that were to take place. Here now was a spacious, ungarrisoned territory, abundantly stocked with fruit, vegetables and animals, providing an expanse of coastline from which to trade in provisions and animal by-products. Here, too, was a new challenge for the breed of men who have been attracted by untamed frontiers throughout history. From amongst these frontiersmen were to emerge the buccaneers.

Cimmarones or maroons, runaways who sought freedom from nearly a century of slavery under the Spanish, were to occupy the more remote mountainsides and valleys of northwestern Hispaniola. And to its coast came shipwrecked and marooned sailors as well as deserters to seek their fortunes.

Gradually their numbers increased as they were joined by others escaping religious persecution, including the Huguenots and other Protestants. After St Christopher (St Kitts) and Nevis were sacked by the Spanish some of the English and French colonists fled to Hispaniola. Social persecution in the Caribbean produced English bondsmen and French engagés, indentured servants sold into near slavery for a period of years. If they were able to escape their masters they could take up a life of boucaniering. As time went by, still another category of individual emerged on the Caribbean frontier: the freebooter or flibustier (from the Dutch 'fly' boats in which they often sailed). The freebooters were not European-based pirates who returned home after raiding ventures but men who emigrated indefinitely to the West Indies and who eventually used as their bases the settlements around northern Hispaniola – Léogane, Petit Goâve and Gonâve in the Cul-de-Sac, Cape St Nicholas, Isle à Vache and, most significantly, Tortuga, and later Port Royal, Jamaica.

To survive on the frontier in the West Indies, Europeans had to adapt to an unfamiliar environment and climate. Inevitably the best teachers were the original inhabitants, the Taino Indians. To cook meat that could be eaten either immediately, or, alternatively, safely preserved, Tainos devised a method of successfully curing it over a fire.

They dug a shallow pit in which to keep a slow-burning fire. Four stakes were driven into the ground on the corners about two to three feet above the surface to support a grill. The grill, or boucan, was made from the branches of a hardwood tree, perhaps *lignum vitae*. The flesh of hogs or cattle was cut into strips up to six feet in length. Salt was sprinkled over them and left to penetrate for three or four hours. The meat was then laid on the boucan, either inside an ajoupa, a primitive dwelling, or outdoors, and smoked slowly over a low burning fire stoked with fat, bones and entrails from the slaughtered animal. Cooked over flames from an aromatic wood like pimento the meat proved remarkably flavourful.

The process known as boucanning was easily the most common method of preparing meat. It produced food smoke-cured so it could be eaten several days later and was convenient to carry. The huntsmen who boucanned their meat were known as 'boucaniers'.

Boucaniers learnt the art of curing and slow-cooking meat to preserve it from the Taino Indians. They usually hunted in small bands, accompanied by packs of dogs and equipped with guns and knives.

The boucaniers usually hunted in small bands of between five to eight men but up to as many as 40. A temporary campsite called a 'rendezvous' would be set up in clearings in the woods close to the grasslands where their prey dwelt. To catch the prevailing north and east winds and so reduce the discomfort of mosquitoes, a slightly elevated site was preferred. Here the boucans for cooking and the ajoupas for sleeping or storage were erected.

Boucaniers prepared the hides of the animals they hunted to trade with passing vessels.

Rising early in the cool Caribbean dawn, the hunters smeared their faces with hog grease to discourage pests. They wore a smock-like shirt with coarse cloth trousers or a skirt resembling a brewer's apron – both stiff with blood and grease as if they had been tarred – and tied with a strip of bull's hide. They carried around their waists a sack in which a boucanier slept to fend off the mosquitoes and other annoying insects. Around their feet they wrapped cowskin or pigskin and they wore a cap with a peak to keep off the sun.

A well-equipped boucanier carried several knives, usually of Flemish origin, a cutlass primarily for clearing trails, and a large bore, single-shot musket with a four-foot long barrel that fired one-ounce lead balls. A powder bag or horn and a bullet pouch completed his gear.

Wild dogs, trapped when puppies and trained, were used in packs of 20 or 30. Alexander Exquemelin, in his book *Bucaniers of America*, claimed young piglets were also domesticated and used on hunting expeditions to seek out wild hogs which they did by grunting and squealing. There is mention, too, of the taming of forest horses for use hauling meat and hides from the hunting grounds.

When the hunt was on, one man stayed at the rendezvous to carry out the daily chores whilst the others, led by an experienced boucanier and his dog, penetrated the forest and savanna. Once a victim was located and encircled by the dog pack, one of the hunters would be chosen to aim or kill it with a musket shot. The men would then set about butchering the animal, first breaking the bones and sucking out the warm marrow for sustenance. This completed, one man would remain behind to skin the carcass for its valuable hide and cut up choice pieces of meat before returning to camp.

The hunt continued until every man had at least one kill. However, frequently many more cattle or hogs were slaughtered than could be carried away. A full morning's hunt might take the band nearly ten miles before the hunters returned to eat their first full meal of the day.

A French missionary, Pere Labat, who recorded his experiences in the Caribbean in the late seventeenth century, described a boucanier meal as consisting of roasted bananas and broth with meat followed by the boucanned flesh of a hog spiced with sauce made from pimento berries. Pork, being more popular than beef, was usually roasted on a spit and possibly stewed in the 'pepper pot' fashion of the Amerindians.

Life was physically harsh and hunting a rigorous discipline. To amuse themselves in the forests the boucaniers would test the skill most crucial to their survival – sharpshooting. Shooting birds such as parrots, pigeons, turkeys and wood-fowl or picking off oranges by nicking the stem was extremely difficult using a cumbersome musket. This skill was to serve them admirably when they turned to buccaneering. Like their predecessors the Tainos, the boucaniers found the recreation of smoking tobacco served a two-fold purpose providing both relaxation and a way of warding off mosquitoes.

The absence of women on the hunt must have been conducive to the practice of homosexuality but there is no documented evidence to this effect. When the boucaniers paid a visit to coastal settlements they were known to boisterously seek the services of prostitutes. The hunter's life was one of strenuous exertion, abundant sun and clean air, fresh meat and fruit, occasionally endangered by an on-rushing wounded boar but most likely threatened by a variety of tropical diseases generally described in contemporary literature as fevers. Personal hygiene was often minimal and the scourge of body lice commonplace. When a boucanier died he was likely to be interred under a cairn of stones with the simplest of ceremonies.

Hunting wild boars could be a particularly dangerous endeavour for boucaniers.

15

Boucaniers hunted animals for their own consumption as well as for trading for other basic needs. Their routine was simple: setting up a boucan, they would normally hunt game for hides, tallow (for lamp oil) and meat over a period of several months and up to a year or two. Descending to the coast, they would set up makeshift trading posts accessible to coastal trading vessels and where safe anchorage as well as ample fresh water and other foodstuffs such as fruit were available.

The boucanier had little use for money, even when it was offered. Barter was the common and most acceptable method of doing business. Exquemelin reports the bartering of two pounds of tobacco for one pot of tallow lamp oil. The boucanier exchanged his products for guns, ammunition and knives in order to continue hunting; for utensils and cloth for daily living; and for wine, brandy, dice and playing cards for diversion. Later in the seventeenth century it is recorded that they even acquired servants to carry out manual labour. Although there is no mention of them ever owning African slaves, Africans were said to be present in Spanish-settled northwestern Hispaniola in the early part of the seventeenth century.

As time went by the provision of hides, tallow, meat and even hunting dogs (sought after by planters) became better organised, with the introduction of specific contracts between purchasers and traders.

Some of their temporary coastal settlements became permanent. The leading amongst these was Basse Terre on Tortuga. It was to become well-known as a trading settlement and a place of recreation with its taverns, brothels and gaming tables. Exquemelin recorded:

'… they squander in a month all the money which has taken them a year or 18 months to earn. They drink brandy like water, and will buy a whole case of wine, broach it, and drink it until there's not a drop left. Day and night they roam the town, keeping the feast of Bacchus so long as they can drink for money. The service of Venus is not forgotten either. In fact, the tavern keepers and whores make ready for the coming of the hunters and the privateers in the same way as their fellows in Amsterdam prepared for the arrival of the East India ships and men-of-war. Once their money is all spent and they've had all they can on credit, back they go to the woods again …'

This settlement on Tortuga has been described as possibly the earliest independent community in the Caribbean because it was not protected by or allied to any sovereign nation. Instead, it thrived on free trade and appears to have managed its own affairs in a more or less democratic fashion. To understand how this unique condition emerged it is necessary to trace the transition of boucanier to buccaneer.

'Once their money is all spent and they've had all they can on credit, back they go to the woods again …'

These pioneers were highly individualistic and non-conformist; to survive they had to be tough, enterprising and determined. The boucaniers mastered their environment by organising themselves in bands, primarily for the mutual advantage of seeking a livelihood with some degree of security. They developed a style of communal property. But, most importantly, the boucaniers depended on a unique formal system of comradeship known as 'matelotage' for their social and economic security. With so few women on the Caribbean frontier in the seventeenth century, this special form of friendship also provided in its own way a substitute for the institution of marriage or cohabitation and, although there may have been instances of homosexuality, matelotage did not exist for this purpose specifically.

For instance two young men, 'matelots' – or comrades – who had finished serving their terms as indentured servants agreed to merge their resources and sign a document which covered the disposal of any inheritance left by one or the other. This instrument was applied on the infrequent occasions a boucanier got married and parted company from his matelot. Louis Le Golif, in a book 'discovered' in the last century, dubiously claimed to have lived the life of a boucanier. He maintained that a married man had to make his spouse sexually available to his matelot to conform with the original arrangement of each to defend, support and work alongside the other.

Out of this dependence one for the other came a mutual respect for characteristics such as sincerity, integrity, courage and resourcefulness. These were to prove invaluable assets as the ever-persistent threat of Spanish attack grew and the boucanier, seeing the wild cattle and hogs becoming scarcer, had to seek other ways to survive. Wasteful practices in the early years combined with the proliferation of wild dog packs had exacerbated this problem. The situation deteriorated further when the Spanish authorities in Santo Domingo ordered the wholesale slaughter of livestock in the northwest in an effort to starve out the hunters of Hispaniola.

The presence of the boucaniers had always been a threat to the Spanish authorities in Santo Domingo. In the 1630s a force of some 500 lancers was formed and organised into troops of 50 men on horseback. These troops were divided into patrols of a dozen men with an officer. Their strategy was to reconnoitre an area in order to identify boucan sites and gauge the size of the hunting party. By attacking a boucan at night with a superior fighting force the Spanish held a distinct advantage. However, when confronted by a patrol in the forest during daylight, the boucanier was a formidable foe not only because of his accurate marksmanship but also because of his ferocious determination to avoid capture.

The persistence of the Spanish attempts to rid the land of the boucaniers eventually produced two results: first, the hunters began congregating in larger numbers to give themselves a better chance of survival; secondly, more permanent coastal boucans were set up from which the hunters would depart daily to the mainland to hunt, returning to these more defensible bases before sundown. These places also became trading camps and began lending a greater degree of permanence to the boucanier's presence in northwestern Hispaniola and, over time, Tortuga.

"The Spaniards, seeing the pirates aboard their ship, without scarce seeing them at sea, cried out: "Jesus bless us! Are these devils or what are they?""

Relentless Spanish efforts to suppress them led to retaliation in the name of self-defence, revenge and, inevitably, the prospect of spoils. The boucaniers fought in the knowledge that capture would mean imprisonment, torture, slavery or even death. They showed no mercy because they received none.

In 1663 another Spanish royal decree ordering their eviction resulted in the only pitched battle recorded between the boucaniers and the Spanish. A force of 500 experienced troops set out for the largest boucan situated in the Savane Burlee. Spotted before they arrived, the Spanish were confronted by a far smaller band of hunters in a mountain pass between the Petits Fonds and the Grands Fonds. After a full day of fighting, the Spanish broke and fled in confusion, their commander and many others dead on the field of battle.

Alexander Exquemelin credits a French pirate, Pierre le Grand, for setting the example for the boucaniers. Le Grand with a small boat and a crew of 28 captured the vice-admiral of the Spanish fleet off Cape Tiburon in western Hispaniola. Exquemelin explained:

'The boat wherein Pierre le Grand was with his companions, had now been at sea a long time, without finding anything, according to his intent of piracy suitable to make a prey. And now, their provisions beginning to fail, they could keep themselves no longer upon the ocean or they must of necessity starve.'

The vessel le Grand sailed in was probably no larger than the galleon's own longboat and was barely seaworthy. His strategy was to pick out a galleon that had strayed from the main fleet. The Spanish vice-admiral, when warned that the tiny vessel was on his horizon and might pose a threat, dismissed the suggestion contemptuously.

Le Grand's tactics were simple and seemingly suicidal as his crew was armed with only pistols and cutlasses. Relying on the element of surprise, he approached the galleon in near darkness and, having bored a hole in the bottom of his own vessel to scuttle it, led his men on to the Spaniard's deck. Exquemelin continues:

'The Spaniards, seeing the pirates aboard their ship, without scarce seeing them at sea, cried out: "Jesus bless us! Are these devils or what are they?" In the meanwhile some of them took possession of the gunroom and military affairs they found there, killing as many of the ship as made any opposition.'

Le Grand kept those of the Spaniards as he needed to sail the ship and set the rest ashore. Having obtained a royal commission after the event to legitimise his venture, he sailed into his French home port with his prize and was reputed never to have gone to sea again.

Exquemelin suggests that the success of le Grand's daring endeavour was what persuaded boucaniers of Hispaniola to take up 'buccaneering'. More likely is the fact that the seafaring predators who were already in the Caribbean became their logical allies with whom they were to form a loose alliance. What is certain, however, is that le Grand's strategy and tactics, the type of vessel he used and the strategy of hand-to-hand fighting all typified the way in which the early buccaneers pursued and captured their prey at sea.

The boucaniers had, Exquemelin put it, 'no sooner understood this happy event and rich prizes those pirates had obtained, but they resolved to follow their example'.

The settlement of Basse Terre was to become the headquarters of the boucaniers-turned-buccaneers on Tortuga.

At first Spanish galleons were more ambitious targets than most men would contemplate. The earliest sea-going boucaniers from Hispaniola used dug-out canoes, or pirogues, up to 40 feet long to intercept small barques carrying out coastal trade. Seizing cargoes of hides, logwood, tobacco and other agricultural produce and commandeering these vessels for future exploits, they would return to Tortuga and supply interloping trading ships anchored in the roadstead at Basse Terre. Inevitably the buccaneers began seeking out richer vessels, sometimes merchantmen with wines, cloth, grain, weapons, implements and other commodities imported from Spain and, before long, outward-bound treasure ships with their immensely valuable cargoes of precious metals, jewels and dyewoods.

Exquemelin recorded in detail the comprehensive social contract and conditions for participation in such expeditions as well as the modus operandi which the boucaniers adopted in those early years. In many respects the spirit of loyalty, cooperation and respect for democratic principles that was acknowledged by the boucaniers was embodied in the rules by which the later buccaneers were to govern themselves.

Having decided to go to sea, a leader would put out the word and soon a body of men, armed with their own weapons, powder and shot, gathered. Some of the men undertook to make the vessel, probably a captured Spanish barque, seaworthy whilst the others joined a hunting party in search of boucanned meat which was to be the mainstay of their diet at sea. The alternative method of stocking the vessel with food was to raid a Spanish settlement, stealing domesticated pigs from the hog pen, cattle from the savanna and turtles from crawls kept at the sea's edge.

Before sailing an agreement, or *chasse-partie*, was drawn up setting out how the proceeds of any prize secured would be divided. The hunter who provided the boucanned meat, for instance, would receive 200 pieces of eight, the carpenter 100 to 150 pieces of eight for making the craft seaworthy and the surgeon 200 to 250 according to the quantity of medical supplies dictated by the size of the crew.

Next came a scale of awards as compensation for bodily injury or loss. For the loss of a right arm, 600 pieces of eight or six slaves; a left arm or a right leg, 500 pieces of eight or five slaves; a left leg, 400 pieces of eight or four slaves; an eye or a finger, 100 pieces of eight or one slave. Even severe internal injuries were compensated. If a pipe had to be inserted into a man's windpipe in order to allow him to breathe, 500 pieces of eight were to be paid.

The fees and injury awards were deducted before the prize was divided. The captain drew at least four or five portions for providing the vessel and then two for himself, if in fact the owner of the vessel was also the chosen leader of the expedition. The remainder of the crew received a portion each and boys a half share.

When a prize ship was captured, the entire crew would be party to the decision as to whether or not to keep it, exchange it for the vessel in which they were sailing or destroy it by fire. Everything plundered from the luckless victim was first gathered together and then distributed according to the rules set out. An oath was said to be taken by each man before the booty was given out by which he swore that he had kept nothing for himself. Any man proven to have sworn falsely ran the risk of banishment or even death. Justice amongst the buccaneers was quick and merciless. For theft, an ear or a nose might be chopped off. A more severe case of treachery could result in a flogging followed by being marooned on a deserted beach with only a musket, a small amount of ammunition, and a bottle of water. Quarrelling ultimately led to the wrongdoer being flogged, although duels were condoned as a means of settling bitter disputes. However, to even the score in which a man had been shot before he had a chance to defend himself was punishable by death.

Captured prisoners were considered a nuisance. Of those who survived the taking of their vessel, most were usually set ashore whilst a handful were kept on board to perform menial tasks.

Before sailing and guided by a democratic vote, the buccaneers chose a leader and decided on a course of action. Off the nearby coasts of Jamaica, Cuba, Hispaniola and Puerto Rico they could find coastal traders and, within the vicinity of their ports, merchant vessels of Spanish origin. However, richer pickings plied the waters between Cuba and the Yucatan, in the Florida Straits as well as off the coast of present-day Venezuela, Colombia, Nicaragua and Honduras.

If they did not have a captured vessel, the boucaniers preferred to sail in a single-masted sloop or a barque, the best of which were reputed to have been built in Jamaica or Bermuda. A barque was equipped with a single mast, two triangular forward sails and one main sail and could be manoeuvred close to the wind giving its speed. At first their remarkable marksmanship as hunters provided the buccaneers with their only firepower. The Jesuit priest-historian, Jean-Baptiste Labat, said they considered four muskets more effective than one cannon. When they later employed cannons it was few, from six to a dozen. At the best of times their vessels, even when they used a larger corvette or brigantine, were crowded and carried provisions enough for only a limited voyage.

Although a broadside from a larger but more cumbersome Spanish ship could be fatal, the buccaneers manoeuvred skilfully, trying to keep their vessels at a right angle to their intended prey to reduce the likelihood of being hit. Meanwhile, with their muskets, they would pick off as many men as possible on deck or in the rigging. When the moment was opportune they would board, brandishing knives, cutlasses and pistols, their outlandish garb and terrifying antics as much a weapon as their arms.

A buccaneer preferred to dictate the circumstances in which to confront his adversary. Clearly, it was essential to challenge a lone vessel or a galleon that had strayed too far from the fleet. The tricky waters around small islands or cays with their shallow reefs and narrow channels gave the buccaneers a distinct tactical advantage. A sudden change in wind could spell disaster for the large Spanish vessels. The close proximity of a narrow river mouth or a lagoon camouflaged by dense tropical vegetation was useful for springing a surprise attack as well as providing a hiding place or a safe harbour to careen and refit their vessels.

Earliest attacks on Spanish vessels were carried out from pirogues by men armed only with pistols, swords and muskets.

Islands like Tortuga, Jamaica and the Bay Islands became popular with the buccaneers because they offered secure refuge from the Spanish. But there were to be repeated occasions when attempts were made to drive them out. On these islands they would trade, refit their vessels and prepare for their assaults on the Spanish. The emergence of the buccaneer - part hunter, part soldier, part outlaw and part adventurer – apparently did not end the era of the original boucanier.

As late as 1701, the priest Pere Labat records in his journal that on a stopover at the westernmost tip of Hispaniola the ship on which he was travelling traded with a settlement of boucaniers. In exchange for pork, bacon, ham and 300 pounds of lard, the boucaniers received powder and shot, cloth and haberdashery. Labat said that in dress and appearance these men looked no different than the boucaniers from whom they had descended 70 years earlier.

Chapter 3

TORTUGA

BIRTHPLACE OF THE BUCCANEERS

~

A t the northern end of the Windward Passage separating Cuba and Haiti lies the island of La Tortue, or Tortuga, which can authentically claim to be the birthplace of the buccaneers and where their story begins. Once a busy buccaneer seaport, its main settlement is now a small tropical village supported by boat-building and inter-island trade.

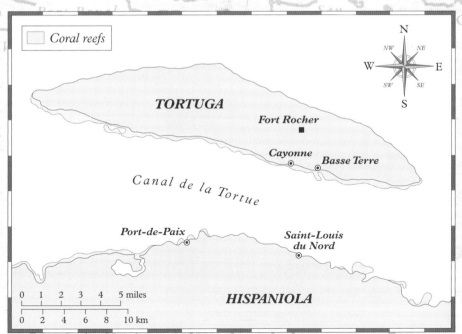

Sighted by Christopher Columbus in 1492, the island of Tortuga lies off the northwestern coast of Haiti and can rightfully claim to be the birthplace of the buccaneers.

A few walls still remain of what was the imposing Fort de la Roche, or Fort Rocher, built by Jean LeVasseur in the 1640s. Cannons of the colonial era are scattered in the undergrowth, some at the water's edge. A visitor today would be hard pressed to imagine what Tortuga was like nearly 400 years ago. Probably only its geographical location and unique topography reminds us why this birth was possible.

Christopher Columbus, sailing southeast following his discovery of the Bahamas islands and Cuba in 1492, sighted a small, oval-shaped island with a high ridge rising to its centre. Covered with dense green tropical vegetation, it was named Tortuga by the Admiral 'because it looks like a monster sea turtle above the waves'. The island lies two miles off the north coast of present-day Haiti, a part of the island called L'Isla Espagnola, or Hispaniola, by Columbus. The hump of the turtle's shell

A few remains of seventeenth-century battlements and cannons scattered in the undergrowth provide meagre contemporary evidence of Tortuga's buccaneering heyday.

is a ridge running east to west, its highest point being Morne Monde, 1,400 feet, near its eastern end. The island is four miles wide and 24 miles long.

Morne Monde falls steeply and rapidly to the present-day south coast settlements of Cayonne and Basse Terre, with their reef-protected anchorages. To the south and west there are broad savannas. The lowlands are characterised by sparse vegetation while grasslands cover the savannas. The northern side is virtually uninhabitable. The steep volcanic rock combined with persistent Atlantic swells make landings from the sea treacherous. It is the aptly named Côte de Fer. These peculiar topographical conditions, allied with historical circumstance, contributed significantly to Tortuga becoming the birthplace of buccaneering.

At the time of Columbus' voyage, Hispaniola and Tortuga were inhabited by Tainos, an Amerindian people who had migrated north from South America centuries before Europeans penetrated the region. The hot tropical climate with its seasonal but ample rainfall created a bountiful environment. Only nature's occasional destructive storms, known as hurricanes, disturbed their habitat. These hurricanes were later to ravage the treasure fleets of Spain resulting in costly losses. Tainos lived off the land, planting and harvesting indigenous vegetables such as cassava, corn, sweet potatoes, yams and peanuts and fruits like soursops, guavas, pineapples and papaya. They planted tobacco which they used for medicinal purposes, in religious ceremonies or smoked for its euphoric effect.

Their diet also included birds: ducks, parrots and pigeons caught in simple traps or with bow and arrow. The meat of the iguana, a large lizard, was a delicacy, while a variety of indigenous Caribbean rodents provided an alternative source of edible flesh. Both salt and fresh water fish were hooked or speared. The mammal sea cow, the manatee, provided succulent meat, fat and bones which had a variety of uses. Curiously, the Tainos, unlike the European settlers, shunned turtle meat because of superstition although they did not hesitate to eat turtle eggs.

Usually the Tainos lived on the coast or on river banks in inland valleys. The types of food they grew, hunted and fished and many other facets of their daily existence were adopted by the Europeans who came later. The shelter of the boucaniers was similar to the Tainos' caneyes or Carib Indians' ajoupa, a conical hut made from leaves and branches on a framework of posts with a central upright pole with a single entrance. They slept in hammocks, hanging beds of woven cotton fibres which were light and cool and suspended the sleeper safely off the ground. To fish or to travel long distances, the Tainos hollowed out huge hardwood trees by skilfully burning out the core. A friendly people, the Tainos led a simple yet peaceful existence, reaping nature's bounty with the most basic of implements.

Tortuga's hot tropical climate and ample rainfall allowed indigenous crops and wildlife to flourish.

But from the very first contingent of men left behind at Columbus' first colony, La Navidad, on the north coast of Hispaniola, the Spanish treated the indigenous population brutally. If not slaughtered for opposing the invaders, the Tainos were enslaved to labour in the fields and mines. Disease and warfare inevitably took its fatal toll.

There is no record of how long the Tainos survived on Tortuga, similarly there is no record of when the island was first populated by Europeans. Spanish settlements in northwest Hispaniola far removed from Santo Domingo, the centre of Hispaniola's administrative authority, gradually spread further in the north in the sixteenth century. But as early as 1537 French pirates carried out a series of devastating raids on Hispaniola. The Elizabethan privateer, Sir Francis Drake, commanded a force that captured Santo Domingo 20 years later contributing to the growing realisation that it was not just the vast, mountainous expanses of Hispaniola that were difficult to defend.

As well as pirates and privateers intruding in Spain's domain, English, Dutch and French armed trading ships were regularly seen at Cape St Nicholas on the northernmost tip of Hispaniola by 1599. These isolated settlements welcomed the illicit traders as they provided much needed merchandise for day-to-day living. In return the settlers, often boucaniers, exchanged products of their domestic enterprise and offered safe anchorage for repairing vessels.

But the Spanish authorities finally conceded that persistent pillaging and trading in contraband had to be stamped out. Unable to provide an effective defence for the entire island of Hispaniola, Spain's King Philip III decreed that the northern and western coasts – which would include Tortuga – should be abandoned and all settlements destroyed. The population was to be relocated to the southeast plain near Santo Domingo where its safety could be ensured. Those who resisted were designated renegades left to fend for themselves in territory effectively open to occupation by anyone. The Dutch, for one, frequented Léogane to obtain wood and water, and at Cape St Nicholas they engaged in collecting salt for curing fish.

Boucaniers crossed the two-mile channel separating the mainland and the island of Tortuga some time before 1630 to put their Spanish enemies at a distance and to take advantage of the wild hogs that roamed the forest and savanna. So abundant were the swine that the island was often referred to as 'L'Isle de Porceaux', the island of pigs.

The first English-documented establishment of a formal settlement on Tortuga had a curious origin. A young ship's captain, Anthony Hilton, was despatched by a group of English West Country merchants in 1623 to Virginia to explore the Hudson River with the object of finding the elusive Northwest Passage to the Orient. He began by taking the usual westward course across the Atlantic, making landfall at St Kitts in the Caribbean where he met a fellow countryman, Thomas Warner, who had himself arrived only a year before and was successfully growing tobacco.

Hilton's Hudson River expedition which followed proved a disaster but on his return to England he recruited a handful of followers and returned to St Kitts where Warner granted him a plantation. Warlike Carib Indians, reputed to eat human flesh, attacked and destroyed Hilton's first landholding. Fortunately he managed to escape unharmed and return to start over again growing tobacco which he sold profitably in Ireland. But Hilton's relationship with Warner deteriorated drastically. He attempted to settle on the islands of Barbuda, Antigua and Montserrat before putting down roots at Nevis, close to St Kitts in 1628. Within a year he was accusing Warner of plotting his murder and had become regarded by his patron, the Earl of Carlisle, as a liability.

Hilton fled to England in 1629 and attempted to reconcile himself with Carlisle. His timing was fortuitous because, during his absence, a Spanish fleet of 30 vessels under Don Federico de Toledo devastated both St Kitts and Nevis. Hilton never went back to Nevis but Warner, knighted for his services to the crown, did return along with those of the settlers who had not been captured and resumed the governorship of the English half of St Kitts that it shared with the French.

Anthony Hilton took advantage of his growing familiarity with the buccaneers when he decided that a brighter future lay on the more defensible island of Tortuga. Taking his remaining Nevisian followers with him he settled there. A safe distance from the Spanish authorities on the mainland, Tortuga was stocked with ample game, promised a rich harvest of valuable tropical woods and could be made into a trading outpost with unlimited potential. All that he and his supporters needed was financial backing but even the ambitious Hilton could never have imagined from where it would eventually come. The Providence Company, a group of Puritan aristocrats and merchants whose ventures were to stretch from Bermuda to New England to the West Indies in the first half of the seventeenth century, reacted enthusiastically to his proposals.

The company had already settled the island of Providence, or Santa Catalina (now Providencia), off present-day Nicaragua and by 1631 had persuaded King Charles II to extend the limits of their royal patent for colonisation which, for all practical purposes, stretched to include most of the central West Indies.

Plans for fortifying the settlement were drawn up and provision made for six cannons with a supply of ammunition. It was resolved that the island should be renamed the 'Island of Association'. Before long the new colony, governed by Captain Hilton, began attracting fugitives from many nations who sought to sail in pursuit of Spanish booty and who could alternate such employment hunting cattle and swine or cutting wood in the heavily forested interior.

Before long, however, dissension amongst the English and French made the colony vulnerable. Learning of this the Spanish saw an opportunity to terminate this growing threat to Spain's domination of the Caribbean. A disgruntled Irishman, John Murphy, who described himself to the Spanish as 'sargento-mayor' of Tortuga, deserted to Cartagena with the objective of persuading the Spanish authorities that with his help they could bring about Hilton's downfall.

In December 1634, 250 foot soldiers under Ruiz Fernandez de Fuemayor were despatched to take Tortuga. At the time, according to Spanish accounts, 600 men bearing arms occupied the island although the Providence Company claimed there were as few as 150 permanent inhabitants. The Spanish flotilla, due to the ignorance of the pilot, struck the offshore reefs but Ruiz Fernandez somehow managed to land 30 soldiers on the shore and at dawn seized the fort without any difficulty. When they realised they were under attack the English, purportedly led by Governor Hilton, confronted the invaders. According to Spanish reports, he was stabbed to death by the Irishman Murphy. The records of the Providence Company, however, showed that Hilton had died earlier and Christopher Wormeley had been appointed governor. In the fray some of the inhabitants, believing they could not hold the island, regained the fort, spiked the guns, then carried away what they could in several ships anchored in the harbour.

Ruiz Fernandez defeated a second body of armed inhabitants who had stayed behind then sacked their houses and destroyed the tobacco plantation. He took 70 prisoners and returned to Santo Domingo after a month's occupation. The Spanish general had ruthlessly put to the sword whoever opposed him. Those who had fled to the woods and returned, compelled by hunger, were hanged. Amongst those who got away was Christopher Wormeley who was accused of cowardice and banished from the colony. However, on reaching Virginia he ultimately married and regained respectability as the captain of Fort Comfort there. Ruiz Fernandez, for his part, later became governor of the province of Venezuela.

A little more than a year later, a new governor appointed by the Providence

Company regained control of the island. Captain Nicholas Riskinner, who had been chosen to revive the fortunes of Tortuga, came from a Flemish family long settled in England. Described as a soldier and a gentleman, Riskinner was most likely chosen on the basis that his most obvious attribute was his familiarity with the buccaneers. His employers supplied him with 30 muskets, ten pistols, two artillery pieces, 33 barrels of powder, shot and matches, 30 swords, a drum, a flag, assorted tools and £20 in cash for his own use.

Captain Riskinner turned out to be quite unfit for the post assigned him and he died of fever not long after his arrival in the Caribbean. By this time 80-odd English and 150 Negroes inhabited the island but the French were beginning to frequent it with regularity to harvest the valuable brazilwood. The Providence Company took time to choose a suitable replacement and, when a decision was finally made in late 1630, reports arrived in London that the English settlers had already decided to relocate to the mainland of Hispaniola.

A small French contingent remained behind and once again, in 1638, the Spanish ravaged the settlement, then departed without leaving a garrison to prevent further encroachment. And once again the English, 300 in number, sailed from Nevis for Tortuga led by a Captain Roger Flood. The French eighteenth-century historian, P F X Charlevoix, wrote 90 years later that the French and English population on Tortuga could be split into four categories: boucaniers, who were hunters; flibustiers who were in fact pirates; habitants or planters; and engagés, servants supplied by merchants in Dieppe. Remarkably this unlikely mix of nationalities and personalities democratically elected a William James in place of Roger Flood. James decided to title himself 'president' because he felt it more appropriate than 'governor', in a self-governing community. Unfortunately, his rule was anything but democratic as the French inhabitants soon began complaining of discrimination since he reserved power solely for the English.

Within four months President James was disarming the French and marooning them on the opposite shore on the mainland. Before long the news that the English were making Tortuga an English colony reached the ears of the French governor-general of the French islands, Lonvilliers de Poincy. As fate would have it, de Poincy also had another problem: he was under pressure from France to get rid of the French Protestant Huguenots, who were troublesome rivals of the Roman Catholics in St Kitts. De Poincy struck on a solution to resolve both his dilemmas by asking Captain Jean LeVasseur to head a force of the Huguenots to retake Tortuga in the name of France. It was LeVasseur who was to make the island secure for the French buccaneers and facilitate its use as their base, which it remained until late in the seventeenth century.

De Poincy recognised LeVasseur's qualities of intelligence, initiative and courage and took into account the fact that he had lived for over 20 years in the region. He invited him to take charge of the government of Tortuga subject to conditions which LeVasseur quickly ignored.

His proposal was enthusiastically received and in the summer of 1640 LeVasseur took 50 men from St Kitts to Port Margot, on the north coast of Hispaniola and near enough for an assault on Tortuga. During the three months he was there he persuaded 50 French buccaneers to join his venture. Using the excuse that French settlers had been mistreated and a vessel of de Poincy's seized, LeVasseur gave the English 24 hours to leave. Abetted by the French settlers, he executed a surprise attack, taking the island without a blow being landed and capturing President James. Ten days later the inhabitants who had fled to Hispaniola counter-attacked without success and retired to Providence Island, thus ending the Puritan era.

LeVasseur wrote to Cardinal Richelieu in France proposing: 'If it please Your Excellency to make me governor of this island I will do everything possible to hold it, in the hope that it will be useful to us in the conquest of Santo Domingo …' However, it was generally accepted that Catholic France wanted to rid its colony in St Kitts of the heretics and LeVasseur's expedition was really more of a matter of expediency than political strategy. On November 4, 1641, de Poincy and LeVasseur signed an agreement in St Kitts recognising the latter as governor and setting out 13 articles for regulating the colonisation of Tortuga.

Jean LeVasseur, now a man in his 40s, clearly saw this as the moment to achieve his destiny. He appears to have had few scruples. Before very long he was deliberately ignoring the terms of his agreement and was setting out to exploit the newly-founded colony for personal profit. Being an experienced man of war, his first priority was to fortify the main settlement of Basse Terre in case of the return of the English or, more likely, the Spanish. He was acknowledged to be an excellent engineer and Fort Rocher that he built over 1,000 feet above the island's principal anchorage proved in its own right to be about as inaccessible as the far more ambitious fortifications protecting Havana, San Juan and Cartagena.

On a narrow plateau overlooking the roadstead he created a series of terraces that could accommodate 300 to 400 men. From the centre of this plateau a massive rock rose 30 feet. Steps led half way up the slope but access to the top was restricted to an iron ladder which could be detached whenever prudent. He is also believed to have designed and built a chimney-like escape from the rock to the terraces. At the base of the rock an inexhaustible spring supplied the defenders with fresh water.

On the top of the rock LeVasseur established his personal residence as well as storage for ammunition. A row of cannons on the terrace was carefully placed to guard the entrance to the bay. In making the fortress virtually impregnable, LeVasseur aroused the anxiety of de Poincy who was fearful that his second-in-command was beginning to act in his own best interests and not those of his country. These concerns were justified. De Poincy sent his nephew, M de Lanvilliers, and an associate by the name of LaVernade with a contingent of about 40 men to settle in

Tortuga and reconfirm its relationship with St Kitts. LeVasseur summarily prevented them from landing on the island.

In another display of arrogance, LeVasseur dismissed a demand by de Poincy to return a silver statue of the Virgin Mary stolen from a Spanish vessel by the buccaneers which he desired for his chapel. Instead, LeVasseur sent him a wooden replica. In a letter accompanying the Madonna, he sarcastically argued that as Catholics were spiritual and did not care for material objects he would keep the silver original which he more preferred.

But barely had the engineer completed what he called his 'dove-cote' in 1643, than it was to receive a baptism of fire from the Spanish. A force of 600 men in ten ships was dispatched from Santo Domingo. A barrage of artillery fire from the fort greeted the approaching vessels, sinking one and forcing the remainder to retreat. When the Spaniards finally landed, they walked into an ambush losing 100 men before hastily retreating. The news of LeVasseur's conclusive victory spread throughout the Caribbean – it was ten years before the Spanish attempted to take the buccaneers' island again.

Built by LeVasseur over 1,000 feet above the island's principal anchorage, Fort Rocher was virtually impregnable.

31

'... they returned immediately to Santo Domingo where they did twice as much damage as usual.'

From then on LeVasseur's Tortuga became a permanent and very welcoming base for both buccaneering expeditions as well as those trading in contraband. J B Duterte in his book, *Histoire des Antilles Francais*, published in Paris in 1667 explained the new phenomenon:

'… since the buccaneers of Santo Domingo had to do no more than take their skins to this island and in a very short time collect their gunpowder, lead, whisky and whatever else they needed, they returned immediately to Santo Domingo where they did twice as much damage as usual. As the adventurers got hold of booty, instead of taking it to the islands and spending two or three months enroute they took it to the port of Tortuga, and by the following day they were on their way back to the mouth of the rivers and bays of Santo Domingo'.

Situated as it was in close proximity to the new European colonies in the Caribbean, Tortuga became a warehouse for captured merchandise – goods brought mainly from Europe – as well as boucanned meat, hides and tallow supplied by the boucaniers. Trade thrived, as did the establishments that provided provisions and recreation for those who found Tortuga a convenient, if not permanent, address.

Flushed with success and perhaps mesmerised by his self-importance – a suspicion that de Poincy harboured – LeVasseur became paranoid, intolerant and often violent. In a campaign of persecution against the Catholics, he had a chapel that he had built at his own expense burnt to the ground and forbade them to practise their religion. Contemporary accounts by the Jesuits reported that he kept his enemies in a cage on his rock where they could neither stand up nor lie down, a torture from which offenders never recovered. He also maintained a prison he nicknamed 'Purgatory'.

Jean LeVasseur had his own system of taxation on trade and made himself excessively rich with a relatively lavish lifestyle. Inevitably after 12 years of his cruelty and despotic rule, de Poincy was left with no choice but to plot his downfall.

The opportunity presented itself when a French nobleman, the Chevalier de Fontenay, arrived in St Kitts with a 22-gun frigate in search of men to replace those he had recently lost in battle. De Fontenay had won a reputation as an astute naval commander in conflicts in the Mediterranean and was now seeking his fortune against the Spanish.

De Fontenay eagerly accepted de Poincy's offer and volunteers were raised on St Kitts in the belief that he was leading an attack on the coast of Central America so as to avoid detection by LeVasseur. He rendezvoused with another nephew of de Poincy, de Treval, who commanded a frigate equally well-prepared for an invasion of Tortuga. However, before departing they learnt of LeVasseur's assassination at the hands of two men, Martin and Thibault, who had been adopted by the tyrant as his successors. It seems that Thibault possessed a beautiful prostitute of whom LeVasseur disapproved. As his hatred and malice grew, Thibault plotted his mentor's demise. One morning when LeVasseur ascended from the dove-cote and was approaching his storehouses at the water's edge, Thibault and Martin with half a dozen men fired at him with muskets. The historian, du Terte, recorded that LeVasseur's figure was first reflected in a mirror, which image his murderers mistook initially for him. However, when LeVasseur reached for a sword being carried by a servant, Thibault stepped out and stabbed him to death.

According to the French historian, on recognising his assassin, LeVasseur borrowed Julius Caesar's appeal to Brutus: 'Can it be you, Thibault, who has taken my life?' before, ironically, requesting a priest in order to die a Roman Catholic. On hearing of LeVasseur's murder, de Fontenay sailed for Tortuga. The assassins, who had taken possession of 'the Rock', realised that they did not have the support of the populace and handed over the fortress on condition that they would not be prosecuted for LeVasseur's death and that they would be allowed to retain the inherited fortune from the man they had betrayed.

De Fontenay formally assumed the title of 'Governor for the King of Tortuga and the Coast of Santo Domingo', restored the rights of the Catholics and encouraged the traders and buccaneers to continue their activities. He built a new chapel and created an environment that attracted an increasing number of settlers. La Tortue began to flourish once again. But perhaps LeVasseur had the last laugh from his grave. In November, 1653 Don Juan Francisco de Montemayor, president of Santo Domingo, sent a new expedition to recapture the island.

Under the command of Don Gabriel Roxas de Valle-Figueroa, five vessels and 400 soldiers embarked for the invasion. A storm devastated the flotilla and only the capitana and almirante of the fleet reached their destination on January 10. Like its predecessor, this Spanish force also came under fire from the fortress as it approached the harbour, forcing the invaders to land at a distance. To dislodge the defenders the Spanish mounted cannons on sled-like wooden frames and hauled them to positions above the fort.

For several days the bombardment continued whilst the besieged attempted to capture the battery. De Fontenay, seemingly not the fighting man that LeVasseur was, capitulated on terms that would allow him and his retainers to depart. This time the Spanish left behind a garrison of 150 men and returned to Santo Domingo with guns, ammunitions and slaves, having burnt most of the island's settlements to the ground.

The French dispersed, with de Fontenay going to Port Margot to await the release of his brother who was held hostage by Don Gabriel until the Spaniard's return to Santo Domingo. Most of the rest of his followers abandoned him to join the buccaneers elsewhere along the coast of Hispaniola including Petit Goâve in the Cul-de-Sac. Thibault and Martin reputedly commandeered a vessel carrying women and children which became marooned on one of the Cayman Islands and had to be rescued by a passing Dutch vessel. De Fontenay was to make an unsuccessful attempt to recapture Tortuga with an inadequate force and eventually sailed for France, having the misfortune to be shipwrecked near the Azores. Shortly after his return to France he died.

It took only 18 months before the Spanish concluded that in determining priorities for the defence of their Caribbean possessions, Santo Domingo was significantly more important than Tortuga. With the approach of an English expedition under Admiral William Penn and General Robert Venables in 1655, the president of Santo Domingo, the Conde de Penalva, ordered the destruction of Fort Rocher rendering useless any artillery that could not be carried away, and returned his troops to assist in the defence of the mainland capital, fearful that England was hungry for territory in the Caribbean.

The see-saw saga of settlement in Tortuga continued in a curious fashion. An Englishman by the name of Elias Watts, hearing that the island was deserted, sailed from the recently-acquired English colony of Jamaica and with a commission from General Brayne, governor of Jamaica, claimed Tortuga for England. On the ruins of LeVasseur's fort he installed a battery of four cannons and before long had attracted 150 English and French inhabitants.

Meanwhile with a commission from the English governor, 400 mainly French buccaneers from Tortuga compelled the captain of a frigate recently arrived from Nantes in France to carry them to Puerto Plata in northern Hispaniola. From there they marched inland surprising the inhabitants of the unsuspecting and prosperous town of Santiago de los Caballeros by attacking at dawn. Even the governor was caught in his bed. For the next 24 hours they ravaged the town and terrified the populace. Hatred of the Spanish, which had become a major motivation behind the buccaneers' depredations, led them to looting the bells, crosses and other sacred ornaments in the churches and taking hostages from amongst the leading citizens. With their booty as well as their prisoners in tow, they set out to return to Puerto Plata.

However, a hastily-organised force of nearly 1,000 men who had been rallied around from the countryside set an ambush. The buccaneers resisted stubbornly and, through their superior marksmanship and by threatening to mutilate their captives, drove off their attackers. They remained on the coast waiting for the ransom they had demanded but when it did not materialise they reluctantly released the hostages and returned to Tortuga, barely satisfied with 300 crowns each as a share of the booty.

By 1659 an enterprising Frenchman, Jérémie Deschamps, Seigneur du Rausset, who had lived in Tortuga under LeVasseur, had successfully petitioned the English government to give him a commission to govern Tortuga and hold in the English interest. Watts, on learning that he was to be replaced, packed up his family and belongings and resettled in New England. As in the instance of LeVasseur's dealings with de Poincy, duplicity was once again the order of the day. Deschamps, on being reprimanded by Jamaica's Governor D'Oyley for legitimising buccaneers to perform acts of piracy, maintained he had a commission from the French authorities which to his way of thinking superseded the English instrument of power. With more French on the island than English, Deschamps hoisted the French colours and once again Tortuga was claimed for France.

James Arundell, a former colonel in Charles II's ill-fated army in England and who had married Watts' daughter, was given permission by Governor D'Oyley to regain Tortuga, which he did in Deschamps' absence from the island. He surprised Deschamps' deputy, Sieur de la Place, and briefly held power before being disarmed and put on a boat back to Jamaica. Arundell's bad luck pursued him. Off Matanzas in Cuba the Spanish seized the vessel and he was executed, his head being publicly displayed in the town of Puerto Principe.

De la Place had succeeded Deschamps after the latter had returned to France in ill-health where he was arrested, seemingly for having entered into negotiation with the English to return Tortuga to their ownership on condition that he was reimbursed with £6,000, a substantial amount at that time. Deschamps wisely changed his mind after a short stay in the notorious Bastille prison and afterwards ceded his rights to the French West India Company which had become the agent for France's Caribbean colonies.

Profit was now the foremost consideration in the administration of the island for the new governor, an ex-buccaneer, Bertrand d'Ogeron. History has subsequently acknowledged the significant role d'Ogeron played in advancing the colonisation of western Hispaniola and consolidating French power in the Caribbean. He has been described as generous, resourceful, imaginative, and possessing an indomitable will. First establishing himself at Port Margot, opposite Tortuga, in 1665, he set about wooing buccaneers, settlers and traders alike.

Writing to Jean-Baptiste Colbert, founder of the new French West India Company, d'Ogeron, in an effort to consolidate the French position in Tortuga, wrote:

'Seven or eight hundred Frenchmen are living along the shores of this Spanish island (Hispaniola) in inaccessible places surrounded by mountains, or huge rocks, or the sea and go abroad everywhere in little canoes. They live three or four or six or ten together, more or less separated one group from the other by distances of two or three or six or eight leagues wherever they find suitable places, and live like savages without recognising any authority, without a leader of their own, and they commit a thousand robberies. They have stolen several Dutch and English ships which has caused us much trouble; they live on the meat of wild boars and cattle, and grow a little tobacco which they trade for arms, munitions, and supplies. Thus it will be necessary for His Majesty to give an order which would compel these men to leave the Spanish island. They should be ordered under the pain of death to settle in Tortuga which they would do without doubt if it were fortified.'

He encouraged trade by providing two ships to sail between France and the colony, at the same time levying a five per cent customs duty to please his employers. When France made peace with Spain, he obtained commissions from Portugal and attracted French buccaneers back from Port Royal. But his most ingenious manoeuvre, designed to persuade the buccaneers to settle on the land, was to bring several batches of 50 women, prostitutes and petty criminals, from the prisons of France. They were not obliged to marry but if they did their partner had two responsibilities: to pay for her transportation and to treat his woman suitably as a companion or run the risk of having the marriage dissolved by the governor.

The first contingent arrived in 1666. This was how the event was described:

'The men formed a semicircle on the beach; many of them had shaved. The women were made to disembark in tens. When the canoe ran aground on the sand they jumped into the water with their skirts raised halfway up their thighs and there they waited for the rest of their companions. Everyone remained silent until the last woman had stepped off onto the land. The women did not dare to look the men in the face and the latter seemed indifferent. Suddenly one of the brotherhood stepped out from among the others and leaning on his rifle began a long, ceremonious, grave and grandiloquent speech. He spoke of good behaviour, honesty, fidelity and even redemption. Ultimately he said to the women that since they had chosen this line of conduct they should follow it at all costs and correct their base instincts. The sale was conducted absolutely calmly.'

Under d'Ogeron's resourceful leadership, the colony grew but there was a growing number of settlers on the Atlantic coast of Hispaniola and within the Cul-de-Sac that encompassed Léogane, Petit Goâve and the small village that was to become Haiti's capital, Port-au-Prince. He gradually transferred the seat of authority to the mainland town of Port-de-Paix. As the soil of Tortuga became overworked, farming on the mainland became more profitable. Meanwhile an increasing number of buccaneers began receiving their commissions and gathering at Petit Goâve.

~

'Suddenly one of the brotherhood stepped out from among the others and leaning on his rifle began a long, ceremonious, grave and grandiloquent speech. He spoke of good behaviour, honesty, fidelity and even redemption.'

Amongst the ranks of the buccaneers who sailed from Tortuga it would be hard to find one who gained as much notoriety as Nau L'Ollonais in the fact and fiction recorded during their era.

An imaginative artist's impression of a batch of prostitutes arriving in Tortuga from France in 1666.

Probably Exquemelin's account in *The Bucaniers of America*, written to be a popular best-seller, is the most colourful but undoubtedly there are moments in his telling of L'Ollonais' violent career that are exaggerated and quite possibly untrue.

He was probably born about 1630, the son of a small tradesman in Les Sables d'Olonne on the coast of France, and shipped out to the West Indies as an engagé. The master to whom he was indentured in Martinique apparently mistreated him brutally as did the buccaneer with whom he later escaped to Hispaniola. In one account of his early experiences, L'Ollonais was savagely beaten and left for dead in the woods only to survive and return to the camp where he dealt his tormentor a fatal blow with an axe.

He is next heard of taking part in a number of buccaneering voyages that brought him to the attention of M de la Place, then governor of Tortuga. The governor entrusted him with a small ship to carry out attacks on the Spanish. Perhaps hardened by the ill-treatment he had received as a young man, he quickly earned a reputation for cruelty which spread amongst the Spanish in the region.

When foul weather drove his ship on-shore off the coast of Campeche, he and his men were attacked by the waiting Spanish. The Frenchman, smearing himself with blood and lying beneath the corpses on the beach, was able to escape detection. After he had recovered, disguised in Spanish clothing he entered Campeche where he was able to convince some slaves, in exchange for their freedom, to steal a small boat with which they sailed back to Tortuga. Meanwhile his captured shipmates unwittingly swore to the Spanish that their captain had died on the beach.

Undeterred L'Ollonais set off again, this time to the coast of Cuba in a small vessel 'obtained by trickery' according to Exquemelin. Word got back to the governor of Havana that L'Ollonais was indeed alive. Alarmed by the prospect of L'Ollonais seeking revenge in his domain, the governor sent a ten-gun ship to intercept him.

The buccaneers had seized some barques used for coastal trading and, knowing of the Spanish ship's whereabouts, they took it by surprise, boarding their adversary with terrifying curses in a wild assault. L'Ollonais drove all his prisoners below deck and then, on learning that the governor had given instructions to hang every buccaneer, he brought them back on deck and beheaded them one by one. A single Spanish seaman was given a reprieve and a letter to the governor of Havana saying that he also hoped to give no quarter to the governor should he be given the chance.

Now in possession of a suitable vessel for a more ambitious excursion, L'Ollonais returned to Tortuga. With eight vessels, nearly 700 men in his fleet and a commission from Governor d'Ogeron, he sailed for Maracaibo on the lake of Venezuela in 1667. As Henry Morgan was later to learn, the entrance from the Caribbean Sea into the lake was not only narrow and seemingly easy to defend but also treacherous due to the shallow channels and sandbars. But by advancing on the Isla de las Palomas fort from the rear, the buccaneers took just four hours to subdue the defenders with only muskets and hand arms, destroying the cannons and walls of the fort as they departed.

A day later they entered the city of Maracaibo which was not, to their astonishment, prepared to 'fight to the last man' but in fact was absolutely deserted. The Spanish had taken their wives, their children and whatever possessions they could transport into the surrounding countryside. The buccaneers' first response was to gorge themselves on the food and drink left behind, occupying the finest residences as their billets. Next day L'Ollonais sent a party of 150 men to scour the outskirts. Several mules carrying goods including 20,000 pieces of eight, and a number of men and women were brought in. According to Exquemelin, L'Ollonais took his sword and hacked one of the prisoners to pieces in front of the others promising to repeat this bloodthirsty act if they would not reveal where their valuables were hidden. After two weeks the buccaneers then crossed the lake to ransack the prosperous farming town of Gibraltar.

Thanks to his determination and adequately forewarned of L'Ollonais' approach, the governor of nearby Merida had mustered a force of 800 men supported by a battery of 22 cannons. Blocking the main road to Gibraltar, the governor forced the invaders to use the marshlands to approach the town. By cutting down the trees before the settlement, the Spanish gunners were able to inflict severe losses on the buccaneers from behind their defensive line. The conflict was a stalemate bordering on a defeat until the quick-witted L'Ollonais used a not-unfamiliar ploy to deceive his enemies. He had his men pretend to retreat and, without stopping to consider the implications, the Spanish rushed out from behind their barricades only to be confronted by a renewed attack by the buccaneers.

With the Spanish gunners unable to engage their cannons for fear of firing on their own men, the buccaneers swarmed forward and soon had Gibraltar at their mercy. The intensity of the fighting and the ruthlessness of L'Ollonais' men left more than 500 Spanish dead, many wounded and hundreds of inhabitants and slaves soon in captivity. Against this, Exquemelin claims, only 40 dead and 30 were wounded on the opposing side.

As well as collecting what spoils they could find, the buccaneers demanded ransom in terms of money and supplies, largely cattle. With the use of torture – stretching a person on the rack was commonplace or burning the soles of their feet – and by threatening to demolish the town, they eventually produced results they wanted. Although only a few buildings were damaged, the looting of churches and convents was widespread. An unlikely explanation was given to the Spanish authorities that the sacred vessels, pictures, religious artefacts and bells were being taken to install in a new church to be dedicated to Our Lady of Victories on Tortuga.

The fleet sailed across the Caribbean to the familiar Isle à Vache where the booty was shared: 260,000 pieces of eight in coins, silver, gold and precious stones divided in the agreed manner of the Brotherhood of the Coast. Exquemelin also reveals that once the men were installed in the brothels and taverns of Basse Terre, their booty lasted a very short time.

By now L'Ollonais' reputation was reaching mythic proportions. He soon gathered another squadron of ships and several hundred men to raid the settlements on Lake Nicaragua. From the beginning this expedition had the stamp of disaster. Due to unfavourable weather and prevailing currents, they drifted past the San Juan River (which would have taken them to Lake Nicaragua) and entered the Gulf of Honduras. Capturing a Spanish merchant ship with 24 cannons at Puerto Cabello, they proceeded inland towards San Pedro but were subjected to a series of ambushes by troops of Spaniards. It was after facing one of these bloody diversions that, as recorded by Exquemelin in his book, L'Ollonais demonstrated how evil a man he had become. He was convinced that there must be an alternative road to his objective and, frustrated by his inability to get a positive answer from captured prisoners, he went berserk. As Exquemelin tells it: '... L'Ollonais, being possessed of a devil's fury, ripped open one of the prisoners with his cutlass, tore the living heart out of his body, gnawed at it, and then hurled it in the face of one of the others, saying, "show me another way or I will do the same to you".'

The buccaneers did eventually take San Pedro but gained little in the way of spoils. His fortunes barely improved over the next several months, fellow-captains deserting him one by one until he himself had the misfortune to land on the Gulf of Darien in search of supplies and was captured by Indians. One of his crew who managed to escape said L'Ollonais suffered an atrocity worthy of his own making when he was tortured, hacked to pieces, roasted and devoured by his captors. Perhaps not a typical buccaneer but L'Ollonais was the kind of man whose exploits became legendary.

One of Tortuga's most notorious inhabitants was Nau L'Ollonais whose cruelty was the stuff of legends.

Tortuga's population at its zenith may have exceeded 2,000 men, women and children with hundreds more slaves. In all, Tortuga's buccaneering era extended for 50 years from the early 1630s until the end of the century. Tortuga had proved the ideal gathering point for attacking Spanish shipping and possessions. The French and English authorities had recognised and exploited this. Only Port Royal in Jamaica came close to Tortuga in this regard and flourished for a much shorter period.

Before he died in 1675 in France, Governor d'Ogeron undertook one final task for his king. With war declared between France and Holland, he embarked with 300 buccaneers to join a French naval force intent on taking Curaçao. A storm drove them into the hands of the Spanish and those who did not drown were sentenced to serve in the silver mines of Peru. Fortunately for d'Ogeron, he managed to escape when the fort in which he was being held temporarily was assaulted by English buccaneers.

After the Treaty of Madrid in 1670, as a result of which the English in the Caribbean, albeit hesitatingly, acknowledged that they were at peace with Spain, Tortuga once again rose to prominence as the homeport of the buccaneers. Between 1678 and 1685, under official patronage, the French buccaneers carried on an extensive campaign of privateering. As the governor of French Hispaniola put it: 'The manner of life is very singular. They only raid the Spaniards and cruise to get something with which to come and eat and drink at Petit Goâve or in Tortuga.'

In 1678 Sieur de Grammont was leading the French buccaneers in a series of assaults on the Gulf of Venezuela whilst others were attacking the pearl fisheries at Margarita. Others who frequented Tortuga and northwestern Hispaniola included the Dutch buccaneers Nicholas Van Hoorn and Laurens de Graaf who, in 1683, carried out a spectacular raid on the Mexican port of Vera Cruz with its massive fortification, San Juan de Ulua.

The last quarter of the seventeenth century saw Tortuga decline in importance as several mainland ports such as Cape Haitien, Léogane, Gonâve and Petit Goâve further gained in importance. But while they lasted, Tortuga's 50 colourful years spanning both boucaniers and buccaneers left an indelible stamp on the history and heritage of the West Indies. An enduring legacy was the evolution of the modern-day state of Haiti which owes much to the skilful manipulation of the buccaneers by the foresighted governor, Bertrand d'Ogeron.

FRANCIS LOLONOIS.
Part. 2. Page. 1.

The depredations of Nau L'Ollonais reached mythic proportions after his sacking of Maracaibo and Gibraltar in Venezuela.

Chapter 4

PORT ROYAL

THE WICKEDEST CITY IN THE WORLD

~

The capture of the Spanish colony Jamaica in 1655 by the English marked the beginning of the heyday of buccaneering. As we shall see, there were a variety of reasons for this. What is most remarkable about the rise of 'the wickedest city in the world' is that two-thirds of its structures and 2,000 souls disappeared into the sea in less than 40 years.

Although Port Royal was the buccaneers' home port, they often rendezvoused at Bluefields Bay.

An incredible repository of seventeenth-century structures and artefacts still exists at Port Royal but unfortunately most of it is below the sea and some beneath the ground, which itself has an extremely shallow water table. The earthquake of 1692 was particularly destructive because many buildings suffered not only from the earthquake itself but also from the aftermath of wave activity. When the earthquake struck, the wharves toppled into 30 or 40 feet of water but many other structures slid or sank into the harbour. However, some buildings were close enough to the surface to be entered and their contents removed. The remains of Fort Rupert, built by Henry Morgan when he was lieutenant-governor in 1678, can still be seen on approaching the town from Kingston. Out in a lagoon is a part of its brick battery wall.

Fort James and Fort Carlisle disappeared under the waves but Fort Charles on the eastern side of the spit survived. Although extensively remodelled in the eighteenth century, a section of the fort's very early exterior wall can be seen at ground level. Archaeological searches in the second half of the twentieth century unearthed a wealth of articles used in daily life at the time the buccaneers were in residence. Regrettably, very few are on display for the visitors.

Fort Charles, considerably modified after it was originally erected in the seventeenth century, is the only remaining structure of that period in Port Royal still in use.

Aerial view of Port Royal today.

The Anglican church of St Peters, built after the earthquake, contains the grave of Lewis Galdy, a French Huguenot refugee who, according to the inscription, was 'swallowed up and spewed out by the earth in 1692' to live a while longer. The church also holds a set of communion plate alleged to be a gift of Sir Henry Morgan but it has been more accurately identified as early eighteenth-century North American silverware.

The bustling buccaneer port has given way to a quiet little town, home to fishermen, the coastguard and Kingston harbour's pilotage, which, while still taking pride in its heritage, offers little by way of insights into its raffish past.

If Tortuga can lay claim to be the birthplace of buccaneering, Port Royal was where it blossomed and flourished. Between 1657, when Governor Edward D'Oyley began luring buccaneers from Tortuga, and 1671, when Henry Morgan sacked Panama, Port Royal provided a secure safe harbour, a convenient port to repair and victual vessels, a marketplace for plunder and an amply-supplied fleshpot for the enjoyment of the profits of their endeavours.

Oliver Cromwell, who had deposed King Charles I, persuaded the English parliament to undertake his Western Design which identified Santo Domingo as the initial objective of a plan to encroach on Spain's American possessions. When this venture failed miserably, Jamaica was taken as a consolation prize and Port Royal built as a foothold.

Not that the English were unaware of the desirability of settling on the island. Sir Anthony Shirley in 1596 had easily surprised and overwhelmed Jamaica's Spanish capital, St Jago de la Vega. Again in 1643, the English privateer William Jackson, with a commission from the Puritan merchants in London, ended his Caribbean expedition by landing in what is now Kingston harbour. With 500 men he marched on the capital, overcoming the Spanish defences after several sharp encounters. With a ransom of 200 cattle, 10,000 pounds of cassava bread and 7,000 pieces of eight, Jackson waxed lyrical to his employers: 'Whatsoever is fabled by Ye Poets, or maintained by Historians, concerning ye Arcadian Plaines, or ye Thessalian Tempe, may here be verified and truly affirmed, touching ye delight and plenty of all necessaries conferred by nature upon this terrestrial Paradise, Jamaica ...' Despite the fact that his argument to establish a colony was quickly rebuffed, 23 of Jackson's own men deserted to the Spaniards in 'Paradise'.

A Spanish account of Jamaica written in 1652 by a former governor observed that unwelcome vessels made use of the many bays around Jamaica to be careened and refitted while supplying themselves '... with water, wood, oranges, limes and other wild fruits that abound and have sometimes got meat which is of much comfort to them'. Importantly, the Spanish recognised that Jamaica lay too conveniently close to the paths of their treasure galleons as they sailed from Cartagena and Vera Cruz to Havana en route to Spain and was a short sailing distance from their colonial settlements in Cuba, the Yucatan and Honduras.

The site of the future Port Royal at the end of a peninsula almost enclosing what is now the Kingston harbour had been retained by the Spanish solely for beaching their ships to rid the undersides of the avaricious teredos which ate into the wooden planking. But located as it was on the last of a series of cays, the English invaders recognised its primary importance for the defence of the harbour which had contained the Spanish settlement of Caguaya, the doorway to the original Spanish capital on its western perimeter.

General Robert Venables, commander-in-chief of the English invasion force, began the task of building fortifications within a month of landing. The work was accomplished at a slow pace, hampered by a shortage of provisions to feed his men and the onslaught of disease ranging from dysentery to yellow fever in the unfamiliar and debilitating tropical climate.

Barely a year later, Fort Cromwell, as it was called, comprised a circular stone tower around which, in a rectangular shape, there were primitive gun platforms mounted with 20 guns. Some had been brought from England and others taken following a raid on Santa Marta using the dozen ships left behind by Admiral William Penn, who with Venables had been assigned to carry out Cromwell's Western Design.

Having failed to capture Santo Domingo, Admiral William Penn and General Robert Venables sought compensation by invading Jamaica.

~

Over a period of five years both the fort and the settlement of 'the Point', or Cagway as it was called, took shape. The fort attracted military personnel as well as artisans responsible for its upkeep and improvement; merchants given licences to sell provisions and strong drink; storehouses, a dwelling place for the commander-in-chief, a forge, a church and a courthouse soon added for the use of the growing number of residents.

Progress was slow because almost all components for building had to be brought across the harbour from the official colonial warehousing situated at Passage Fort, as the English had renamed Caguaya. The nearby hills supplied limestone where the Spanish had built a lime kiln. The clay soil, near the old Spanish capital of St Jago de la Vega, made suitable bricks. Even potable water had to be transported over to the Point by seamen who usually quoted their tariff in gallons of brandy.

1660 saw the restoration of the monarchy in England and the renaming in 1662 of the fort, Fort Charles. With the settlement, soon to become Port Royal instead of the Point, the town was well on its way to assuming its legendary status. Four years later the 200 dwelling places had doubled in number and by 1672 doubled again. The area of the town was never greater than 60 acres in total. Squeezed into that space were houses, taverns, brothels, prisons, business places, artisans' workshops, public buildings, churches and warehouses. Land was reclaimed out of the sea on which to build private wharves by the increasing number of merchants. The southernmost point of land, in a hook-like formation, contained Chocolata Hole where shallow draft boats and turtle crawls, or pens, were accommodated.

The town's principal defence, Fort Charles with 38 guns near the end of the peninsula, was eventually complemented by Walker's Fort with 18 guns to the north. A vessel passing the point would have faced Fort James and its 26 guns in 1673 and five years later Fort Carlisle (14 guns) named in honour of the new governor, to the north. Morgan's Line (16 guns) and Fort Rupert (22 guns) at the southern end of the township were built largely as a result of Henry Morgan's energetic efforts when he was appointed lieutenant-governor. Port Royal was never to come under attack from land or sea but of its substantial fortifications only Fort Charles was to survive the catastrophic earthquake of 1692 intact.

Once the monarchy was restored in England in 1660, King Charles II gave his name to Fort Charles in a settlement now called Port Royal.

47

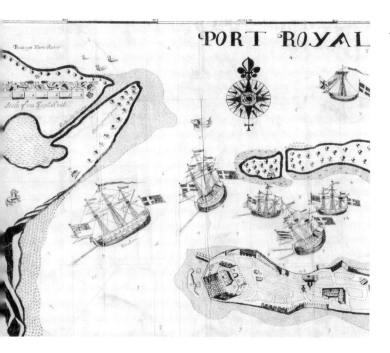

John Taylor's plan of Port Royal before 1692. Ringed as it was by six fortifications, Port Royal never came under attack.

The town's grid grew from a single thoroughfare, Thames Street, on the harbour across Queen, High, New, York, Tower and Church Streets to the Caribbean Sea on the southern extremity. Lime Street and Fishers' Row marked the western boundary. The streets were remarkably wide, from 20 to 30 feet in width, with lanes and alleys at irregular intervals but surfaced only in loose sand.

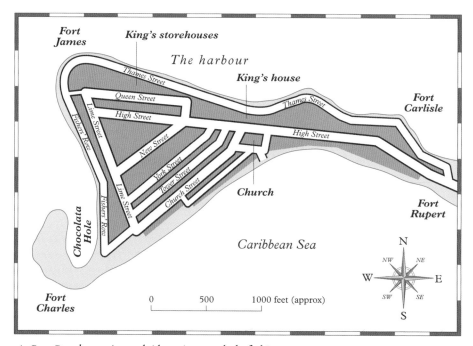

As Port Royal grew it was laid out in an orderly fashion.

Whilst the more impressive private and public structures were to be built of stone, three and four stories high, the less imposing buildings were constructed of timber, usually a single storey, with roofs thatched from palm leaves. Contemporary opinion is that Port Royal probably looked like a provincial English town in design and took little into consideration to compensate for the tropical climate. Its clutter and closeness led the 'fyremaster', Nicholas Keen, to be seriously concerned about its inflammability.

Port Royal was to become a bustling, thriving seaport town only just exceeded in population in the English-speaking Americas by Boston. John Taylor in his lively (unpublished) manuscript complains that rents were as high as in Cheapside, the business district of London. The shortage of land on this narrow spit, surrounded as it was by the sea on three sides, forced owners of land to build upwards as many as four storeys. The houses of affluent merchants would have cellars, a tiled roof, glazed sash windows, a porch and a separate entity in which to cook, all built on an area as cramped as 30 square feet.

The structures in Port Royal were built in close proximity to each other in much the same way as they were in London.

As well as having suitable if tight living quarters, most inhabitants of Port Royal enjoyed a comfortable, leisured life. At best, as John Taylor describes it, 'The Merchants and Gentry live here to the Height of Splendor, in full ease and plenty, being sumptuously arrayed, and attended on, and served by their Negro slaves ...' Allowing for his tendency to embroider the truth, Taylor made an assessment that was not entirely misleading. Situated as it was on a peninsula, Port Royal boasted a climate that was generally temperate by tropical standards enjoying constant light breezes. Even so, at midday businesses were shuttered for three hours during the heat of the day to allow for joining acquaintances in a tavern followed by a leisurely lunch, and a snooze in a hammock.

Far from being a remote outpost dependent on often-overdue supply vessels, living off the limited produce a newly-colonised territory could provide, Port Royal offered an astonishing range of foodstuffs and alcoholic drinks. Only fresh water posed a problem as it had no supply of its own. Although not cheap, food was available in variety, some imported from New England and Europe, the rest home-grown. Three markets offered three different types of provisions. At the central market on High Street they sold vegetables, fruits and herbs, in addition to fowls such as turkeys, ducks, pigeons, doves and parrots. At the western end of High Street

Port Royal's houses were built in close proximity to each other.

where the turtle crawls were maintained in Chocolata Hole, the market for meat was kept. Because meat had to be cooked quickly (or otherwise salted or dried) so that it would not rot in the tropical humidity, cows, pigs and sheep were slaughtered on the mainland side before daybreak and shipped across the harbour. The fish market was held on the wharf where local fare as well as cured fish from North America and England were purveyed.

What the colonists probably missed most was flour. It was seldom fit to eat after the Atlantic crossing and when it was it made a poor quality biscuit. Instead cassava, pressed to rid it of its poisonous juice, dried, grated and pressed into a wafer, was to prove an acceptable substitute. Taylor, despite lamenting the absence of English bread, said of the Port Royallers '... they live with full feed tables, not wanting anything requisite to satisfie, delight, and please curious appetites.' The problem of limited drinking water was resolved by making do from a wide choice of alcoholic drinks, in particular Madeira, brandy, French and German wine, beer and rum punch.

The composition of its population made Port Royal a distinctive urban community. As was the case with Barbados, it had a surprisingly higher percentage of women settlers to men. In less than 20 years after the taking of Jamaica, Port Royal had 529 women to 714 men, in addition to an astonishing 426 children. By the 1692 earthquake this number had increased to 1,600 men, 1,400 women and around 1,000 children. The number of slaves gradually grew as a proportion of the population so that by 1692 in a town of 6,500, 2,500 souls were slaves.

A substantial number of the white men were indentured servants, individuals transported to Jamaica as an outcome of their criminal sentencing or because they took part in political uprisings. Legally bonded for ten years, they were virtually slaves and often lived in worse conditions with even less privileges than the Africans who gradually replaced them. Even after their terms of servitude had expired, unless they possessed a tradesman's skill they were often forced by poverty to continue working for a callous and uncaring master.

John Taylor, who provided a vivid and sometimes exaggerated account of life in Port Royal, recalled the arrival and sale of indentured servants, including his own, on the ship *Saint George* on which he arrived on January 3, 1688. On the appointed day, Captain

Merchant ships brought merchandise and comestibles from England and New England to Port Royal.

51

James at ten in the morning fired a gun to indicate the commencement of the sale 'of the convicts and servants'. Taylor disposed of two women and a man for a return of $145 and, after paying the ship's captain $72 for his passage, he retained $73 which he describes as 'a profit not so considerable'.

The fact that Port Royal soon boasted an Anglican church, Jewish synagogue, Quaker meeting house, Presbyterian meeting house and Roman Catholic chapel suggests that a remarkable level of religious freedom was tolerated amongst its diverse population and, by the standards of the day, it must have been considered a haven for the persecuted. The Jews, however, although some dutifully joined the militia, still had to pay a special tax.

The bulk of the Port Royal population was initially made up of seamen, fishermen and those employed in the defence of the town. The profile of the population began to change as, for instance, merchants exporting the planters' agricultural products, selling imported goods or trading in the buccaneers' spoils required more slaves and servants. Records show that one sailmaker, Robert Phillips, had as many as 14 slaves. When he occupied the governor's house, Sir Henry Morgan kept ten white servants and 14 black slaves.

The largest single category of inhabitants of Port Royal, albeit peripatetic, was the men of many nations who became known collectively as buccaneers. Mainly English and French, their number also included Scots, Welsh, Portuguese, Dutch, Danes, Germans, Miskito Indians, Africans and even renegade Spaniards. In the 1660s and 1670s as many as 1200 of these 'wild, dissolute and tattered fellows' would roam the town.

Certainly for the decade of the 1660s the economy of Port Royal very much depended on the spoils that were brought to shore. Even after this period, the practice was encouraged for good financial reasons. The stolen cargoes gradually changed from precious metals, weapons and slaves to include merchandise such as cloth, wine, cacao, indigo, logwood and sugar. To serve the needs of the buccaneers, there existed '… Sodom fill'd with all manner of debauchery.' A wealthy planter, John Style, in 1670 protested that the number of 'tippling houses' had doubly increased, with more than a hundred licensed establishments as well as sugar works and rum distilleries which sold spirits without a licence.

As well as taverns the town had numerous 'punch or music houses', as brothels were euphemistically called, where John Taylor's 'vile strumpets and common prostitutes' plied their trade. Probably the most famous of these was English-born Mary Carleton, who became known as 'the German Princess' as a result of a brief visit to Germany. She married twice, the second time without legally disposing of her first husband for which she was charged with bigamy. Her skilful explanation earned her an acquittal by public proclamation. A play, 'The German Princess', celebrated her notoriety but in February, 1671, she was convicted of stealing and transported to Jamaica. Mary soon returned to her infamous ways earning a living by prostitution and theft. She made her mark in historical literature writing 'News from Jamaica in a letter from Port Royal, to her fellow collegiates and friends in Newgate' (the infamous London prison). Impatient for the lights of London, she rashly returned to England despite being originally sentenced to servitude for life in Jamaica. Soon she was arrested again for stealing and her identity revealed. This time she was condemned to hang from the notorious Tyburn gallows. Her career spawned a spate of sensational literature including one account that described her as '… common as a barber chair: no sooner was one out, but another was in. Cunning, crafty, subtle and hot in the pursuit of her intended designs …' Many of the buccaneers' female companions were probably not unlike Mary Carleton in disposition.

There is no doubt that prostitution thrived and, although Port Royal's otherwise comprehensive records are statistically silent on the subject, it is recorded that John Starre had an establishment noted by the 1680 census as having 21 white and two black women. The boisterous activities of the buccaneers have to be largely imagined although Exquemelin describes how they would spend 2,000 or 3,000 pieces of eight in a night without leaving themselves a good shirt to wear on their backs in the morning. He observed: 'I saw one of them give unto a common strumpet 500 pieces of eight only that he may see her naked.' On another occasion a buccaneer bought a cask of wine, placed it in the middle of the street and insisted that everyone passing should drink with him, brandishing a pistol to enforce his hospitality.

The most celebrated of Port Royal's denizens of the night was Mary Carleton, banished to Jamaica for thievery, who thrived on her immoral activities in the town.

It is no wonder that one man of God who witnessed the debauchery left on the same boat on which he had arrived, exclaiming: 'This town is the Sodom of the New World and since the majority of its population consists of pirates, cut-throats, whores and some of the vilest persons in the whole of the world, I felt my permanence there was of no use and I could better preach the Word of God elsewhere among a better sort of folk.'

Although drinking appears to have been one of the most habitual of recreations for townspeople and buccaneers alike, the choice of entertainment venues in Port Royal included coffee houses, a bear-baiting garden, a cockpit for cockfighting, with billiard rooms and shuttleboard in the taverns. Those who would finally take excess to extreme would either spend the night sobering up in a cage in the turtle market or be committed for more violent behaviour to Bridewell Prison for women and Marshallsea for men. Lesser offences resulted in time in a ducking stool or stocks. Ever present was the row of gibbets at nearby Gallows Point, normally reserved for pirates who committed an offence against the state.

Despite its relatively healthy location, its inhabitants succumbed to a variety of diseases common in the tropics. Dysentery, or the bloody flux as it was known, was often exacerbated by the heavy consumption of alcohol and could kill a person in four days. Yellow fever, tuberculosis, smallpox and other contagious illnesses were a constant threat and newcomers could not expect a long life. John Taylor notes that towards the end of the 1680s 'it hath pleased God to bestow on this place some few honest chirurgeons' (surgeons or, more specifically, the doctors of the era). Those who died were buried in a cemetery outside the Palisadoes gate at the northern end of the peninsula.

During the heyday of buccaneering Port Royal provided the perfect home port for the buccaneers. As well as having facilities for building and repairing ships, Port Royal could supply shipwrights and sailmakers. But more importantly still was the availability of vessels seized as prizes and put up for sale, either to be English merchantmen or more often to sail on marauding expeditions.

Jamaican-built vessels of less than 60 tons cost as little as a £100 and could be fully fitted out for the same again. This was a quantum leap from the pirogues and small sailing craft that the earliest buccaneers adopted. Larger vessels came into the buccaneers' hands as prizes and often sold for as little as a tenth of their original cost. When Captain Maurice Williams in 1664 brought in the *Santo Christo*, a small Spanish vessel separated from the galleon fleet in a hurricane, and had it sold by the Jamaican court for just £50, its owner Ximenes de Bohorques protested that it was worth several thousand pounds. Even Henry Morgan's flagship on his Portobelo and Panama expeditions was a Spanish prize.

Once equipped with a vessel a buccaneer captain, often in partnership with a Port Royaller like the governor or other prominent citizens, enlisted a crew. Whilst a merchant vessel strictly operating as a legitimate cargo carrier might have only one crew member for every eight tons of its weight, the buccaneers carried a man for every half a ton on vessels under 20 tons and more than the equivalent of a man per ton on one larger. The reason for this was simple: the captain of a vessel under attack was likely to capitulate faster if he saw the manpower odds were heavily stacked against him. In addition, a buccaneer captain would attempt to complete his assault as quickly as possible to avoid damaging his prize and then be able to man it with an adequate crew without seriously depleting his own ship.

Before departing Port Royal it was wise for the buccaneer captain to get a commission or letter of marque. These legally authorised him to seize enemy ships and goods and were conventionally issued in times of war. In peacetime they were an instrument of private redress whereby a country could authorise its citizens to seek compensation for injury at the hands of foreigners by giving them the authority to obtain recompense at the expense of the offending country's subjects. To the Spanish all intruders in the Caribbean were pirates and treated as such although other European nations normally recognised these commissions.

The governors of Jamaica were known to charge for issuing a commission. Sir Thomas Modyford, who was governor between 1664 and 1670, claimed his commissions cost £20 and demanded that the recipient return to port with his prize and surrender it to an admiralty court appointed by the crown. The court took one-fifteenth of the vessel's value for the king, a tenth for the admiralty and required that owners' expenses and profit be paid first before a distribution to the crew. Publicly Modyford even acknowledged that he earned at least £1,000 a year from the buccaneers, a useful sum in those days.

However, prizes taken at sea might be transporting mundane cargoes such as hides and agricultural products which would sell for only a few pounds. It was the forays on land which proved more lucrative. But because so many men were necessary for the undertaking, the return could be disappointing. Even if the captain ultimately disembarked in Port Royal, with a little skulduggery his benefactors could be cheated out of their portion by distributing the spoils en route.

Henry Morgan's 1668 raid on Portobelo proved particularly profitable and gave each man a £120 share, yet his remarkable feat of taking Maracaibo in 1669 produced only £30 a share. Lawrence Prince, who navigated the San Juan River and Lake Nicaragua to sack Granada, paid out no more than a £26 share. Whilst most buccaneers spent their earnings recklessly in the taverns and brothels of Port Royal, astute men like Henry Morgan and Lawrence Prince invested extensively in land in Jamaica and died wealthy men. In fact the profits secured off buccaneers and their prizes allowed many a Port Royal merchant to become an owner of a Jamaican plantation.

No comprehensive account exists of the changing fortunes of a buccaneer of Port Royal. However one historian, Nuala Zahedieh, recorded that of 12 out of 26 captains holding commissions between September 1662 and July 1663, six had been killed, one taken prisoner, two were cutting logwood, two had become planters and a few were still at sea eight years later.

~

The roll call of buccaneer captains who were part-time residents of Port Royal could fill a volume of its own. At the very height of the buccaneering era the English were in the majority but French and Dutch were amongst others who tasted the pleasures and sold their booty on the streets of the town, earning it briefly the title of 'the wickedest city in the world'.

Like the German Princess, many of the personalities who stamped their imprint on Port Royal's history were opportunists and adventurers. A naval captain, Abraham Langford, at Governor Windsor's behest made an abortive attempt to win over the Tortuga buccaneers in 1663 and then somehow persuaded their counterparts at Petit Goâve on the Hispaniola mainland to make him their chief. He then went to the court in London to petition Charles II to appoint him governor of 'Tortuga and the coasts of Hispaniola'. He was rebuffed and soon faded into obscurity but not before a contemporary observed '... he speaks no French, nor does he understand it; he is a man of no wisdom, his interest in Jamaica and person is despicable, his fortune forlorn, his honesty questionable'. Langford lived out his life in well-deserved obscurity.

The first acknowledged leader of the buccaneers, Edward Mansfield, first appeared at Port Royal when Governor D'Oyley granted him a 'let-pass', a simple licence to pass through Port Royal to wherever he wished to go. He was to lead the buccaneers on Christopher Myngs's assault on Campeche, about which we will hear more, and assumed command after Myngs was severely wounded.

One of Port Royal's more notorious temporary residents was Dutch-born Rock Brasiliano, so-called by the English when he found his way there in the late 1650s after being driven out of Bahia by the Spanish and Portuguese. Exquemelin provides an account of Brasiliano's Port Royal years from his rise as a newly-recruited buccaneer through his first success as captain of a small barque capturing a rich Spanish treasure ship and winning the acclaim of all Port Royal. His career was notable for the role he played in Morgan's sacking of Portobelo and Panama. According to his biographer '... in his domestic affairs he had no good behavior nor government over himself; for in these he would often times shew himself either brutish or foolish'. Apparently when drunk, Rock Brasiliano would be seen on the streets of Port Royal wilfully beating or wounding whomsoever he met. His Spanish victims suffered even more severely. Says Exquemelin, 'Unto the Spaniards he always showed himself very barbarous and cruel, only out of an inveterate hatred he had against the nation'. If Exquemelin is to be believed he ordered several of his captives to be roasted alive on wooden spits for little more than refusing to show him the whereabouts of hog pens where he could steal swine.

Another of Exquemelin's brief biographies is of Bartholomew Portuguese, who took a small vessel with 30 men and four guns out of Port Royal in search of a Spanish trophy. Luck and, later, determination led to his triumph over a richly-laden, Havana-bound galleon bearing 20 guns and 70 men. The same luck ran out when he crossed the path of three more Spanish ships and he and his men, along with their prize, were taken to Campeche where he was put on trial. Fearful that their notorious

Rock Brasiliano, a Dutch-born buccaneer, made Port Royal his home. His barbarity, it is said, extended to roasting one of his captives alive on a spit.

Another occasional inhabitant of Port Royal was Bartholomew Portuguese whose choice for pillaging was Campeche.

buccaneer might escape before his trial and sentencing, the authorities kept him on board a ship in the harbour. He escaped by secretly purchasing a knife, according to Exquemelin, and waiting until dark took the life of his sleeping guard. Not being able to swim, he fashioned two wine jars as floats and leapt overboard.

Portuguese made his way to the Bay of Campeche where he found several of his old comrades and persuaded them to return to Campeche intent on recovering his prize. Arriving after several days, he tricked the prize vessel's officers into believing he was simply transporting contraband cargo to the anchored vessel. Once on board, Portuguese and his men seized the ship and set sail for Port Royal. But again adversity prevailed and in a turbulent storm off Cuba's Isle of Pines his ship broke up and sank. Although he reached Jamaica in a canoe, says Exquemelin, in his further exploits Portuguese continued to meet nothing but misfortune which was more often than not the buccaneer's lot.

Port Royal would never have flourished as a buccaneer port without the sympathetic connivance and often overt support of the island's governors. Seldom in the seventeenth century was the English government able to provide adequate naval protection for its West Indian colonies which meant that the authorities had to use their ingenuity. Whilst some governors during the period had to acknowledge, usually belatedly, that there were periods when Spain was at peace with England, their efforts were less than successful in reining-in buccaneers. Other governors not only encouraged attacks on the Spanish but sought opportunities to profit from them personally.

The instructions that had been given by Oliver Cromwell in 1655 to Admiral William Penn and General Robert Venables were, simply put, to seize and destroy all Spanish ships and settlements. Spurred on by their ignominious defeat in Santo Domingo and bolstered by the facile conquest of Jamaica, the English only weeks later dispatched Penn's vice-admiral, William Goodson, into the Spanish Caribbean. With the few naval vessels left behind after Penn's hurried departure from Jamaica (for which he was briefly incarcerated in the Tower of London), Goodson seized Santa Marta on the coast of present-day Venezuela in the autumn of 1655, contemplated attacking Cartagena but lacked the forces, and in the following year sacked nearby Riohacha.

Two years after the capture of Jamaica the island received its first formal governor, Edward D'Oyley. He inherited an army with no way of paying them, a guerrilla force of Spanish still at large and the ever-present threat of a renewed attempt by the Spanish to recapture the island. As early as 1657 D'Oyley had begun wooing the Tortuga buccaneers to Port Royal, intending to create some sort of seaborne defence as well as savouring the prospect of handling their loot. Soon he was actively handing out commissions authorising attacks on Spanish vessels to the buccaneers.

It was Captain Christopher Myngs, Goodson's successor as the commander of Port Royal's dwindling naval squadron, who attracted the attention of the French buccaneers. After his own stunning success in 1658 at Santa Marta and Tolu in the following year, Myngs outdid himself on an expedition against Cumana, then Puerto Cabello and, finally, Coro, where his good fortune was to unearth 22 chests each containing 400 pounds of silver, with a value of over half a million pounds. By this time word of Myngs's successes had spread. When he was seeking support for a long-anticipated attack on Santiago de Cuba, he attracted the French buccaneers from Tortuga to Port Royal.

One of the earliest prizes to be incorporated into the navy at Port Royal was the Spanish prize *Angel Gabriell* which the governor acquired in 1659. Governor D'Oyley went out of his way to accommodate free enterprise at sea when Captain Maurice Williams was able to pay £120 for a Spanish merchant ship in an auction where he was the last bidder before a marked candle burned out. This was known as sale 'by inch of candle'. By proclamation, D'Oyley even allowed Captain Williams to recruit men from Myngs's naval frigate, *Marston Moor*. Williams was then granted permission to purchase five cannons from the royal warehouse to arm the vessel.

Shortly after Charles II was restored to the throne in 1662, D'Oyley was succeeded by Thomas, Lord Windsor. Windsor, albeit residing in Port Royal for a very short period, took a pragmatic view. It was he who would take the responsibility for Myngs's attack on Santiago de Cuba, the logical jumping-off point from which Spain would reclaim its former Jamaican colony. The Tortuga buccaneers were to play a major role in this assault, as did the soldiers and sailors who were remnants of the English invading force left behind by Penn and Venables.

The appointment of Sir Thomas Modyford in 1664 as governor of Jamaica not surprisingly coincided with the period in which Port Royal buccaneering reached its zenith, 1664-71. Born in Exeter, England, one of six sisters and five brothers, he was a barrister by profession and served on the Royalist side in the Civil War. He emigrated to Barbados when he was 27 years old and there was able to purchase a 500-acre plantation.

He soon became involved in the administration of the island's affairs and, despite opposition from many of his Royalist contemporaries, he threw his lot in with Cromwell's faction. For a period of six months after the restoration of the monarchy he held the position of governor but controversy followed as his Royalist predecessor was rumoured to be being brought back and Modyford was to be charged with treasonous behaviour. Fortunately Modyford was a kinsman of George Monck, Cromwell's foremost general who had managed to change sides and, elevated to the peerage of Duke of Albemarle, was held in high regard by Charles II. Modyford was never charged and, through Albemarle's influence, he was appointed Speaker of the

Assembly in Bridgetown. It was the Duke of Albemarle who proposed Modyford to replace Lord Windsor as governor of Jamaica in 1664 and in February, 1664, Thomas Modyford was knighted.

Modyford early on expressed a concern about Spain's dominance in the Caribbean. He had played a role in influencing Cromwell to undertake his Western Design and when the English fleet stopped in Barbados before sailing to Santo Domingo he was one of the men, as commander of a militia regiment, who helped General Venables raise recruits to join the expedition. Eight days after his 1664 arrival at Port Royal, one of his first duties was to carry out King Charles II's edict that 'for the future all acts of hostility against the Spaniards should cease'. Modyford initially acted in good faith to carry out his instructions. Spanish ships and their cargoes were returned to their owners if they were brought into Port Royal. Piracy was not to be indulged either. A Captain Munro, sailing with an earlier Jamaican commission, turned pirate and unwisely plundered several English ships off the island. When he was captured after putting up fierce resistance, Modyford saw that Munro and his men were tried and hung at Gallows Point for all to witness.

Modyford's other principal directive was to approach the Spanish colonies with the objective of encouraging trade with Jamaica. This was an unlikely prospect and quickly deemed to be unacceptable by the Spanish. This created the incentive to end the post-Restoration truce. His own brother-in-law, Thomas Kendall, bluntly put forward the case for once again issuing of commissions to the buccaneers: 'This must be done by fair means and giving them leave to dispose of their prizes when they come in, otherwise they will be alarmed and go to the French in Tortuga and his Majesty will lose 1,000 to 1,500 stout men …' This advice was taken and after nearly two months Modyford was able to report to the English authorities '… upon my gentleness to them, the privateers come in a-pace and cheerfully offer life and fortune to his Majesty's service'. Not a moment too soon as Lord Windsor, on instruction, had disbanded the remains of Venables's army and almost all royal naval vessels had been recalled to England.

However, Modyford's efforts to restrain the buccaneers were proving fruitless. Colonel Edward Morgan's buccaneer-supported expedition to St Eustatius and Saba aborted its mission to capture Curaçao. Later Modyford thought he had persuaded the acknowledged leader of the buccaneers, Edward Mansfield, to sail again against the principal Dutch island. Hardly had Mansfield's flotilla lost sight of Jamaica than it changed course for Cuba and then the Central American coast in search of Spanish plunder. The buccaneers were to prove recalcitrant on other occasions when their hunger for booty took precedence over political priorities.

Governor Modyford was all powerful in the young colony. He only summoned the Assembly together once and could rule by governor-in-council or proclamation. He frequently disregarded the authorities in England, controlled domestic revenue and dispensed judicial and military posts within his family. No governor after him ruled with such impunity. It could be said that on several occasions Governor Modyford launched a private war against the Spanish to justify attacks on England's possessions. During these times he sent Henry Morgan, admiral of the buccaneers after Mansfield's death, against Granada in Nicaragua, Puerto Principe in Cuba, Portobelo, Maracaibo and Panama. For a second time, in 1669, as governor he was ordered to proclaim on the streets of Port Royal that hostilities against the Spanish should cease but on this occasion the Spanish in the Caribbean themselves gave him an excuse for hostilities to resume when they actively began harassing English and French shipping.

Ironically, hardly had the Council of Jamaica passed a vote of thanks for Morgan's execution of his Panama victory (which is the subject of Chapter 10) than both Sir Thomas and Morgan were arrested. In July, 1670, the Treaty of Madrid had been signed between England and Spain acknowledging the sovereignty of the King of England over its West Indian colonies with the intention of settling the differences between the two nations in the Caribbean, imposing peace and ending attacks on land and at sea. But by May of the next year, Modyford had not yet received formal notification of the treaty from London and was able to argue with justification that Morgan's last expedition was carried out without his knowledge of any peace treaty.

To placate the Spanish Sir Thomas Modyford was replaced in 1671, arrested by the new governor, Sir Thomas Lynch, lured on board a vessel bound for England, and sent to England where he was incarcerated in the Tower of London until 1674. By this time his advocate, the Duke of Albemarle, had passed away. Modyford's son, unknown to his father, had earlier been held as a hostage in England in the Tower until his father's arrival, and Henry Morgan was to follow.

Lynch later boasted that he had been instrumental in eradicating piracy and ending the activities of the buccaneers in Port Royal. The Spanish made only half-hearted concessions to English traders in the Caribbean and continued to attack English shipping. The buccaneers were once again permitted to take up Port Royal commissions against the Dutch but English captains could always obtain a French commission in Tortuga or Petit Goâve to 'legitimately' attack the Spanish.

Much to Lynch's disgust, Henry Morgan was released from prison and knighted for his services to the crown. He was sent back as lieutenant-governor of Jamaica under the Earl of Carlisle after his friends had succeeded in clearing his name. A year later, Sir Thomas Modyford also returned, appointed as chief justice, where he lived quietly until his death four years later.

Modyford has been described as a creative politician and certainly for the nearly 20 years he held public office his contribution to the evolution of England's colonies of Barbados and Jamaica was substantial. This book does not address his successful initiatives to settle the land and create a viable agricultural economy but these were considerable. It was for his deft handling of the buccaneers that an eminent English historian declared in 1774: 'It is to the buccaneers we owe the possession of Jamaica to this hour'.

The epitaph on his tombstone in Spanish Town (St Jago de la Vega) brought his career to a fitting conclusion: 'Mistake not reader, for here lyes not only the

On June 7, 1692, two-thirds of Port Royal toppled, slid or sank into the sea in a cataclysmic earthquake.

deceased body of the honorable Sir Thomas Modyford Barronett, but even the soule and life of all Jamaica, who first made it what it now is. Here lyes the best and longest governor, the most considerable planter, the ablest and upright judge this island ever enjoyed'.

Despite the 1670 Treaty of Madrid, Port Royal continued to attract the custom of the buccaneers but now Tortuga and ports on northwestern Hispaniola once again became the likely place to secure commissions against the Spanish. Port Royal had begun to thrive more on trade, including the slave commerce, and the plunder taken from the Spanish in the colony's early years had in many cases been converted into profitable sugar estates. Even so, in 1689, John Taylor was still able to describe Port Royal as 'a Sodom filled with all manner of debauchery'.

It was no surprise to the god-fearing that on Wednesday, June 7, 1692, a massive earthquake struck the island of Jamaica as the residents of Port Royal were beginning their noon siesta. In a matter of minutes, two-thirds of the town had slid or sunk into the sea and at the end of a series of aftershocks and tidal waves nearly 2,000 people had died, many crushed under their own buildings. In the days that passed another 2,000 inhabitants were to perish from injury and disease. Of the 60 acres only 25 remained. Fort Charles was the only defence left unscathed as all the warehouses and the entire waterfront disappeared into the murky water. If there was ever to be a dramatic grand and spectacular finale to an era in English buccaneering history, it was to be the Great Earthquake of 1692.

Chapter 5

THE 'OTHER BUCCANEERS'

~

From the day that the English captured Jamaica, successive governors expected Spain to reclaim their former colony. Not only had the Spanish who escaped from Jamaica fled to Santiago de Cuba, then Cuba's capital, at the eastern end of the country, but the city was also the closest geographical point to the island they had lost. Virtually deprived of an effective naval presence in the West Indies, the English quickly recognised that the Tortuga buccaneers could be useful in protecting their new colony. It was on Christopher Myngs's expedition to Santiago de Cuba that their mettle was first tested in this role.

Already nearly 140 years old in 1655, Santiago de Cuba was a city of considerable size. Its original centre, the Plaza de Armas, now named Parque Cespedes, proudly retains evidence of its colonial heritage. More of a plaza than a park, it is bordered on one side by the oldest residential building in Cuba, the home and office of Diego Velazquez, its first governor, which has been maintained as the Museo de Ambiente Historico Cubano.

In the 1600s it was the so-called House of Transactions and the ground floor still has an old furnace in which gold ingots were made. A fascinating collection of colonial furniture, weapons and bric-a-brac includes two first-floor rooms representing the latter half of the seventeenth century with an elegant carved mahogany chest, Velazquez's portrait and a number of attractive ceramic pieces. As a reminder of its vulnerability, the building houses a small cannon covering the approach from the harbour.

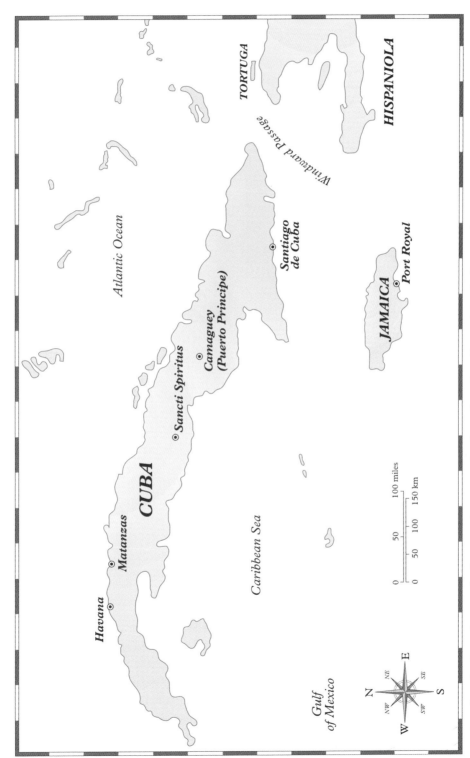

Santiago de Cuba, located 150 miles from Jamaica, expected to be used as a base for regaining its former colony.

The Museo de Ambiente Historico Cubano in the Parque Cespedes (the original Plaza de Armas) was the residence of the first governor, Diego Velazquez.

On the south side of the square is the Cathedral de Nuestra Senora de la Asuncion. Velazquez oversaw the construction of the first cathedral in 1522 but thanks to the depredations of pirates, buccaneers and earthquakes it has been rebuilt several times. On the northern perimeter of Parque Cespedes sits the town hall, an architectural reproduction of the original colonial building.

Approximately three blocks away is the Balcon de Velazquez which was originally a sixteenth-century lookout point monitoring vessels entering the harbour. The fortification contains a semi-circle of cannons and in the centre of the patio there was the entrance to a tunnel running down to the waterfront for besieged residents.

Eight miles south of the city stands El Castillo de Morro San Pedro de la Roca – commonly referred to as El Morro – built between 1633 and 1639 but restored after Christopher Myngs's attack.

This massive stone edifice stretches down the cliff on five different levels and overlooks the entrance to the bay. It consists of a maze of gun batteries, an ammunition storeroom, a chapel and dormitories for 150 soldiers. Rooms have been set aside for an exhibition about the 'corsarios'. Perhaps it is the magnitude of the castle's outer walls and massive drawbridge with its deep moat that convinces one of its impregnability. The original fort and four bastions were built in 1638 after a visit by the legendary Italian-born military engineer, Juan Bautista Antonelli. Between 1663 and 1669 it was expanded and reinforced to look more or less as it does today.

El Castillo still stands at the entrance to the harbour of Santiago de Cuba.

The first governor of Santiago de Cuba, Diego Velazquez, originally founded a village on the hill overlooking the harbour in 1515 and seven years later the first cathedral was begun. Although its early population barely numbered 50, it had all the administrative trappings of a well-ordered Spanish colonial city (a designation granted early in its existence): a civic council, a treasury, a formal residence for the civil and military governor and la casa de contraction (the board of trade). The settlers lived in simple dwellings made of sun-dried bricks, and palm leaves. The economy of Santiago and surrounding settlements grew in large part thanks to legal and illegal trading with other Europeans. Sugar, cattle, gold and copper allowed the population to prosper despite the ever-present threat of tropical hurricanes and French and English pirates.

A French corsair, who had earlier captured a valuable Spanish galleon heading home, sailed into port to be met by a well-known dealer in contraband slaves and horses, Diego Perez, on board his vessel the *Magdalena*, an armed merchant-ship. In a naval engagement that lasted only a few hours, Perez repulsed the Frenchmen using guns against crossbows for a loss of only three dead. The pirates counted six dead and over 80 wounded. For his contribution to the defence of Santiago it seems Perez appealed for recognition from the crown in the form of a heraldic coat of arms. Another Spanish report of French audacity tells of a pirate, possibly a Gascon by the name of Hallebarde, who entered Santiago harbour and seized a Spanish caravel at anchor. Locking the crew up below deck, he took the vessel out of the harbour and he left the luckless men up the coast before disappearing with the boat and its cargo.

Probably the most devastating raid on Santiago prior to that of the Englishman Christopher Myngs over a century later took place in October, 1554, when a notorious peg-legged Frenchman Francois le Clerc, better known as Jambe de Bois (or Pie de Palo by the Spanish), stormed the town with 300 men and a fleet of eight ships. Staying for a month, Le Clerc's men reputedly extorted 80,000 pieces of eight from its inhabitants.

A son's decision to avenge his French pirate father resulted in the eventual sacking of Santiago de Cuba in 1586 and almost led to the abandonment of the city. The father, known as Ricarte by the French and Mota by the Spanish, a Portuguese pirate actually living in Cuba, captured a Spanish coastal trading vessel captained by a Captain Casanova. Ricarte demanded a ransom and sent Casanova to collect the money. Meanwhile, hearing of the presence of the French, Captain Gomez de Rojas retrieved Casanova's ship killing a number of pirates and arresting their leader. Ricarte's son, a member of the crew, somehow managed to escape. The Spanish captain took the heads of the dead and displayed them on pikes in nearby Bayamo, jailing ten prisoners. The church demanded that they face the dreaded Inquisition but Gomez de Rojas, fearing that they knew Cuba's coast too well and might abscond, took them out at midnight and hung them.

The younger Ricarte entered Santiago harbour with two vessels in search of his father but was defeated and took flight to Tortuga. The Frenchman returned, now strengthened by six ships and purportedly 800 men, intent on attacking by land and sea. Despite desperate resistance from the Spanish militia and a heavy loss of casualties, the pirates took control of the town and laid it to waste, destroying the dwellings and smashing the religious icons in the church, monastery and cathedral.

After their departure, serious consideration was given to abandoning the town because of its vulnerability. Repeated attacks over half a century were disheartening to say the least and Spain was unable to provide the resources for Santiago's defence. Captain Alonso de Miranda, one of the town's oldest residents, led the argument to rebuild, to which the colonial authorities finally acquiesced. Gomez de Rojas called for markets to open, artisans to return to work, organised for the city to be cleaned up and ordered Mass to be sung. It took some time for Santiago to recover, with the women and children returning from the nearby town of El Caney where they had taken refuge. On hearing of the disaster, the Spanish king granted funds to restore the sacred buildings. But it was to take decades before Santiago de Cuba achieved any semblance of a continuously peaceful existence and by that time Havana had been designated the capital of Cuba.

Santiago de Cuba drew the attention of one of the most notorious Dutch sea-rovers, Cornelius Jol, also known as Pie de Palo because of his peg-leg. Under the flag of the powerful West India Company, he set out from Holland with two small craft with Santiago on his target. He cunningly dressed crew members as monks and priests of the Roman Catholic faith in order to enter the harbour without raising an alarm. Taken in by the ruse, the governor sent out a sloop to meet them but realising his error it turned about face. In the skirmish that followed the crew were captured, the captain killed and several other ships in the harbour seized. Jol began negotiating with the governor to ransom his captives. Despite commanding only a small militia, the governor indignantly refused to discuss such a possibility and after an extended barrage of fire from both sides the Dutch withdrew.

The proximity of Santiago to Jamaica profited it from the time the latter was first settled. Tobacco, timber, cattle and sugar were exported to Jamaica during its years as a Spanish colony. Soon Santiago de Cuba also became a hub for slave-trading. Ideally situated geographically, Santiago became the ideal point for launching the invasion of Mexico. Possessing one of the best harbours in the Caribbean was to make it an attractive port for trading which soon developed as a consequence of the demand for the contraband cargo carried by Dutch, French and eventually English ships in defiance of the authorities in Spain. By the middle of the sixteenth century every port in eastern Cuba was being used for illegal trading and Santiago de Cuba was a prime example. Indeed, a Captain Francisco de Godoy who commanded its garrison of 50 men was executed by the local authorities on trumped-up charges because he had dared to prevent this trade in the harbour.

When work began on a battery at the mouth of the harbour in 1567, the residents forced it to stop because of its potential effect on illegal trading. It was even suggested that the corsairs might actually make Santiago de Cuba a permanent base. Despite this, the powerful Audencia in Santo Domingo refused to finance its defence. Whilst the inhabitants initially had to depend almost entirely on their own resources to provide the manpower for the defence of their town, the crown finally granted funds to build fortifications to protect the harbour. Castillo de Morro was constructed with a battery, La Estrella, below it almost at sea level, at the entrance to the port overlooking the 60-yard entrance from the Caribbean Sea. Santa Catalina fortress was added to make access to the harbour supposedly impossible. It was the invasion of Jamaica by the English a century later that reinforced the need for the defences of Santiago to be continuously revived.

Cromwell's force under Penn and Venables did not stay long enough on the island to witness the final defeat of the Spanish. It took eight years to drive the Spanish out of Jamaica once and for all. During that time there were numerous occasions on which the remaining Spanish were supplied from Santiago de Cuba and at least two major troop landings began there intended to initiate the process of recapturing the island for Spain.

Ironically it was the experience of guerrilla warfare in Jamaica opposing the Spanish (who were initially assisted by their former slaves) that was one of two factors that turned the English army survivors in Jamaica into men capable of fighting in tropical conditions. The other factor was their gradual acclimatisation to the heat, humidity and disease-ridden conditions in which they found themselves.

These were the men who were to accompany Christopher Myngs on his ventures in the Caribbean. They joined ships commissioned by the English authorities to serve under leaders like Mansfield and Morgan, becoming 'the other buccaneers', fighting alongside the former boucaniers from Tortuga. Before we accompany these new buccaneers in the attack on Santiago some understanding of who they were will help to understand their motivation.

Contrary to the little knowledge we have of the boucaniers turned buccaneers, we know much more about the pedigree of the soldiers who arrived in Jamaica with Penn and Venables. Oliver Cromwell had given his brother-in-law, Major-General Desborough, the task of raising 2,500 men to fulfil his Western Design and terminate the Spanish colonial monopoly in the Caribbean. Constrained by time, Desborough, instead of drawing from regiments in Ireland as proposed by the expedition's military leader, General Venables, sought volunteers from the army in England. This offered the ideal opportunity for commanding officers to get rid of their undesirables and troublemakers. When insufficient numbers were gathered, the shortfall was made up by recruiting gangs who marched through the streets of London seeking 'volunteers'.

These recruits were sarcastically described in a contemporary report by one of their number as 'hectors, and knights of the blade, with common cheats, thieves, cutpurses, and such lewd persons, who had long time lived by sleight of hand, and dexterity of wit, and were now making a fair progress unto Newgate from whence they were to proceed towards Tyburn'.

Daily provisions were quickly put on board the invasion flotilla: half a pound of bread per man per day, a pint of oatmeal, a pint of peas, or a pound of flour per day for four men and a butt of brandy for each regiment. But these were to be remorselessly depleted by weevils, rats, cockroaches, ants, earwigs and, quite simply, spoilage.

Accompanying the fleet under Admiral Penn was Vice-Admiral William Goodson, commanding a sea regiment of 1,000 men. Goodson was said to have lived for a time in Cartagena and have had some knowledge of Spain's Caribbean colonies. Dissatisfied with the size of his fighting force, Venables arrived in Barbados at the end of January, 1655, seeking more recruits. Several thousand men volunteered from Barbados and the other English-settled islands of St Christopher, Nevis and Montserrat. Although largely unskilled in military technique, these recruits had the advantage of at least being acclimatised and less susceptible to tropical disease. Many were indentured servants bonded to work for many years before earning their freedom. To them General Venables offered their release if they enlisted for the campaign. This severely distressed the plantation owners who themselves desperately needed labour. Amongst their number it was said that several prostitutes dressed as men managed to board Penn's ships.

A total of seven regiments numbering almost 8,000 men sailed to Santo Domingo where, in the ensuing debacle, over a thousand died in battle or from sickness. Worse was to come. The English force landed at Passage Fort on Hunt's Bay near present-day Kingston on May 10, 1655, easily overwhelming the Spanish resistance before marching six miles to the capital, St Jago de la Vega (Spanish Town).

The invading force carried inadequate supplies and, to add to the dilemma, the Spanish population was a third of its size and, although the Spanish were largely settled around the capital, they were also scattered across the island. This meant that the local supply of livestock and crops was very quickly consumed. The English invasion had taken place in the dry season, a time when seed could not be planted although officers were directed to put their men to work as farmers. Those who had been bondsmen in the other islands found themselves once more tilling the soil instead of reaping the fortunes of war by ravaging lucrative Spanish outposts in the Caribbean. Many preferred to be returned to England and, as this did not materialise, they were encouraged to sabotage the farming in the hope of achieving the desired result.

They found themselves foraging for food, hunting wild boar and abandoned cattle, exposing themselves to ambush by the Spanish guerrillas when they travelled too far from their encampments. At times they were reduced to eating rats, lizards and the large iguanas that populated Jamaica. Major-General Robert Sedgwick wrote to the Navy Commissioners: 'The state of our army is sad, as God has visited us with a sore hand of sickness, tearing and snatching us away with much displeasure … what God will do with us he knoweth best'. Tragically it was dysentery and malaria which had travelled with them from Santo Domingo that took the lives of the troops more often than a shortage of food. After the invasion 140 men were dying each week. In November only 3,710 of the original 7,000 were still alive. By May, 1656, approximately 5,000 army officers and men had perished.

Although Cromwell dispatched another 1,200 seasoned veterans under Major-General William Brayne in the same year, by the time the English army in Jamaica was formally disbanded in October, 1662, it numbered just 1,523. Of these, 400 foot soldiers and 150 cavalry were to form Jamaica's colonial defence force. Those who were redundant were attracted by the prospect of Spanish plunder and flocked to Port Royal to join in the buccaneering exploits that dominated Caribbean history for the next 30 years. Wearing their battered tricorn hats and faded red coats issued to them by Oliver Cromwell, they sharply contrasted with the ragged but more suitably attired boucaniers.

The men who served in Vice-Admiral Goodson's fleet fared considerably better, not only thanks to the seaborne climate but also because they were subject to tight naval discipline. Because Cromwell had decreed that all Spanish colonial possessions should be the target of attack, plunder and destruction, Goodson quickly seized the opportunity to take to the high seas. Santiago was the first objective contemplated because of the likelihood that a counter-attack on Jamaica would emanate from there. However, within two months of the successful capture of Jamaica he had sailed to Santa Marta on the Spanish colonial mainland and seized the town with only 120 men. The populace had fled with their possessions and Goodson's ransom demand was denied. After two weeks of pillaging his men loaded 32 pieces of ordnance on board, put the town to the torch and departed. Less than a year later he inflicted a similar blow on Riohacha. He considered meting out similar treatment again to Santa Marta and nearby Cartagena. It was at Riohacha that Christopher Myngs was to have his first taste of naval warfare in the tropics, barely six years before he took Santiago de Cuba with the largest force of English buccaneers ever assembled.

Christopher Myngs (also spelt 'Mings') was born in 1625 into a prosperous Norfolk family and is believed to have gone to sea in his youth in a coastal trading vessel. He joined the navy and served with Thomas Brooks, a chaplain to Admiral Rainsborough, who was to become Myngs's mentor. Brooks wrote to the Admiralty Commissioner seeking promotion for young Myngs on the grounds that 'he found him religious and of much valour'. As it happened, Myngs had had to bring home the naval vessel *Elizabeth* from the Mediterranean when her captain was killed during a skirmish with a Dutch warship in May, 1653. Myngs was given the vacancy on the *Elizabeth* and in the October 1655, thanks to his mentor again, he was promoted to the command of the *Marston Moor* which had recently returned from Jamaica transporting General Robert Venables.

Ordered back to Jamaica, the crew of the *Marston Moor*, who had not been paid or suitably rewarded with any spoils from their earlier West Indian excursion, threatened to mutiny. Myngs took swift, decisive action ejecting many of the men and moving anchorage from Portsmouth to Spithead where he paid the men he had retained over the objection of the local admiralty agent. His strength of personality would prove to serve him well in his taking of Santiago de Cuba.

Christopher Myngs, the senior naval commander in Jamaica, was able to seize Santiago de Cuba by enrolling the remnants of General Venables's army.

In a continuing endeavour to relieve the Spanish treasure galleons of their valuable cargo after Riohacha, Goodson and Myngs plied the Caribbean in search of the treasure galleons without success. Later in 1656 this fleet, led by Governor Luke Stokes, was used to transport 1,400 settlers from Nevis to populate the much larger island of Jamaica. Early in the New Year Goodson, complaining of ill-health, departed for England. Myngs followed in the *Marston Moor* which required refitting, arriving in Dover in July. He was granted leave of absence to get married, after which he left for Jamaica once again in December with three supply ships and, according to naval records, the sum of £2,572.17.11½d to fortify the island.

He arrived in Bridgetown, Barbados, on February 20, 1658, where he confiscated six Dutch merchant vessels which he maintained were trading contrary to English regulations. These he carried into Cagway where he claimed them as his prizes. Much to his disgust, the authorities ruled that five of them should be released on technicalities.

Captain Myngs was now the senior naval officer in command in Jamaica with a small squadron, as the eighteenth-century historian Edward Long declared '… maintained at Jamaica to finally compel the Spaniards into a solid, durable peace, by annoying them in every quarter and interrupting their navigation'.

But his first priority had to be defence and one of his earliest missions was to confront 500 soldiers landed off four Spanish transports on Jamaica's north coast. With a substantial contingent carried in ten ships, Myngs crushed the invaders in a brief pitched battle. The Spanish artillery captured proved useful in equipping Cagway's primitive fortifications.

More to Christopher Myngs's liking was the offensive aspect of his responsibilities. He assaulted Santa Marta, following in the footsteps of his predecessor, and Tolu with little loss of men. A Spanish account of these incidents describes the Englishman as 'the terrible Cristobal Myngs, whose mere presence would inspire terror'. Setting sail for home, he intercepted three Spanish merchant ships and sold them as prizes

The naval warship Marston Moor *played an integral role in Admiral Myngs's life, carrying him to England on trumped-up charges of defrauding the state.*

to men who were to become well-known buccaneer captains in their own right: Robert Searle, John Morris and a Dutchman, Laurens Prins, or Lawrence Prince.

By the beginning of 1659 Captain Christopher Myngs, his seamen and his Jamaican recruits were attracting the attention of not only the Spanish colonial authorities but also numbers of adventurers and pirates who wanted to enrich themselves under the legal protection of commissions from Jamaica's governor. These commissions were primarily intended to save Cromwell's government the cost of maintaining a large naval presence in the West Indies. It was expected that the type of individual who would respond to a buccaneer captain's call would come from society's lower strata. In fact, the governor of Nottingham goal wrote that he had 'some very drunken men and quarrelsome' who would fit the bill perfectly.

With a commission from the governor, Colonel Edward D'Oyley, Myngs set off in his frigates, *Marston Moor*, *Hector* and John Searle's *Cagway* in early 1659. He sailed east, tacking as he did, to fall upon the unsuspecting and ill-prepared town of Cumana. With the wind now in his favour, he quickly set off westward for Puerto Cabello before a warning could reach them and then, once again sailing west, he surprised the town of Coro. Here his good fortune proved greater than he might have anticipated.

In the harbour were two Dutch ships flying Spanish colours carrying 22 or more chests each containing 400 pounds of silver ingots as well as coins, the property of the King of Spain. Whilst the populace of Cagway enthusiastically welcomed the return of the buccaneers, the authorities were not entirely pleased. It was evident that the chests had been opened and part of their contents removed. When challenged about the disappearance of some of the booty, Christopher Myngs did not deny the charge but contended that it was a standard practice during expeditions such as his to expect such losses.

Governor D'Oyley was not persuaded and, suspending Myngs from duty, ordered the *Marston Moor* back to England for him to stand trial for defrauding the state. In official despatches he sarcastically referred to Myngs as 'the wonder-doing captain of the *Marston Moor*'. To the dismay of the other captains, D'Oyley also withdrew the commissions he had issued. In Jamaica, too, Myngs had his enemies, probably at least in part because his sympathies were with the Royalists. One outspoken planter described him as '… a proud, plain speaking fool, and a knave in cheating the state and robbing the merchants'. Opinion of him was better in London where a council of war cleared him of all charges in June, 1660, a time when England was going through the throes of restoring the monarchy. His case was probably helped when it was revealed that Governor D'Oyley and his cohorts had also helped themselves to some of the spoils unknown to Myngs at the time. Events appear to have delayed the return of Myngs, once again restored to his naval command, until April, 1662 when he accompanied the new governor Thomas, Lord Windsor, in the 46-gun warship *Centurion*. But what would be England's new policy towards colonial Spain now that the monarchy had been restored?

~

Charles II had been crowned on May 8, 1660. Cromwell's opposition to Spain had been essentially about religion: Puritanism versus Catholicism. The new king was indeed an acknowledged Roman Catholic but he was not inclined to allow religious differences to dictate foreign policy. During his years in the wilderness, he had permitted a secret treaty to be negotiated with the Spanish which would have handed back Jamaica to Spain. Although after the Restoration he was pressured to honour the agreement, he was less than enthusiastic as the Spanish throne had done little to assist his return to the throne. The situation became more complicated when Charles married the Portuguese princess, Catherine of Braganza, which led to an alliance with Portugal with whom Spain was at war.

It was not long before he put the secret treaty behind him with a series of directives to his colonial governors. The Council in Jamaica was of the opinion that Spain forbidding other nations to trade in its domain did not apply to the Caribbean. Lord Windsor effectively confirmed this when he arrived in Jamaica with Captain Myngs in August, 1662, with specific instructions 'to endeavour to obtain and preserve a good correspondence and free commence with the plantation belonging to the King of Spain' even resorting to force if necessary.

When Spanish governors in Santo Domingo and Puerto Rico replied to Windsor's 'good correspondence' and denied England permission to trade with their colonies, the die was cast. The Council of Jamaica passed two resolutions, one in August declaring that '… according to his Majesty's instructions to Lord Windsor, a trade by force or otherwise be endeavoured'. Another resolution in the following month stated '… that men be enlisted for a design by sea with the *Centurion* and other vessels'.

Santiago de Cuba was of continuing concern to Jamaica. Situated only 150 miles away, it was the source of supplies for the last of the guerrillas before they were finally withdrawn to a Cuba still harbouring a desire to return and restore the island to Spanish sovereignty. The English for their part realised they were not strong enough at the time to attack and hold Santiago, particularly as disease had reduced their numbers to a point

During his short tenure of the governorship of Jamaica, Lord Windsor had instructions to force the Spanish, if necessary, to allow the English to trade in the Caribbean.

where Vice-Admiral Goodson had said they '… had not enough men to secure their own quarters'. The arrival of Lord Windsor with his royal instructions and the return of Captain Myngs with his appetite for fighting the Spanish in August, 1662, suggested that the time was finally right.

It took less than a week to draw 1,300 volunteers to Port Royal (as Lord Windsor had renamed it), many of whom were disbanded soldiers whose attempts to live off the land had left them impoverished and eager to rejoin a fighting force. Commodore Myngs sailing in the *Centurion* was to be in command of a fleet of 11 buccaneers' vessels including a small one captained by Henry Morgan. Stores of fresh fruit and vegetables, salted beef, boucanned pork and casks of water drawn from the Rio Cobre across the harbour from Port Royal were put on board. Muskets, pikes, pistols and swords were distributed and armour issued. On September 21, 1662, the small armada sailed west to Negril Point. What transpired thereafter was well documented by Myngs himself in a report to Lord Windsor. The Spanish had their own somewhat conflicting accounts.

Don Pedro Morales was the governor of Santiago in 1662. It was anticipated at the time that sooner or later the English would seek to avenge the attacks on Jamaica and end Spanish hopes of retaking the island. The issue of the Spanish trading monopoly – already effectively ignored by the Spanish settlements themselves – was also going to be a challenge for the authorities. Morales had been warned from the start of the year that he should prepare for an English attack. Despite being a soldier, he seemed to be more concerned with enhancing his own fortunes and those of his family and colleagues than strengthening the defences of his city. His negligence was to prove fatal.

Myngs found that the prevailing wind blowing from the east made progress slow and it was not until September 25 that the fleet approached the Cuban coast. Here they came across a renegade royalist turned buccaneer, Sir Thomas Whetstone. Sir Thomas, curiously a nephew of Oliver Cromwell, had been confined in London's Marshallsea Prison for debt as a result of his self-indulgent lifestyle. His petition for £100 to satisfy his creditors and free him to depart for Jamaica was fortunately looked on with favour by King Charles II. Whetstone provided intelligence that Santiago had received no significant additional reinforcements in recent times. Myngs's captains met in a council of war to determine how best to take the town. There were bitter memories amongst those who had participated in the Santo Domingo campaign where they had been put on shore 30 miles from their objective and been decimated by sickness and ambush during the long march. The decision was to force their way past the heavily fortified entrance to the harbour and attack the town frontally.

In the end this strategy did not prove to be feasible. On October 5, when the Morro came into view, the wind was not sufficient to approach the narrow harbour entrance. Once the land breeze rose in the early evening it was impossible to enter. Not only were the guns of the castle intimidating but also the prospect of a safe passage through the channel was daunting at best.

By the time a new course of action was decided upon another six vessels had arrived from Port Royal, further strengthening Myngs's hand. He advised his captains that as conditions for an attempt to pass the Morro could not be implemented until the next day at the earliest, it was vital that a landing be made whilst night was falling. He chose the village of Aguadores at the mouth of the San Juan River east of the castle. Here 900 men landed unopposed, the few residents having fled to the town. Myngs had found the only accommodating landing site and one which also served the future president of the United States, Theodore Roosevelt, in the Spanish-American War nearly 250 years later.

The trek to the town proved to be a long nine miles across some typically difficult Caribbean terrain. The men moved in single file marching through the night over honeycomb-like limestone rock, up and down narrow gullies and through thick vegetation, bitten by mosquitoes and slashed by sharp rocks. Unlike their disastrous experience in Santo Domingo, this was something they had become used to in pursuit of Spanish guerrillas and while hunting wild boars in the Jamaican interior.

In his report to Governor Windsor, Myngs wrote: 'With much labour by break of day wee recovered a plantation by a river's side some six miles from our landing, and three miles from towne, where being refreshed by water, daylight and a better way: wee very cheerfully advanced for the towne.'

Governor Morales had expected the English to assault the fortresses at the entrance to the harbour. Realising his error in the early hours of the morning of October 6, he recalled 170 regular soldiers from the garrison and rounded up his hastily-formed militia to man barricades on the road along which Myngs was approaching. Meanwhile the populace was frantically removing its families and belongings to the countryside. The condition of near panic combined with Morales's faltering leadership did not augur well for the day.

The barricades, according to Myngs's account, consisted of casks filled with soil and stones, bound together with cowhide, with two cannons in support of the individual weaponry. Don Christopher Ysassi Arnoldo, the last Spanish governor of Jamaica, was in command of the militia. The resistance at the barricades proved short-lived and was rapidly overcome as was the fight put up by Don Christopher's militia. Myngs claimed that the former governor 'fairly ran away' and his contingent was routed. The English force proceeded into Santiago which it systematically ransacked. Six small vessels in the harbour were boarded by men clasping knives and cutlasses between the teeth, a mannerism that had become a hallmark of buccaneering, designed to convince their enemy to flee in terror.

The next day, October 7, 500 men were sent in groups to seek out those inhabitants who had fled and to retrieve their valuables. A coordinated tactic was employed to bring the English ships into the harbour: at 11 a.m. they were to pass through the entrance while a land force would simultaneously attack the castle from the rear. El Morro was considered impregnable when it was built, boasting walls 63 feet high on the landward side and perched as it was on a promontory on the sea side. Thirty-four guns faced the mouth of the harbour and its cavernous interior was believed to have been able to house a thousand men. But when the English advanced it was manned by fewer than 20 men under the command of Governor Morales's 20-year-old nephew, Jeronimo Garci-Ximenez de Morales. Not a single additional soldier or any supplies had reached the fort in anticipation of the English assault.

Edward Long, the historian, gives a melodramatic although substantially accurate description of what took place: '... the troops, who had no sooner drew near the fort, and began to assault, than the enemy, dismayed at their huzzas, and the impetuosity of their manoeuvres, deserted the ramparts, and betook themselves to the inner ramparts; from which also they retreated with precipitation, after firing a few irregular shots, and were pursued as far as the English general thought advisable'. Young Morales, one of his uncle's many nepotistic military appointments, escaped by canoe across the channel and hid in the mountains. An apocryphal and uncorroborated report from Spanish sources maintained that Henry Morgan said he could have defended the castle 'single-handed with a musket and my dog'. Once the ships were safely at anchor in the harbour, the looting of the town and countryside continued. Myngs recorded his difficulty containing the rampaging soldiers and buccaneers, claiming to have at least restrained them from firing the churches. However, the Spanish later maintained that the cathedral, hospital and governor's residence were destroyed.

Don Pedro Morales also retreated to the mountains. He did not attempt to rally any further resistance but proceeded towards the inland town of Bayamo until he reached the Cauto River seven days later, taking with him soldiers and settlers. He only returned to Santiago on October 29, long after the English had departed. The governor of Cuba, Don Juan de Salamanca, on hearing of Myngs's landing, mobilised a force of 200 soldiers and 500 militiamen in Havana. However when they reached Trinidad, less than half way, he turned back because the English had already disembarked.

On October 15 Myngs's fleet had anchored at the entrance to the harbour. The next four days were spent dismantling the fortifications. A thousand pounds of gunpowder and 34 guns were itemised. Of this, 700 pounds of explosives were used to level the Morro to its foundations; the brass and copper guns were carried off and the heavier iron guns toppled into the sea.

The fortress, said to have cost the King of Spain £100,000 which was an enormous amount at the time, was demolished. Myngs's fleet loaded with silver plate, barrels of wine, sacks of sugar, bales of hides, cannons, even several church bells, slaves and a number of Spanish prisoners entered Port Royal on October 21 to an enthusiastic welcome. Out of the Myngs's contingent only six men were killed in battle and another 20 lost from illness or accident.

Losses were put by the Spanish authorities as high as half a million pounds, an exaggerated figure in all likelihood, to underline Santiago de Cuba's vulnerability and gain support for a more viable defence budget in the future. Governor Morales was quickly denounced as the culprit to blame for the disaster. The former governor of Jamaica, Ysassi, accused him of taking away the weapons of the guerrillas he had

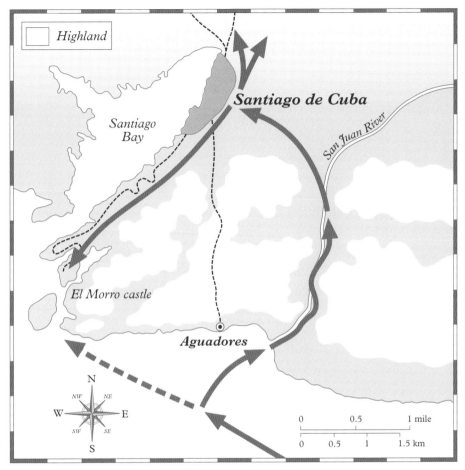

Myngs's assault against Santiago de Cuba.

evacuated from Jamaica and not permitting them to fight. A higher authority, the Count of Banos, Viceroy of Nueva Espana, denounced Morales to the King for a false sense of security '... when he received my letters he never replied'. The viceroy also maintained that Morales had at the time under his command 250 men from a regiment based in Mexico who had been preparing to invade Jamaica.

Serious charges of dereliction of duty were laid against Morales. A legal investigation, which was to last 18 months, revealed not only his corrupt practice of handing out military appointments, but also his mismanagement of the town's affairs which included embezzling 78,000 pesos in public funds. He was impeached, forced out of his governorship and sent to Spain accused of gross incompetence. After a period of recovery Santiago returned to prosperity. Smuggling was still actively carried on with Jamaica to the extent that one bitter Spaniard moaned, 'All that is lacking is for Santiago to declare itself English'.

A curious but unlikely footnote to the event comes by way of Spanish history. A bishop, Morell de Santa Cruz, tells us: 'A priest of nearly 90 years old who was taken prisoner during this invasion and who for that reason got to know him (Commodore Myngs) and spoke of his stay in this city says that he (Myngs) was a Spaniard from Seville, the son of a cobbler whose name was Xptoral Mendez.'

The future of Port Royal as a haven for buccaneers became even rosier with the decision in England to allow colonial governors in the West Indies to establish courts of admiralty under the authority of the Lord High Admiral, the Duke of York, who was Charles II's brother. As a result when Lord Windsor arrived in Jamaica, he appointed his brother-in-law Colonel William Mitchell to hear complaints, condemn lawful prizes and impose penalties for infractions under the new law known as the Navigation Acts. All enemy ships brought into port were henceforth deemed lawful prizes. The king was entitled to a one-fifteenth and the Lord High Admiral a one-tenth of the share of their value. Royalty was now legitimately in business with the buccaneers.

On his arrival, Myngs found that Lord Windsor had returned to England putting in charge his lieutenant-governor, Sir Charles Lyttleton. Now a member of the Council of Jamaica, Myngs began pressing for another raid against the Spanish.

This time his target was San Francisco de Campeche in the Yucatan on the Central American mainland. His exploits at Santiago de Cuba had enhanced his reputation throughout the northern Caribbean and he had no trouble attracting the likes of Edward Mansfield who was later to be recognised as the de facto leader of the English buccaneers.

The expedition sailed on January 21, 1663. The venture was ultimately less lucrative than his Cuban experience and resulted in a heavier loss of life. While leading the charge, Myngs himself received near-fatal wounds to his face and thighs and had to be carried back to his flagship *Centurion*. His deputy, Sir Thomas Morgan, assumed command. Even after victory was secured, the voyage back to Jamaica took nearly eight weeks caused by difficult navigating conditions.

Myngs's convalescence was expected to take a long time as a result of which he returned to England in early July. Fully recovered by 1665, he took part in a battle against the Dutch in the English Channel following which he was knighted for bravery. Promoted to vice-admiral the next year, he was to take part in his final naval engagement on board the *HMS Victory* once again against the Dutch. Known as the 'Four Days Fight', this demonstration of Dutch naval supremacy proved fatal for Christopher Myngs. In a heroic display he refused to leave his command despite a wound in his throat. Staunching the flow of blood with his finger, he continued to rally his men until a second bullet felled him. A few days later he died at his London home in Goodman's Field, Whitechapel.

Samuel Pepys, Secretary of the Navy and accomplished diarist, records that after the funeral sailors who had served under Myngs approached with tears in their eyes and requested assistance to avenge him against the Dutch. 'If you will please get His Royal Highness to give us a fireship among us all ... that (we) shall show our memory of our dead commander and our revenge ...' In the Caribbean it was not only his bravery but also his strategies and tactics that would best serve as an example to the buccaneers who were to continue in his footsteps. There was never an attack on Jamaica mounted from Santiago de Cuba in the seventeenth century; Myngs's success proved that by employing buccaneers the island was assured of a degree of security that it could not otherwise have enjoyed.

Samuel Pepys, Secretary of the Navy at the time of Myngs's funeral, was approached by Myngs's comrades to get them a ship to avenge his death by the Dutch.

Chapter 6

ST EUSTATIUS

DRIVING OUT THE DUTCH

~

The French temporarily occupied St Eustatius, or Statia as it is popularly known, in 1627 and erected a small fortification upon which the Dutch who later settled the island built Fort Oranje in 1636. Once started the fort grew in importance, at first to provide security for the fledgling colony of tobacco farmers but by the eighteenth century to protect the thriving trading port that lay beneath its battlements. However, at the time that Colonel Edward Morgan, supported by his buccaneers, led an assault on St Eustatius, it provided a woefully inadequate defence.

Still today the most distinctive feature of the capital Oranjestad's urban landscape is Fort Oranje situated above the historic waterfront. Although it has undergone changes, the fort remains fundamentally the same as it was centuries ago. The fort was originally square but now has three bastions. The commander of the fort lived above the north bastion which is the entrance. Just inside to the left is one of the barracks used in the eighteenth century and next to it five prison cells opening on to the central courtyard. Three-pound iron guns dating back to the eighteenth century are mounted on the parapet. (Larger guns had to be abandoned, as the recoil had sent some of them over the edge!) The nearby museum of the St Eustatius Historical Society contains little that captures the island's turbulent seventeenth century history but displays many fascinating historical artefacts.

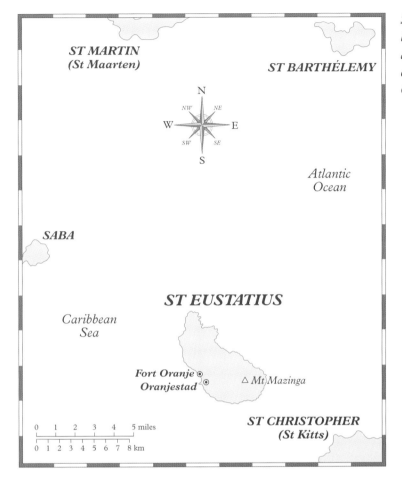

St Eustatius was settled by the Dutch in 1636 and was one of Holland's earliest colonies in the Caribbean.

Fort Oranje overlooks the roadstead that once served a thriving seaport.

~

The English took nearly a decade after capturing Jamaica from the Spanish to realise that the Dutch were also a serious threat to their efforts to trade in the West Indies. It was Colonel Edward Morgan, an uncle of Henry Morgan, who was chosen to end that challenge.

The Dutch had been present in the Caribbean region since the late sixteenth century. Deprived of access by the Portuguese to salt needed for pickling their herring catches, the Dutch crossed the Atlantic to the salt pans at Punta de Araya off Venezuela. Dutch vessels were also selling supplies to Spanish settlements in the eastern Caribbean despite Spain's claim to the exclusive right to trading in the region. Their early incursions were dealt with harshly. The Spaniard Luis Fajardo, with a fleet of 14 galleons and 2,500 men, attacked the interlopers, who included French and English, at Punta de Araya in 1605. He treated his captives as 'pirates and corsairs', beheading or hanging most of them without trial. Early in the following year Fajardo engaged some 24 more unwelcome vessels off the south coast of Cuba.

When a 12-year truce between Spain and the Netherlands ended in 1621, the Dutch West India Company was formed by a group of 19 gentlemen known as the Heeren XIX with what has been described as 'belligerent commerce' in mind. This event also coincided with the end of a period of building costly defences at Havana, Santa Domingo, Cartagena and Vera Cruz which was to severely drain Spain's financial resources. The first time a Dutch flag was raised – but only briefly – over a Caribbean island was in 1625. The Dutch General, Boudwijn Hendricksz successfully evaded the guns of the El Morro fortress at San Juan, Puerto Rico. Despite a five-week siege, his force of 700 men could not breach the battlements and he was obliged to abandon his venture.

Piet Heyn, who eventually became an admiral serving the Dutch West India Company, achieved for his company's shareholders what his predecessor had failed to do. Pieter Pieterszoon Heyn was born in Delfshaven near Rotterdam in 1577. He went to sea at 16 and as a young man was captured by the Spanish and forced to work on their galleys. In the West Indies he was taken prisoner again, gaoled in Havana and made to toil once again on a galley. By 1611 he was captaining vessels sailing to the East Indies and later rose to the rank of general on account of his successful campaigns against the Portuguese in Brazil. His knowledge of the Spanish deployment of vessels in the Caribbean and his hatred of his former captors combined with his charismatic leadership were to prove invaluable when he was chosen to pursue one of the Spanish silver fleets as it sailed from the Caribbean.

In the instruction he received from his employers there was clearly a convenient marriage of pious Protestant righteousness with a hunger for profit: 'This is the fleet which brings to Europe the golden rod which chastises the whole of Christianity

MAGNANIMO VIRO D. PETRO HEINIO PETRIDÆ, SOCIETATIS
INDIÆ OCCIDENTALIS PERMISSÆ, A PROVINCIIS COFOEDERATIS
Præfecto classi, et nunc Hollandiæ atque Occidentalis Frisiæ rerum Maritimarum
Præfecto Vicario, etc

Piet Hein.

Kopergravure van W. Hondius, naar Joh. Dane (1629).

Twice captured by the Spanish and forced to work in their galleys, Piet Heyn sought revenge leading a Dutch fleet into the Caribbean in search of Spanish treasure ships.

and discourages it, a rod the force of which can be subdued by 24 well-armed men-of-war and 12 well-provided dispatch boats armed with guns and ammunition and manned by courageous soldiers whose only wish is to fight the enemy.'

Sending Piet Heyn into the Caribbean in chase of one of Spain's heavily-armed silver fleets was no hit-or-miss adventure. The regularity of the fleets' crossings allowed for a systematic study of their routes, composition, fighting capability, cargoes and crew complements and was the kind of information that enabled Heyn to plan his strategy most effectively. Determined to command a large enough fleet to confront any size Spanish force he might encounter, Admiral Heyn requested 28 ships, six brigantines and 12 large sloops. Significantly some of the ships were 800 tons, bigger than most generally used. The fleet was armed with 129 bronze and 550 iron cannons, 2,300 seamen and 1,000 soldiers.

On July 12, 1628, Heyn's squadron dropped anchor at St Vincent in the Windward Islands before proceeding northwards to Cuba. The Dutchman's objective was Cape San Antonio where he would wait for the homeward-bound treasure ships leaving the Yucatan Channel. Capturing two Spanish dispatch boats in August, he was able to confirm that neither the Tierra Firme nor New Spain fleets had arrived yet in Havana, the last stop before crossing the Atlantic.

Juan de Benavides, who commanded the Flota of St John, had left Spain a year earlier escorting a fleet of merchantmen to the Caribbean. The most important vessels destined to carry the New World treasure to Spain were his flagship, the *Santa Gertrudis*, the *San Juan Bautista* and the *Nuestro Senora de la Antigua*. However, on their return leg they were carrying far more passengers than space allowed, as a result of which the ships' cannons were impeded by baggage, merchandise and temporary accommodation crowding the deck. When the time came to engage the enemy, Spanish firepower was drastically curtailed. The hurricane season weather did Admiral Benavides no favours; after leaving Vera Cruz for Havana a storm widely scattered his fleet.

Informed that the treasure ships were approaching, Heyn sailed on a northeast course until, on the morning of September 8, 1628, he met the vanguard of 12 vessels of which he captured six. Ironically, this advanced contingent of Spanish ships had been mistakenly following the lights of Heyn's Dutch fleet and in turn the rest of the Spanish had been following these vessels. Finding himself east of Havana and at Piet Heyn's mercy, Benavides had the choice of battling his way through the Dutch in an attempt to reach Havana or taking cover in the nearby bay at Matanzas. Here he would hope to defend the mouth of the bay while he unloaded the cargo on shore, if necessary setting fire to his abandoned vessels. He chose to enter Matanzas Bay. Discipline collapsed on board the Spanish ships. Many of the original crew had already deserted in New Spain and passengers had been conscripted to serve as seamen which probably provides the explanation as to why panic broke out, orders were disobeyed and the vessels allowed to run aground.

By nightfall Heyn had done what no one before or after him managed to do – capture an entire Spanish treasure fleet. Four massive galleons and two other ships were caught in Matanzas Bay in addition to those taken earlier. It took eight days to transfer to Dutch holds the chests of silver, gold and merchandise worth nearly five million silver pesos. Heyn returned to Holland in triumph but his men were not to share his success. The Dutch policy of underpaying their sailors and soldiers led to rioting on the streets of Amsterdam by the men who had sailed with him and many probably deserted to join the buccaneers the other side of the Atlantic.

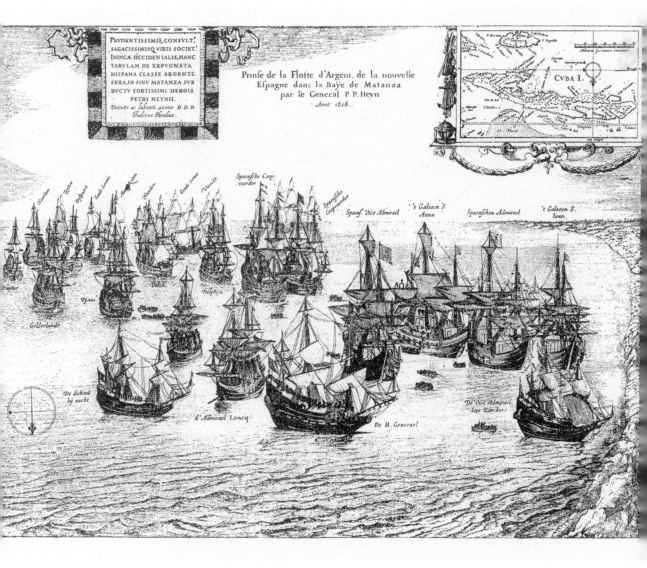

Admiral Heyn cornered and looted an entire Spanish treasure fleet in Matanzas Bay, a feat unequalled in his time.

Juan de Benavides was imprisoned and eventually executed for dereliction of duty. A year later, Piet Heyn died in an engagement with pirates off the coast of France. Heyn's epitaph was to read: 'He has had India, Spain and Flanders as witnesses, first of his slavery, then of his freedom and victories.' Dutch privateering exploits continued in the Caribbean well into the first half of the seventeenth century through the exploits of others. Although his successors were said to have actually inflicted greater damage on the Spanish, Piet Heyn's exploits at Matanzas Bay dealt a crushing blow to Spain's pride and its treasury.

Dutch warships under admirals like Heyn and de Ruyter wreaked havoc in the Caribbean during the middle of the seventeenth century.

The trade in salt continued to be a major attraction for the Dutch West India Company. Removing salt from seawater by collecting from pans in Bonaire, Tortuga (a Venezuelan island by that name) and St Martin (the present-day Dutch/French island of St Maarten/St Martin) frequently aroused Spain's wrath and these islands were to change hands often. In 1634 the Dutch seized Curaçao and its neighbouring islands. Realising that Curaçao possessed an excellent natural harbour, the Dutch made it their permanent trading post in the Caribbean.

St Eustatius was colonised in a less dramatic fashion. Jan Snouck, an entrepreneur from Flushing, got permission in 1636 from the Zeeland Chamber of Commerce to found a colony on any uninhabited West Indian island. The expedition's first stop was St Croix but discovering the English already entrenched. Pieter Van Corselles, the leader who had already established a Dutch colony on Tobago, tried several other islands before disembarking at St Eustatius with 50 settlers. He named it New Zeeland, not knowing that the indigenous Caribs themselves had called it Alo which means cashew tree or St Anastasia as Christopher Columbus had named it.

At Oranjestad, the principal town, Fort Oranje was soon erected by the Zeelanders on the old French foundations. With this secured, the settlers began cultivating tobacco, a profitable West Indian crop until the Virginia leaf being grown in America took over. Cotton then sugar followed and with it the importation of African slaves in ever-increasing numbers. In 1640 nearby Saba was colonised, on which tobacco, cotton, indigo and coffee was grown. Over the next 25 years these colonies expanded modestly in population as well as in economic worth. However, both the English and the Spanish were concerned about the permanence of Holland's presence in the region and took turns confronting the Hollanders. As well as the French, three other European powers were to claim ownership of St Eustatius a total of 22 different times before it was ultimately returned to Dutch hands in 1816.

When the monarchy was restored in England, King Charles II had initially instructed his West Indian governors to suppress privateering activities against the Spanish. However, there were practical concerns for the newly-colonised islands when this edict was issued. In May, 1664, Colonel Lynch, Provost Marshall for Jamaica, wrote:

'The calling in of privateers will be but a remote and hazardous expedient (if the Governor commands and promises a cessation). What compliance can be expected from men so desperate and numerous men, that have no other element but the sea, nor trade but privateering. There may be about 1,500 of them in about 12 vessels, who if they want English commissions can have French and Portugal papers, and if with them they take anything they are sure of a good reception at New Netherlands (Curaçao) and Tortugas. And for this we shall be hated and cursed, for the Spaniards call all the rogues in the seas, of what nation so ever, English. And this will happen, though we live tamely at Jamaica, and sit still and see the French made rich by the prizes, and the Dutch by the trade of the West Indies.'

~

'The calling in of privateers will be but a remote and hazardous expedient (if the Governor commands and promises a cessation).'

These 'desperate and numerous men', called privateers by Lynch but were buccaneers by origin, were soon to be engaged in carrying out English policy in the Caribbean under the command of a military man who was father of Henry Morgan's bride-to-be. Edward and his brother Thomas were professional mercenaries, officers serving in foreign armies at a time when their own countries were at peace. Both fought in the Netherlands and later in Germany. It was in Westphalia that Edward met and married Anna Petronilla, the daughter of Johan Ernst, Feiherr von Pollnitz, the governor of Lippstradt. The two brothers returned to England at the time of the Civil War but experienced very different fortunes. Thomas, an artillery officer, joined Oliver Cromwell. He became second-in-command to Cromwell's outstanding general, George Monck, in 1650. As circumstance would have it, Monck – and Thomas Morgan – successfully made the transition into the administration of Charles II after the Restoration. Monck was eventually made Duke of Albemarle and his son, Christopher, the second duke, briefly held the governorship of Jamaica.

In the final years of the Puritan government in England, Richard Cromwell, who succeeded his father in 1657, had knighted Thomas Morgan somewhat melodramatically, pronouncing him a soldier for 'nearly 40 years and present in the greatest battles and sieges of Christendom for a great part of the time'.

Edward Morgan on the other hand, had opted to fight for Charles I and was captain-general of his forces in South Wales. But when the King was beheaded he sought refuge on his brother-in-law's estate at Asbach in Germany with his young wife. The rule of Richard Cromwell who succeeded his father, Oliver, proved unpopular and it was George Monck who was amongst those who invited Charles II to return to England and regain the throne. General Monck achieved the transition without bloodshed, in the process becoming one of the most influential men in England. His advice to the king was to choose the best men to run the country's affairs and to overlook past political allegiances.

One such man was Sir Thomas Modyford, Monck's cousin, a successful planter and administrator in Barbados for 16 years, who Charles II was to appoint governor of Jamaica. Colonel Edward Morgan was named to be his lieutenant-governor, not only as a reward for his loyalty to the King but apparently also because of his knowledge of the Dutch language and its military systems. Colonel Morgan was to be supplied with arms and ammunitions from England but expected to recruit fighting men in the West Indies. Modyford, who was convinced that Barbados was overpopulated, was authorised to offer colonists free passage and grants of land in Jamaica. From their number and from the remnants of General Venables's army left behind after the 1655 expedition, Colonel Morgan was also to draw his forces.

Whilst Edward Morgan must have been pleased to have received recognition for his support of the crown, his long years in exile had left him almost penniless. He had to borrow to buy his London house. His personal life reached a low ebb when his wife passed away before he departed from the West Indies. He arrived in Barbados on April 21, 1664, on board the *Watergate* with his six children. A seventh, his eldest daughter, described as 'a lady of great beauty and virtues' died on the long voyage and two of his household staff passed on with an illness described as 'a malign distemper caused by the nastiness of the passengers'. In all 30 unfortunates, including 12 seamen, died on the outward passage. It is not surprising that official records show that 1,500 Barbadian settlers who had agreed to emigrate to Jamaica refused to board the ill-fated *Watergate* and alternative transport had to be found.

Whilst at sea Sir Thomas Modyford wrote a letter to the Spanish governor of Santo Domingo informing him that 'His Majesty of Britain, Charles II had commanded him to take charge of the island of Jamaica' and 'strictly enjoined him (Modyford) to restrain all his subjects from molesting the ships or invading his (King Philip of Spain's) possessions'. Colonel Theodore Carey, who was later to assume command of the English at St Eustatius after the tragic events that were to take place there, accompanied by two other officers delivered the message travelling on two men-of-war in a deliberate show of strength.

Colonel Lynch's somewhat cynical comments on King Charles's instruction have already been noted. It did not help that the Spanish governor's reply was evasive and avoided the issue as to whether England had a legitimate right to claim sovereignty over Jamaica. True to his, or more precisely, King Charles II's word, the new governor of Jamaica on his arrival at Port Royal issued the proclamation of peace with Spain. A message to this effect was formally dispatched to the governor of the Tierra Firme at its capital, Cartagena. However, in a letter to his brother in England Modyford criticised his predecessor because he had 'lately sent out so many privateers, which renders my actions very difficult; for I have an account of no less than 1,500 lusty fellows abroad, who, if made desperate by any act of injustice or oppression, may miserably infest this place and much reflect on me'. How to engage the buccaneers in ways that would benefit Jamaica or at least divert them from being a liability to the young colony would be a conundrum for Modyford throughout his term in office.

The committee of the Privy Council on Jamaican affairs that sat in London found a practical solution to the problem of idle buccaneers. It recommended to the Lord High Admiral, the Duke of the York, whose authority in maritime affairs extended to the colonies, that permission be given to those who had previously harried the Spanish, to be engaged in dispossessing the Dutch of Curaçao and their other plantations after which they, the buccaneers, should be invited 'to come and serve His Majesty in these parts'. This the Duke did three weeks even before England declared war on the Dutch in Europe in March, 1665. Modyford quickly took advantage of this turn of events and pardoned 14 men who had recently been tried and condemned to death for piracy.

Meanwhile Colonel Edward Morgan continued to plead his case to Lord Arlington, Secretary of State, for the recovery of the £3,000 he said he had generously spent in the past in the king's service in England, to say nothing of his 'loyalty on the field of battle and in exile'. From the English Exchequer he directly sought money owing to him so he could buy '30 or 40 slaves' for his plantation. He was looking forward to being paid £600 a year as lieutenant-governor in addition to a pension of £300 a year. On reaching Jamaica he received his promised land and assigned his eldest son, Charles, to the running of the plantation. Land title records in Jamaica show that Charles II on September 2, 1664, granted him a house in St Jago de la Vega justifying his generosity as 'encouragement to continue in our land and for diverse other good causes and considerations'.

Modyford meanwhile was planning an ambitious expedition to capture St Eustatius, Saba and Curaçao, then to drive out those Dutch trading at St Kitts and finally on the homeward leg to challenge the buccaneers at Tortuga and mainland Hispaniola. This was presumably to encourage them to seek commissions in Jamaica or to uproot them from their settlements.

The belated departure of the English expedition to St Eustatius ultimately turned out to be fortuitous. Dutch Admiral de Ruyter had amply demonstrated his naval skill and remarkable daring not long before by sailing up the Thames, destroying or capturing many vessels including the royal flagship the *Royal Charles*, in the process panicking the inhabitants of London. In 1665 de Ruyter turned his attention to the West Indies hoping to take the English colonies by surprise. On April 30 he sailed into Carlisle Bay in Barbados. For several hours a fierce gun battle ensued with his fleet bombarded from a nearby fort and determined counter attacks from vessels in the harbour. Carlisle Bay, being narrow, was a difficult place to succeed in an engagement of this type and before long de Ruyter withdrew to the French island of Martinique. De Ruyter never knew how close he had been to victory in Barbados as the English had accidentally spilled 33 barrels of gunpowder and their supplies were almost depleted. He continued north seizing English merchantmen and their cargoes at Montserrat and Nevis but in total showed little return for his efforts. He sold his prizes to Dutch traders at St Kitts and sailed on to St Eustatius. Here he purchased sugar and cotton with the remainder of his spoils and supplied the commander of Fort Oranje with some 7,000 pounds of gunpowder. On May 17, 1665, he left the Caribbean altogether. He had been anchored at St Eustatius barely two months before the English fleet arrived.

Meanwhile Colonel Morgan must have had a premonition because he decided to write his will before setting off. Having had 40 years of military service meant he must have been at least in his late 50s. Once active in the field, he was now overweight and unfit for the conditions of combat that fighting in the tropics imposed. In a memorandum to the governor he left his virtually virgin plantation to his two sons with the instruction that they should increase its size and value in order to be able to maintain their sisters and provide their dowries. His mortgaged London house and a claim he had on an estate in Wales were to pass to Mary Elizabeth, his eldest surviving daughter.

On April 16 Colonel Morgan sailed to the Isle of Pines off Cuba where he was joined by buccaneers who provided his mercenary force. As Governor Modyford put it: 'They are chiefly reformed privateers, scarce a planter among them, being resolute fellows, and well armed with fuses and pistols.' Amongst the captains of the nine vessels were two already of some repute: Captain Robert Searle, sailing as with an earlier Port Royal commission, had recently brought two Spanish vessels into Port Royal as prizes. Unfortunately, because the newly-crowned king had prohibited this type of action, his booty had to be returned. Another of Colonel Morgan's men was the energetic Captain Maurice Williams whose vessel, *Speaker*, was to be the flagship.

After a successful campaign against the English, the Dutch Admiral de Ruyter left St Eustatius just two months before Colonel Morgan's campaign.

When the force mustered on May 16, Morgan had nine ships, 71 guns and 450 men. His fleet comprised:

Captain Maurice Williams	*Speaker*	18 guns
Captain John Harman	*St John*	12 guns
Captain Garret Garrettson	*Civilian*	16 guns
Captain Robert Searle	*Pearl*	9 guns
Captain John Outlaw	*Olive Branch*	6 guns
Captain Albert Bernardson	*Trueman*	6 guns
Captain Nathaniel Cobham	*Susannah*	2 guns
Captain John Bamfield	*Mayflower*	1 gun
Captain Abraham Marlarka (in a galliat)	(name unknown)	1 gun

Modyford was fully aware of the terms under which the buccaneers were taking part – 'no purchase, no pay'. 'Purchase' was the plunder that the expedition was expected to gain and share out as 'pay'. Their continuing commitment and loyalty inevitably depended entirely on the reward they would receive. The voyage of 800 miles against strong east by southeast headwinds of 25 knots with a strong current proved extremely difficult. Off Santo Domingo the fleet put into port intending to buy provisions and take on firewood and water but the Spanish refused them entry. Finally on July 17 after a particularly stormy passage, Colonel Morgan went ashore at Montserrat from the *Speaker* and was met by the governor, Major Nathaniel Reed, from whom he was able to obtain supplies along with a few sloops for the purpose of landing his forces. In the storm two ships had been presumably lost and a third, the *Olive Branch*, was captained by the appropriately named John Outlaw who deserted and sailed to Virginia.

With his contingent reduced to no more than 300 men, Morgan approached St Eustatius. The island, only five miles long and two miles wide, featured an easily recognisable extinct volcano almost 2,000 feet high at its southern end, with a wide plain separating another hilly area extending to the northern tip. The town of Oranjestad was built about 110 feet above the anchorage which was protected by Fort Oranje. A narrow track known as the slave path led up to the town from the beach.

Colonel Morgan sailed into the bay and on July 23 landed with his division first, followed by Colonel Theodore Carey. Captain Harman remained in command of the fleet. After several volleys were fired, Dutch resistance collapsed. Later on the lack of defence attracted the comment that 'it is supposed they (the Dutch) were drunk or mad'. The governor, Peter Adrianson, sent three men to parley after receiving a summons that demanded 'the speedy surrender of the fortress, arms and ammunitions, the submission of the island to such taxes and duties as shall be infused, and the supply of all necessary provisions for the English. These are the only terms that can be offered and if not the "courages" of the soldiers will be put on trial, when the inhabitants may not expect any quarter …'

After the surrender an inventory was taken: 20 cannon, 131 small arms, six barrels of powder, 300 head of cattle, 50 horses, 300 sheep and goats, five ships, 840 Negroes and Indians and 50,000 pounds of cotton. They found six plantations on the island possessing sugar works and cotton fields. Of the settlers, 76 men, 42 women and 132 children – all Dutch – were deported to St Martin. Another 80, including English, Irish and Dutch who took an oath of allegiance to King Charles II were allowed to remain on the island. The island was renamed New Dunkirk.

But success had its price. Sir Thomas Modyford, who only learnt of events in November four months later, reported to the Secretary of State: 'the good, old colonel (Edward Morgan), leaping out of the boat, and being a corpulent man, got a strain, and his spirit being great he pursued over-earnestly the enemy on a hot day, so that he surfeited, and suddenly died to almost of the loss of the whole design.' Where he died was not recorded but it may well have been traversing the steep track leading from the water's edge to the fort above. By general consensus Colonel Carey assumed command, and later when a Major Stevens arrived on the *Mayflower*, which was thought to have been lost in the storm, he was directed to take the nearby island of Saba. Even smaller than St Eustatius, Saba consisted of the core of another extinct volcano rising 3,000 feet out of the sea with a little arable land on its sides and in the cone. Here a small quantity of arms, cattle and other goods was seized along with 85 Negroes and Indians. Eighty-seven Dutch were sent to St Martin; 64 English, Irish and French took the royal oath.

Having incited the buccaneers to capture Saba, Colonel Carey was unable to persuade them to continue on to Curaçao, their 'purchase' having been so disappointing compared with the booty they were used to confiscating from the Spanish. Despite this, the governor of Jamaica wrote home to the colonial authorities that he expected the name of the Dutch would be forgotten in a matter of months in the West Indies. They turned out to hardier than he anticipated.

Leaving Colonel Thomas Morgan and a small contingent behind to occupy St Eustatius and Saba, most of the buccaneers as well as Colonel Carey returned in the direction of Jamaica. Modyford was to report 500 slaves had arrived in Jamaica along with cannons and other armaments, sugar, coppers and stills and sundry goods. In his correspondence, the governor admitted that the buccaneers had connived to steal and hide what plunder they could lay their hands on. However, he was hopeful, 'some of the privateers are well bred, and I hope with good handling to bring them to more humanity and good order, which once obtained his majesty hath 1,500 of the best men in the world belonging to his island …' As a postscript to his report Modyford said of Colonel Morgan '… I fear I shall never meet with one so useful, so complacent and loving as Colonel Morgan was; he died very poor, his great family having little to support them; his eldest daughter is since married to Sergeant-Major Bindlosse of good estate.' His daughter Anna married Robert Byndloss commandant of the garrison at Fort Charles after the customary three months of mourning for her father. The surviving eldest daughter, Mary Elizabeth, married her cousin Henry Morgan not long after and a third sister, Johanna Wilhelmina, too young at the time was later to marry Henry Archbould. The three men, Byndloss, Morgan and Archbould were in different ways to play significant roles in moulding the future of Port Royal and Jamaica.

With England still at war in Europe against the Dutch, Modyford in 1666 engaged his two buccaneer captains, Searle and Stedman, to take the prosperous Dutch colony of Tobago. Having accomplished this with only 80 men they were interrupted in their looting activities a few days later by an expedition under Governor Willoughby of Barbados demanding possession in the name of England's King Charles II. Willoughby agreed to let them sell their plunder in Barbados in exchange for abandoning the eastern Caribbean island without further destruction. In August, 1666, French planters from nearby Grenada drove out the small English garrison in Tobago. Earlier that year, Modyford had sent another buccaneer captain, Edward Mansfield, to capture Curaçao which was increasing in importance as the slave trading centre of the Caribbean. Mansfield was to decide otherwise as we shall see.

It was only a year after Colonel Edward Morgan's misadventure that the Dutch, now firmly united with the French, retook St Eustatius (which by then was garrisoned by just 200 men) only to find their French allies turn around and drive them out of the island. Lieutenant-Colonel Thomas Morgan who had been left behind to govern St Eustatius in April, 1666, had taken a company of buccaneers still in his command to assist Governor Watts at St Kitts which at the time was shared by the English and French. The French on their side of the island were determined to rid the island of the English. In a confrontation, only the buccaneers put up any kind of fight and Thomas Morgan was seriously wounded, shot in both legs, in a shameful defeat.

The French also had designs on Dutch possessions, particularly Curaçao, in the West Indies. Count d'Estrees, vice-admiral of the French fleet in the Caribbean, called on the French buccaneers of Hispaniola to reinforce his forces. Over 30 vessels in May, 1678, sailed towards the Dutch island. As they approached the Isle d'Aves disaster struck when D'Estrees' navy ships and the buccaneers' frigates ran on to the reefs. Heavy seas added to the confusion and after the loss of several vessels the expedition was abandoned. The Dutch were to remain in the West Indies to enjoy a share of its growing prosperity. The English realised that the buccaneers were reluctant to fight England's West Indian conflicts if the prospects of good 'pay' were poor.

Chapter 7

SAN JUAN RIVER

GATEWAY TO GRANADA

~

No Spanish colonial city, other than possibly Panama, underestimated the audacity and determination of the buccaneers more than Granada. Situated as it was at the northwestern end of Lake Nicaragua, 100 miles from the beginning of the San Juan River which was itself well over 100 miles from the Caribbean Sea, Granada seemed safely out of the reach of the marauders. The journey up the San Juan was an arduous one requiring those who mastered it to carry their boats around stretches of the river where rapids made transit dangerous. For the adventurous this experience – without the portaging – is still accessible as the entire length of the river is navigable and the tropical environment setting still resembles what it was in the time of the buccaneers.

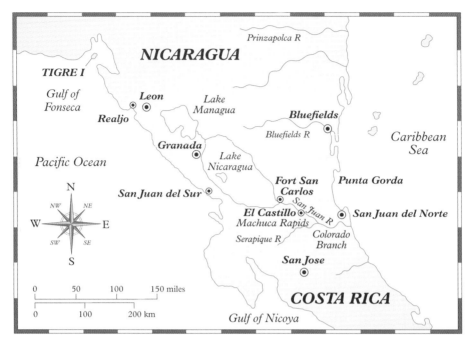

Granada was more than 200 miles from the Caribbean, requiring the buccaneers to travel up the San Juan River and cross Lake Nicaragua.

Granada, the buccaneers' objective, was also the object of the wrath of an American mercenary, William Walker, who torched many of the city's historic buildings in the mid-1800s during a civil war. However, the Convento de San Francisco, originally built in 1529, is now an eclectic museum which includes a small art gallery. Its substantial chapel is being restored to its former glory. The traditional Plaza de Armas, now Parque Central, has also undergone change but the imposing Cathedral de Cartagena still stands on the original site. Iglesia San Francisco, Nicaragua's oldest church dating back to 1585 was also a victim of Walker's fury. One of the most tantalising mysteries in Granada is to speculate on the location of one or more of the tunnels in the city used to escape from the buccaneers that led down from the town to the lake. However, the authorities are said to have sealed them off many years ago. Two fortifications still remain in the city: Fort Polvora, an eighteenth century storehouse for ammunition, and San Pablo, a tiny late-seventeenth-century fort on one of the islands of the Las Isletas archipelago, poised to challenge vessels approaching the city on Lake Nicaragua.

At the head of Lake Nicaragua where the San Juan River originates lies the town of San Carlos. The seventeenth-century fort, or seemingly a recreated version, is being built by the Spanish government.

El Castillo, known formerly as Fortaleza de la Immaculada Concepcion and now well into its fourth century, is approximately two hours down river on an outboard engine-driven boat. Located in front of the El Castillo Rapids, it commands the approach from both ends of the San Juan. It contains an authoritative museum

*Iglesia San Francisco,
Granada's oldest church, is
said to have been destroyed
in William Dampier's time.*

*In an attempt to protect
Granada from intruders
approaching across Lake
Nicaragua, a small fort,
San Pablo, was built in the
Las Isletas archipelago.*

and the local library which is also the repository for documentation on the fort's history. The original fort was remodelled between 1745 and 1746 and contains four bulwarks, a parade ground, a central tower, or caballero, residences for the warden and chaplain, a chapel and barracks. Four staircases descend from the ramparts to the soldiers' quarters and two ramps were built for drawing cannons up to the parapet. Some sections of all these original structures are still identifiable today. A walk along the waterfront roadway through the town takes you to a grassy riverside outcrop clearly marked La Plataforma, the site of the original seventeenth-century gun emplacement at the river's edge.

El Castillo overlooks the El Diablo Rapids on the San Juan River where the buccaneers were forced to portage.

A hill behind the fort is known as Lomas de Nelson as a consequence of young Captain Horatio Nelson's use of this vantage point to bombard it. Despite the ravages of Mansfield, Morgan and Nelson amongst others, El Castillo remains a proud example of how heritage and history can be preserved.

Christopher Columbus might have been somewhat more successful in his search in the Caribbean for a passage to the Orient if he had not passed by the entrance to the San Juan River, or the Desaguadero as it was first known. Sir Francis Drake in 1595, on his last privateering voyage to the region, was probably advised of its existence by the Spanish architect of the fortification at San Juan de Ulua in Vera Cruz, Alberto Ojeda. Drake considered ascending the San Juan in order to surprise the unsuspecting town of Granada on Lake Nicaragua, or even better, to reach the Pacific en route to the rich prize of Panama. Drake died before he had a chance to exercise either option. Despite being only a few miles from the Pacific Ocean, Granada was one of only a few Central American Spanish outposts that did not feel threatened by intruders in the region and certainly not from intruders entering Nicaragua from the Caribbean.

Francisco Hernández de Córdoba had founded Granada in 1524, only a few years after the Spanish had penetrated the west coast of Central America. However, historical lore has it that the Andalusian explorer Gil Gonzalez Davila, on reaching the great interior lake and naming it 'Agua de Nicarao' after an Indian chief, was Granada's founder. Nicarao was subsequently to be the origin of the name of Nicaragua and the lake, Lake Nicaragua. Gonzalez later returned to Hispaniola and in 1524 set out to find the entrance to the San Juan River which he believed would lead him up to Lake Nicaragua to the west, but his search failed. In all likelihood it was Captain Alonso Calero in 1539 who was the first European to navigate the San Juan to the Caribbean, an achievement for which he was summarily arrested by the governor of the territory (which included Panama) who did not want Panama to have to share the cross-isthmus traffic.

Realejo, the most important port on the Pacific coast of Central America was only 125 miles from Granada and almost a quarter of that from Leon, the colonial capital of Nicaragua, which had been settled about the same time as Granada. Puerto de la Posesion, known more commonly as Realejo (which gave way to Corinto), became a shipyard for the Manila galleons and the port for trade with Peru early in the sixteenth century. The harbour lay hidden behind a long island on a small river that led to the town proper. After Sir Francis Drake passed it on his Pacific voyage, fortifications were erected hopefully to deter future marauders.

Founded in 1524 by Francisco Hernández de Córdoba, Granada was more than a hundred miles from the Caribbean yet pirates and buccaneers found their way there by the seventeenth century.

The fertile plains around Lake Nicaragua produced sufficient food supplies for both Peru and Mexico. These commodities were supplied through Realejo as well as through Cartagena by way of the San Juan River which flowed from the south-eastern corner of the lake for over 100 miles to the Caribbean Sea. The wealth of Peru's silver mines was first transported to Spain down the San Juan. When the merchants of Guatemala, who controlled the valuable indigo trade with Spain, were fearful of using Santo Tomas in the Bay of Honduras as a port, they also shipped through Granada down the San Juan.

Aided by a plentiful supply of Indian labour, the populace of Granada as well as Leon thrived over the next century. Although technically under the authority of the Captain-General of Guatemala, Granada enjoyed the kind of autonomy which encouraged unrestricted growth and the accumulation of wealth.

The Irish-born friar, Thomas Gage, in his book *The English-American Survey of the West Indies* published in London in 1655, recorded his vivid impressions of Leon and

Granada after a visit in 1637. Of the inhabitants of Leon, he noted that they lead 'a delicious, lazy and idle life, not aspiring much to trade and traffic "whose chief delight consisted" in their houses and in the pleasure of the country adjoining, and in the abundance of all things for the life of man more than in any extraordinary riches … they are contented with fine gardens, with variety of singing birds, and parrots, with plenty of fish and flesh, which is cheap and with gay houses …'

Granada, he found a 'stately and pleasant town' with 'houses fairer than those of Leon, and the town of more inhabitants, among whom there are some few merchants of very great wealth and many of inferior degree who trade with Cartagena, Guatemala, San Salvador and Comayagua and some by the South Sea to Peru and Panama'. As well as watching the constant flow of goods, ranging from indigo, cochineal and hides to sugar and silver, down to the lake's edge for loading, he also observed the opulence of the religious orders and their cathedral and churches, soon to become the target of the buccaneers' fury.

Thomas Gage visited Granada in 1637 and described the affluence of the city in his 1655 book.

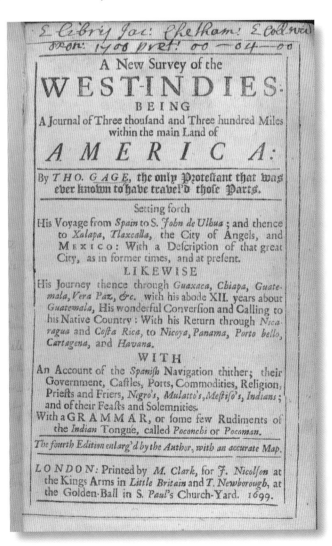

A New Survey of the
WEST-INDIES.
BEING
A Journal of Three thousand and Three hundred Miles within the main Land of
AMERICA:
By *THO. GAGE*, the only Protestant that was ever known to have travel'd those Parts.

Setting forth

His Voyage from *Spain* to S. *John de Ulhua*; and thence to *Xalapa, Tlaxcalla*, the City of Angels, and MEXICO: With a Description of that great City, as in former times, and at present.

LIKEWISE

His Journey thence through *Guaxaca, Chiapa, Guatemala, Vera Paz, &c.* with his abode XII. years about *Guatemala*, His wonderful Conversion and Calling to his Native Country: With his Return through *Nicaragua* and *Costa Rica*, to *Nicoya, Panama, Porto bello, Cartagena*, and *Havana*.

WITH

An Account of the *Spanish* Navigation thither; their Government, Castles, Ports, Commodities, Religion, Priests and Friers, *Negro's, Mulatto's, Mestiso's, Indians*; and of their Feasts and Solemnities.

With a GRAMMAR, or some few Rudiments of the *Indian* Tongue, called *Poconchi* or *Pocoman*.

The fourth Edition enlarg'd by the Author, with an accurate Map.

LONDON: Printed by *M. Clark*, for *J. Nicolson* at the Kings Arms in *Little Britain* and *T. Newborough*, at the Golden-Ball in S. *Paul's* Church-Yard. 1699.

'For although, whilst they sail upon the lake they go securely ...'

He learnt of the difficulties to be encountered in sailing down the San Juan River to reach the Caribbean but declared that he was neither disheartened nor discouraged by the information.

'For although, whilst they sail upon the lake they go securely, and without trouble, yet when they fall from the lake to the river (which there they called El Desaguadero) to go out to the sea, here is nothing but trouble, which sometimes makes that short voyage to last two months, for such is the fall of the waters in many places amongst the rocks that many times they are forced to unlade the frigates, and lade them again with the help of mules which are there kept for that purpose by a few Indians that live about the river ...'

He describes this need to portage around the rapids as tedious to the passenger and goes on to anticipate 'the abundance of gnats' (mosquitoes) and heat so intolerable 'that many die before they get out to sea'. Despite all this he writes, '... yet I am comforted myself that my life was in the hands of the Lord, and that the frigates did commonly every year pass that way, and seldom any were lost'.

Granada being at the southwestern end of Lake Nicaragua was approximately 100 miles from the entrance to the San Juan. One hundred and twenty miles in length, the river varied in width from over 550 yards to a fifth of that and flowed between two to three miles per hour, faster where there were rapids.

In his original report Calero had identified seven rapids, the first 30 miles from Lake Nicaragua which he called El Toro. Another ten miles further on was a second set known as La Casa del Diablo where the river fell seven feet. A few miles below, a series of several rapids named Machuca contained the most dangerous of them all being the longest, often very shallow and extremely rocky.

Ironically, Thomas Gage was not in the end destined to travel the San Juan River route. Although his passage had been previously arranged, he was informed that the authorities in Guatemala had curtailed at least temporarily the use of the route because English and Dutch ships were waiting at the Caribbean mouth of the river for the Granada frigates: '... which made all the merchants of the country to fear and sweat with a cold sweat, and the President to be careful for the King's revenues, lest the loss of them should be imputed to his wilful negligence ...' Although Gage was never able to tell us specifically what he saw and felt on a voyage across Lake Nicaragua and down the San Juan, he described the environment the buccaneers would be encountering quite accurately.

The success of the buccaneering expeditions that plagued Granada between 1665 and 1670 had as its common factor the role played by the Indians of the Mosquito Coast which spreads from present-day Honduras south to Nicaragua, to the town of San Juan del Norte at the end of the San Juan River and finally into Costa Rica.

~

Spanish colonisation on the Caribbean coast of Central America south of Trujillo, Honduras, extending to Panama's Portobelo was extremely limited in the early colonial days. The inhospitality of the landscape and the antipathy of the indigenous Indian tribes towards the Spanish were to serve the buccaneers' purpose admirably. The low-lying coastal mangrove swamp soon became dense tropical jungle until the terrain rises into the rugged mountainous interior. Giant cedar trees and stands of mahogany, as well as fustic and other dyewoods, were eventually to play a significant part in the history of this region.

The Mosquito Coast was unbearably hot, damp and unpredictable particularly to those unfamiliar with the tropical weather. The rainy season could run from May through to January, with occasional respite in September and October. From November to February high winds prevailed in the north; June and July were the wettest with rivers swelling and flooding low-lying districts. In contemporary times 260 inches of rain a year have been measured at the Caribbean end of the San Juan River. A climate like this was ideal for mosquitoes and sand flies which brought on the deadly scourge of malaria and yellow fever.

Little by the way of agriculture could be practised by the Indians who lived largely on wild bananas and cacao, hunting wildlife like deer with bows and arrows or fishing with lances and harpoons for turtles and manatees. The most ferocious of the tribes were the Ramas who occupied the territory in the vicinity of Bluefields and the San Juan River. But the Indians who were to ultimately give the coast its identity were the enterprising Miskito Indians.

Perhaps it was the inhospitability of their barren, boggy land which stretched a short 60 miles south from Cape Gracias à Dios to Brancman's Bluff that fuelled their aggression. The Miskitos were stocky, muscular and seldom more than five foot eight inches in height. Their fishing excursions in dug-out canoes measuring up to 40 feet in length took them long distances requiring endurance and dexterity. Inevitably they were to encounter Europeans, most probably from Providencia (then Providence Island) which lay 100 miles off the Caribbean coast of Nicaragua near to their fishing grounds.

As hunters they moved silently and swiftly to avoid the attention of the ocelots, jaguars and wildcats that roamed the Nicaraguan jungle where they hunted; along riverbanks they were confronted by crocodiles and alligators in their pursuit of turtles; in turbulent seas they pursued sharks and other prey with only primitive harpoons. Nomadic, predatory and acclimatised to the harshest of tropical conditions, they defied subjugation by the Spanish. It is no wonder that the buccaneers recruited them. An exploratory voyage by Captain Sussex Cammock to the western Caribbean in 1629 was to lead to the opening of the Mosquito Coast to European settlement and the emergence of an enduring alliance between the buccaneers and the Miskitos.

Captain Cammock cautiously anchored offshore on the Mosquito Cays before approaching the coast with his cargo of beads, cloth and trinkets for bartering.

Perhaps guided by rigid Puritan principles, the traders struck up and subsequently maintained congenial relations with the Indians. Probably the earliest of commodities to be exchanged by the Miskitos were turtle shells eagerly sought after in England for ornamentation.

The 1633 trading expedition sent by the Puritan governor of Providence Island resulted in English settlement of Cape Gracias à Dios. Two Dutch traders, Abraham and William Blauvelt, who likely accompanied this new expedition of Cammock's, gave their name to the settlement of Bluefields to the south, not too distant from the entrance to the San Juan River. Abraham Blauvelt was still recorded as having been there as late as 1663. At one point, he was known to have a privateering commission from the English and later roamed the Caribbean as a buccaneer sailing a barque with three guns and 50 men. He is still later believed to have accompanied Henry Morgan on his expedition to Panama. This had most likely taken him to the island of Jamaica which also has a Bluefields.

The presence of the English and the Miskitos' partnership with them contributed to the changing nature of the Indians' culture. Already warlike, the Miskitos eagerly took to European weaponry as well as to Caribbean rum. This heady combination was to make their compatibility with the buccaneers complete. Never before had there been a more perfect fit of aggressiveness and survival skills with a lust for spoils of war and hatred of the Spanish.

As we have heard from Thomas Gage, the reputation of Granada and its growing wealth was being spread by word of mouth throughout the Caribbean. Despite the arduous passage up the San Juan (rowing time was more than three days including hauling the canoes over the rapids) and across Lake Nicaragua in another few days (or less if they seized a boat with a sail), intruders were to find that defenceless Granada was a far easier target than many other Spanish towns in Central America. The first to take advantage of an official 'commission' to seek revenge against the Spanish in Granada was the early seventeenth-century English privateer, Captain William Jackson.

The Puritans who in 1629 settled Providence Island provided commissions for reprisals against the Spanish. Financed by merchants in London and Cornwall, Captain William Jackson set out for the West Indies in 1638 on a privateering voyage. His is the first recorded raid by an Englishman on Granada. John Winthrop, a Puritan merchant in Massachusetts Bay, was to write in his diary afterwards: 'Here came a small bark from the West Indies, one Captain Jackson in her, with commission from the Westminster Company to take prize, etc, from the Spaniard.

He brought much wealth in money, plate, indico (indigo) for 1,440 pounds.' But Jackson's exploits on this occasion were apparently far less impressive than his well-documented pillaging between 1642 and 1644 of Maracaibo, the Spanish capital of Jamaica St Jago de la Vega, Trujillo and Tolu.

John Morris was first mentioned as a buccaneer captain in 1658 when he bought a prize captured by Christopher Myngs and renamed it *Dolphin*. For the next few years he probably sailed with Myngs and shared in his successes at Santiago de Cuba and Campeche. Morris was to join forces with the Dutch buccaneer David Martien and other captains, including young Henry Morgan, for a raid on Central America. He later argued that having been away from Port Royal and unaware of any political change, he was still operating under a commission from an earlier governor, Lord Windsor. This foray into Spanish waters began in January, 1665, and almost came to a premature and disastrous end. Having disembarked at the mouth of the Grijalva River and made their way 50 miles to the unsuspecting provincial capital of Villahermosa de Tabasco in Mexico which they sacked, they returned to their waiting vessels on the Caribbean to find that they had been seized by Spanish frigates in pursuit of them.

The buccaneers employed the two small vessels they had used for navigating the shallow Grijalva, released their hostages and attempted to slip away along another river channel only to be bottled up by their own flagship – a ten-gun vessel – and the Spanish eight-gun prize they themselves had earlier seized off Campeche. The Spanish commander, Jose Aldana, demanded their surrender. The buccaneers by now had built a temporary barricade on shore and equipped it with seven small cannons earlier removed from Villahermosa. Aldana decided to avoid an immediate confrontation. Fortuitously next day it was discovered that the Spanish ships had run aground allowing the buccaneers to depart unscathed.

Eventually they turned south, picking up 20 Sambo-Miskitos with their canoes at Cape Gracias à Dios at Monkey Point, south of Bluefields. Here they anchored their vessels and transferred their combined forces, weapons and supplies to the canoes. For four days they ascended the swift-flowing San Juan River, bypassing the rapids, defying the humid air and torrential rain. With enormous relief they reached Lake Nicaragua, marvelling at the abundance of fish and 'sweet' fresh water, as well as the cattle and horses roaming the surrounding savanna. Now they pressed forward only at night, keeping out of sight by day amongst the small islands to maintain the element of surprise.

But by June 30 when they attacked, surprise was scarcely necessary to ensure success. Marching into the city in broad daylight and meeting only a cursory display of firepower, they entered the central plaza, seized 18 large cannons and captured the town hall containing arms and ammunition. They rounded up 300 male prisoners, including many clergy, and imprisoned them in the cathedral while they looted and pillaged for 16 hours assisted, it is said, by a thousand Indians who came down from the mountains to take part in the orgy of destruction. The Indians mistakenly assumed that the buccaneers would remain as conquering occupiers.

Sinking any Spanish vessel they believed might pursue them, they left with a quantity of Negro slaves and 6,000 pesos in coin and bullion in a 100-ton ship that they had captured. Guided by their Miskito companions, John Morris and the buccaneer captains returned to the coast where their ships waited. By August, William Beeston, a member of Jamaica's House of Assembly, was recording their return to Port Royal in his journal. In seven months they had travelled an astounding 3,000 miles and assaulted five large towns.

John Morris went on to become a loyal lieutenant to Henry Morgan in his campaigns at Maracaibo, Portobelo and Panama before accepting an assignment in 1672 from Jamaica's governor, Sir Thomas Lynch, to rein in the old buccaneers turned pirate. The Dutchman David Martien became the object of Lynch's wrath by making Tortuga his refuge because now Holland was at war with England and Spain. However, Governor Modyford later recruited Martien with his two frigates and issued him a commission ostensibly in defence of Jamaica describing him as 'the best man in Tortuga'.

As for Henry Morgan, his apprenticeship was over. The audacious assault on Granada led by John Morris and David Martien stunned the Spanish Crown. The occupation of Jamaica only ten years earlier was proving to present a permanent threat to Spain's hegemony in the Caribbean as well as its security in Central America.

Before his death in 1665, King Philip IV had appointed the former General of the Armada, Martin Carlos de Mencos, to the captaincy-general of the Kingdom of Guatemala with a mandate to prepare it for a possible invasion by the English. The attacks on Granada had accelerated the need for action. The merchants of Guatemala, who required the Lake Nicaragua–San Juan River route as an alternative way to ship their exports, were prepared to submit to a tax to defray the cost of a fort on the river. Assured of the necessary funding, Mencos ordered the governor of Nicaragua, Juan Fernandez de Salinas, to survey the San Juan for the appropriate site. His choice proved to be a poor one and the structure he erected an even poorer one.

Fernandez's location for this defensive obstruction was a small island about 40 miles up from the Caribbean where the Pocosol River, now called the San Carlos, empties into the San Juan from the Costa Rican plateau. Completed in 1667 and named San Carlos after Philip IV's successor, Charles II, it had congenital weaknesses as did its namesake. More a stockade than a fort, it was constructed of wood which began rotting in the devastating humidity from the day it was completed. Seventy soldiers armed with muskets and four light cannon would face the enemy as they came upstream. Reinforcements were nearly 200 miles away in Granada, virtually guaranteeing defeat as soon as the next contingent of buccaneers was to appear.

Laurens Prins – known by the English as Lawrence Prince – like John Morris also acquired a vessel after Christopher Myngs's raid on the Spanish Main in 1658. Prince purchased a vessel of 50 tons with four cannon and renamed it *Pearl*. Although born in Amsterdam, Prince accepted a commission from Sir Thomas Modyford to attack the Dutch island of Bonaire in February, 1665. The expedition earned him little in the way of reward for his efforts – largely cattle – but did considerable damage. The greatest humiliation was the fact that it was led by a Dutchman, on whose head the Dutch West India Company in Curaçao put a price. Prince continued to operate from Jamaica. In the summer of 1670 he engaged Captain Thomas Harris and a Captain Ludbury to join him in harassing the Spanish mainland. His first daring venture was to navigate the Magdalena River in Colombia for 150 miles in an effort to attack the inland town of Mompos but a newly-constructed fort prevented him from succeeding.

His next objective was Granada. Negotiating the San Juan River, he sacked the fort at San Carlos in order to enter Lake Nicaragua. Here with 200 men Prince confronted Gonzalo Noguera y Rebolledo commanding a company of 70, almost half of whom were too ill to resist or were already dead. Noguera put up stout resistance killing 16 and wounding 18 buccaneers but ultimately had to surrender. Unfortunately the fort's captain told Prince that he had despatched a messenger earlier to warn the citizens of Granada hoping, possibly, to persuade the buccaneers to abandon their plans. Prince's reaction was to send his fastest canoe crew to pursue the messenger which they did, capturing him in three days.

Leaving 20 men in control of Fort San Carlos, the others reached Granada undetected. Spanish accounts of Prince's sacking of the city describe him as a violent enemy who accompanied a ransom demand for 70,000 pesos with the head of a

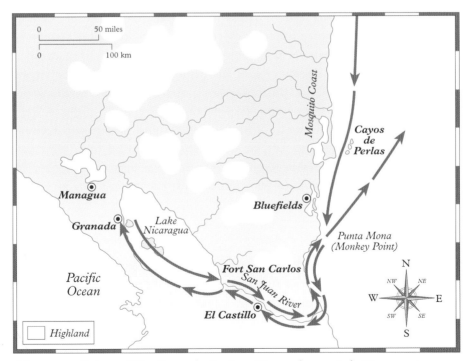

Morgan travelled over 200 miles up the San Juan River and across Lake Nicaragua to plunder Granada.

priest in a basket and a threat to execute the rest of his prisoners if it was not met. However, Governor Modyford in a report to London recorded that their plunder only amounted to '... but seven pounds of silver and £12 in money per head, which is nothing to what they had five years since, but the town is much decayed, and the principal men gone to Guatemala, as being more secure'. The fate of the captured citizens is not mentioned. Modyford went on to reprove the captains '... for daring to do this without permission, but not deeming it prudent to press the matter too far at this juncture, commanded them to attend the Admiral, which they were very ready to do and will be gone in five days'. The 'admiral' of course was Henry Morgan.

The fate of Lawrence Prince, like John Morris, was to be deputised by Governor Lynch to suppress buccaneering and by 1672 Prince had become a considerable landowner in Jamaica. Lynch had described him in official reports as 'one of the great privateers ... a sober man, very brave and an exact pilot. I thought it not amiss for that reason to employ him, and to let the Spaniards see the privateers are subjects to the King's orders, and have not all left the island, but take it as an honour to serve the King in any capacity.'

The buccaneers' continuing depredations in their Central American colonies caused increasing anxiety to the Spanish. The failure of Fort San Carlos to deter Prince led to a review of the defence of the waterway. This time the captain-general of Guatemala, Francisco de Escobedo, decided to make the 600-mile journey from his capital, Santiago de Guatemala, to evaluate personally the prospects for a more effective fortification. Escobedo, previously the governor of Yucatan, was a general of the artillery and, combining the experience of both positions and taking into account the weaknesses of the first fort, he identified a site on a high bluff just above the La Casa del Diablo Rapids where the river narrows and only 40 miles from Lake Nicaragua. In accordance with Escobedo's directives and over a three-year period ending in 1676, Nicaragua's Governor Pablo de Loyola built Fort Immaculada Concepcion.

The fort was to be rectangular with four bastions, 90 feet wide by 195 feet long. Its walls, four feet thick, stood four feet above the ramparts for a total of 15 feet. When finished the fort had a ten-foot wide, three-foot deep moat with a drawbridge to the entrance. Any vessel on the river was within the reach of the fort's 14 cannons facing downstream with falconets and stone throwers so that the curtains could be raked by crossfire in the event of an attempted escalade. The garrison comprised 100 musketeers, a company of artillerymen and a supply of 300 small arms. To thwart or delay a surprise attack a redoubt called La Plataforma, manned by seven soldiers with two four-pound cannons, was established on a small island near the rapids.

Fort Immaculada was the largest fort built in Central America until the eighteenth century. Even then it was not impregnable. If an opposing force put sufficient firepower in position on the other side of the river or on the hill to the southwest, it could dominate the fort. Perhaps as serious was the fact that the fort lacked an adequate water supply and depended primarily on drawing water from the river. But the garrison's worst enemy was to be nature. Muskets and cannons did not wear out, instead they rusted away. And at any one time the number of able-bodied men in the garrison depended on how many were dying or had died from disease and how many replacements had arrived.

Fortaleza de la Immaculada Concepcion, known today as El Castillo, was completed in 1676 to deter the buccaneers.

Because of its close proximity to the Pacific, the towns of Leon and Granada inevitably became the object of the plundering expeditions launched from that ocean. William Dampier, who published an account of his adventures in *A New Voyage Round the World* in 1697, recounted marching the ten miles from the Pacific coast through what he quotes as 'the pleasantest place in the Americas and the paradise of the Indies'. Despite easily taking the town with the militia leaving after showing little resistance, they were outsmarted by the governor of Leon who delayed the ransom negotiations until he built up a sufficient body of men and horses. The buccaneers demanded 300,000 pieces of eight and provisions enough for a thousand men for four months. Concerned about the growing threat of retaliation, the invaders set the town on fire and departed.

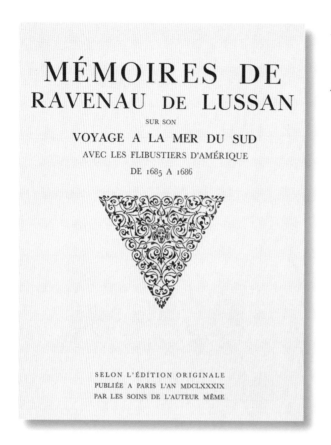

MÉMOIRES DE
RAVENAU DE LUSSAN

SUR SON

VOYAGE A LA MER DU SUD

AVEC LES FLIBUSTIERS D'AMÉRIQUE

DE 1685 A 1686

SELON L'ÉDITION ORIGINALE
PUBLIÉE A PARIS L'AN MDCLXXXIX
PAR LES SOINS DE L'AUTEUR MÊME

Ravenau de Lussan vividly recounted an attack on Granada in which he took part.

Another such campaign was waged by an uncomfortable alliance of French and English buccaneers who had crossed the Isthmus east to west in search of new, lucrative targets. Amongst them were such notable South Seas buccaneers as the English Captains Edward Davis, Charles Swan, William Knight and Francis Townley; their French counterparts included Captains Lescuyer, Francois Grognier and Ravenau de Lussan who wrote himself into buccaneering lore with his *Journal des voyage fait à la Mar du Sud avec les flibustiers de l'Amerique*, published in Paris in 1689.

Only three years earlier, de Lussan had taken part in an attempt by these combined forces against Granada. The force of 346 men, disembarking on the Pacific coast of Nicaragua, marched to the town meeting determined resistance from breastworks armed with cannons that straddled their path. On April 10, 1686, they took Granada only to find that, forewarned, the populace had removed everything valuable to the island of Zapatera on Lake Nicaragua. After the battle, the Catholic French buccaneers sang a Te Deum in the cathedral before departing five days later with little in the way of booty.

This otherwise unmemorable assault on Granada is remarkable for Ravenau de Lussan's account of the events that took place. He gives a fascinating description of the buccaneers' actions with the town and its inhabitants, providing a unique snapshot of the era.

'We had but four killed and eight wounded, though to tell the truth, few of the wounded recovered.'

It appears that the inhabitants of Granada had as much as three weeks advanced notice that the buccaneers were off the coast. When the buccaneers were only three miles from the town approaching from a hill, de Lussan said they actually saw the ships which were carrying the town's wealth away sailing to the island six miles away. Additional evidence of the townspeople's preparedness was revealed when a prisoner seized en route disclosed that a strong wall had been erected around the central plaza and equipped with 14 cannons, six swivel guns and a body of soldiers supported by six troops of horses, whose task it would be to attack the invaders from the rear. This defensive strategy was put in place after the buccaneers' quartermaster had surrendered to the Spanish and forewarned them. Says de Lussan: 'This information, which certainly would have stricken with terror any other but filibustiers, did not make us hesitate a moment, nor did it prevent our reaching the town about two o'clock in the afternoon.'

The defenders of Granada had fortified the central square, blocking the entry roads from each of the four sides. After reconnoitring and deciding that they had insufficient numbers to attack from all four sides, the buccaneers regrouped on the street up which they had originally entered the town. The wall facing them had loopholes for muskets to be fired through, two cannons and six of the lighter swivel guns. As the intruders got closer, they also saw that in several places at the base of the wall space was left to protrude billhooks with the object of scything away at the legs of anyone who got too close!

The Spanish barrage of ball and grapeshot made progress slow, pinning the buccaneers against the walls of the houses on the street. Gradually they forced their way forward until they reached a slight elevation on the lawn of a garden where they fought in the open until they gained the upper hand, According to de Lussan's account the buccaneers began …

'… smothering them with the grenades which we hurled at them incessantly, and finally forced them to the principal church, from whose tower they succeeded in wounding some of our men. Immediately our men upon the heights saw that the enemy were giving way, they called us to jump over the wall, and this we did, they following close upon our heels. In this way we made ourselves masters of the place of arms, and so of the town itself, whence they fled after having lost a great part of their forces. We had but four killed and eight wounded, though to tell the truth, few of the wounded recovered.'

Finding little else in Granada but stores of food and merchandise, the buccaneers sent a detail of 150 men to locate the town's womenfolk in order to place a ransom on them. When this failed, they threatened to burn the town to the ground unless a substantial ransom was forthcoming. By an ironic twist of fate, the Spanish had caught one of de Lussan's compatriots 'whose weariness had made (him) to lag upon the road'. This man assured Granada's defenders that it was the declared intention of the buccaneers to return to the town, equip themselves to cross the lake and go back to the Caribbean down the San Juan so it was unlikely they would destroy it. Says de Lussan: 'this fellow having reassured them, they took no more pains to answer our proposition that they should buy the town back, which obliged some of our people, the most determined, to set fire to it out of spite'.

A young Lieutenant Horatio Nelson made one of the last unsuccessful attempts to secure Fort Immaculada Concepcion.

De Lussan, 50 years after Thomas Gage, comments on the appearance of wealth and well-being in evidence in Granada and environs, singling out its 'magnificent' churches and cathedral, 'well-built houses' and 'several fine sugar factories'. But be that as it may, he laments the buccaneers' lack of good fortune (which had dogged them since they had earlier failed to capture treasure galleons at Panama).

On June 15 the buccaneers abandoned Granada, taking with them what supplies they could scrounge up to sustain them as well as one cannon and four swivel guns. The latter were to prove invaluable as a Spanish force of over 2,500 men from Leon appeared when they had reached a short distance from the town. This was to be one of many skirmishes the buccaneers were forced to endure on their way back to their ships. In prevailing on this occasion, they were to capture a man who claimed that a million and a half pieces of eight had been concealed in a wall in Granada just in case the town was held to ransom. Comments de Lussan, '… we had no desire to go back and look for this money, for we were busied enough in escaping from the hands of enemies as great as that with which we had to deal already'.

The San Juan River over the next 250 years continued to attract the attention of the Europeans. In the eighteenth century the English made several attempts to dominate the river and Horatio Nelson, later the English naval hero of the Napoleonic Wars, was unsuccessful in capturing El Castillo. During the California Gold Rush the American entrepreneur, Cornelius Vanderbilt, transported miners up the river, across Lake Nicaragua to Granada and on by steamship from the Pacific coast to San Francisco. At the end of the nineteenth century an abortive attempt to begin a trans-oceanic canal ended after dredging halted only half a mile up the river from the Caribbean. In 1901 the US House of Representatives actually passed a bill in favour of building that canal but when an active volcano erupted, killing thousands on Ometepe – an island in Lake Nicaragua on the canal's proposed route – Panama was chosen as an alternative location.

The merchants of Granada knew the value of the San Juan River and exploited it despite the hazards and hardships of transporting cargo down to the Caribbean. Unfortunately pirates, privateers and then the buccaneers were drawn to it for this very same reason, at first simply waiting for unsuspecting vessels at its mouth but later using it to reach unsuspecting Granada itself.

Chapter 8

PROVIDENCIA

PURITAN BUCCANEERS

~

The tiny Colombian island of Providencia off the east coast of Nicaragua proved a thorn in the side of the Spanish from the day the English Puritans landed in 1661 with high hopes, naming it Providence Island. Lying as it did close to the route of the treasure galleons between Cartagena, Portobelo and Havana, Providencia soon came to be seen as a better place from which to torment the Spanish than to plant cotton and tobacco.

Much like Tortuga, the topography of the island provides a compelling reason why the buccaneers used it as their headquarters to mount campaigns against Portobelo and Panama. The Santa Catalina peninsula at the northwestern extremity of the island is hilly and includes a 40-foot bluff on top of which the Puritans built Fort Warwick to guard the harbour. A mound of stones and loosely-packed rock on its probable site suggests where it was located. There is no evidence of the other small forts perched on Santa Catalina's hillsides but rusting cannons can be found in the undergrowth.

The buccaneers remain a part of local lore. Some say Henry Morgan buried treasure on the island that he had looted sacking Panama City. To date none has been found. On Santa Catalina there is a headland known as Morgan's Head, although it would be difficult to argue that it resembles him. Only six miles long and four wide, fertile, with a good fresh water supply and a salubrious climate, Providencia must have been a very appealing prospect for men weary of life at sea just as much as it is for the visitor today.

~

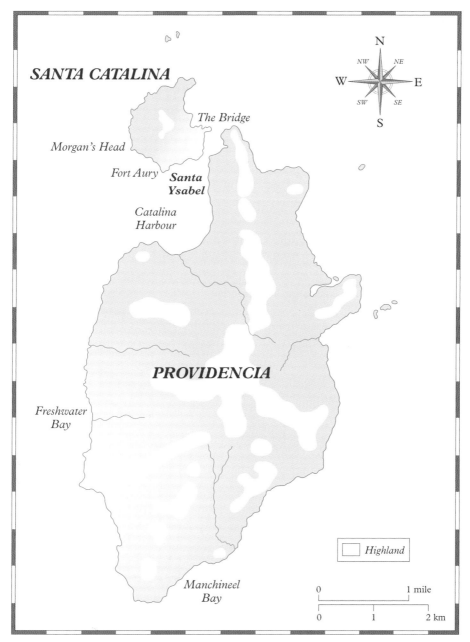

Only six miles long and four miles wide, Providencia's topography made it easy to fortify and use as a base for attacking the Spanish.

Edward Mansfield, the first of the English buccaneer admirals and his successor, Henry Morgan, needed little convincing to agree that the English Puritans' Providence Island, often referred to in history texts as Santa Catalina, was an ideal if precarious outpost from which to harass the Spanish on land and at sea. This tiny Colombian island lies about 110 miles off the Miskito Coast of Nicaragua. Of volcanic origin, it has a central peak 1,990 feet high with verdant valleys stretching between the spines that radiate down to the sea. Despite dry summers, it is a fertile tropical island with a mild climate dominated by easterly tradewinds.

But for the likes of Mansfield and Morgan the island had three primary appeals: it was surrounded by coral reefs which made it difficult to approach, its topography made it easy to fortify, but even more importantly, it lay within reach of the treasure galleons as they began their long voyages home. It was also near enough to the traffic that passed through the mouth of the San Juan River carrying trading vessels from Granada to Cartagena and other coastal towns.

However, it was not the buccaneers who were first attracted to the island but a company of 'gentlemen adventurers', seventeenth century capitalists with a religious mission.

Spain knew of the island in the early sixteenth century but 100 years later it was only occupied by a few Dutch traders, notable amongst them Captain Abraham Blauvelt. The English company of gentlemen adventurers were Puritans, aristocratic men often related by marriage and bonded together by a deep conviction in their religious beliefs. These beliefs would eventually lead to the overthrow of Charles I and the emergence of Oliver Cromwell's Commonwealth, replacing the monarchy. Although they had already undertaken colonising efforts in Virginia and Massachusetts and on Somers Island (Bermuda), they responded eagerly to a proposal for settling the small Western Caribbean outpost. This was to be their initial first step in establishing a much larger English colonial presence in Central America.

In early 1629 Captain Daniel Elfrith put into Somers Island. Employed by Robert Rich, the powerful Earl of Warwick, one of the Puritan gentlemen adventurers, Elfrith probably engaged in the slave trade. He informed the governor, Philip Bell, that he had discovered a group of islands that were fertile and pleasant. He had left a small force under Captain Sussex Cammock on one, San Andres, which the Puritans called Henrietta after Charles I's French wife, and sailed to another referred to as Kathalina which, he said, had the advantage of being able to be made 'invincible'. But the one Governor Bell enthusiastically recommended to his superiors (one Elfrith talked about but had not seen) he called Fonseca. The only problem was that Fonseca did not exist. The Spanish themselves believed in its existence to the extent that it appeared on their maps from the mid-1500s. It was even granted by Charles I to Philip, Earl of Montgomery, in 1628. In 1852 the US government brig *Dolphin* took a sounding of 2,570 feet at its supposed position but found no evidence of an island, thereby exploding the myth once and for all.

In 1630 the Earl of Warwick and several other prominent Puritans formed the Company of Adventurers to settle the island of Providence – Captain Elfrith's Kathalina. The next year Philip Bell arrived from Somers Island appointed governor and Captain Elfrith was named admiral. Elfrith, who had been in the vicinity of the West Indies for over 20 years, came with a colourful if unsavoury reputation. In 1615 he was put in charge of a captured Spanish caravel transporting a cargo of cornmeal which he diverted to Bermuda just in time to save its inhabitants from starvation. His arrival turned out to be a mixed blessing as the vessel also brought a plague of rats that took the colonists several years to eradicate.

He had played the role of the Earl of Warwick's personal privateer in 1618, attempting to use Virginia as his base of operation for the earl's notorious privateering ship *Treasurer*, and causing consternation in the new colony. A year later he put into Virginia with Africans for sale captured from a Spanish vessel and who were said to be the colony's first slaves. After sailing the *Treasurer* to Bermuda, where it was beached as unseaworthy, he settled on the Earl of Warwick's land with the remaining slaves where he stayed for several years. Later he was dispatched on the privateering voyage by his patron that resulted in the occupation of Providence.

The first immigrants arrived on Providence in May, 1631, from England on the *Seaflower*. Philip Bell left the governorship of Somers Island for the governorship of this new colony having married Elfrith's daughter which was not to make his life any easier. Captain Samuel Axe, who had seen military action in Holland, was to be responsible for Providence's fortifications. He sat on the inaugural governing council and soon fell out with his superior, Captain Elfrith. Before long, Elfrith had announced the Puritans' presence on Providence to the Spanish by seizing a frigate of theirs off Cape Gracia à Dios in an unauthorised encounter.

Robert Rich, Earl of Warwick, formed the Company of Adventurers to settle the small island off present-day Nicaragua he optimistically called Providence Island.

The maverick admiral compromised the safety of the island from the Spanish even further by enrolling the renegade Diego Grillo 'El Mulato', whose buccaneering exploits were to continue into the 1670s operating from Tortuga. Diego el Mulato occupies a curious place in English history by being quoted in one of Oliver Cromwell's speeches to parliament. Cromwell had held discussions with Thomas Gage, the Roman Catholic priest referred to earlier. The ship on which Gage was sailing home was captured by Diego el Mulato. The priest pleaded that he was English-born and not sympathetic to the Spanish cause in the hope of getting his possessions back. It was Gage's captor's words that Cromwell repeated in the English parliament on January 22, 1655: 'Oypormi, mananaporti, today fortune hath been for me, tomorrow it may be for thee: or today I have got what tomorrow I may lose again.'

At least Captain Elfrith's assessment of the island's defensibility was accurate. Its natural harbour lay within a peninsula connected to the main island by a narrow neck of land. Some 40 feet above the sea Captain Axe built Warwick Fort on the peninsula commanding the harbour's northern entrance. On the main island the settlement of New Westminster was installed initially at the water's edge. Despite Captain Elfrith's inclinations, the settlers were instructed not to take the offensive against the Spanish but rather to prepare prudently to repel any attacks. Fort Henry was to protect the primary source of water and the southern approach to the harbour whilst on the peninsula Darley's Fort was added east of Warwick Fort as a further deterrent to potential invaders. A fourth fort, Black Rock Fort, was directed to be built by Governor Bell on the main island to complement Warwick Fort.

Providence, so named because its success depended on the providence of God, experienced mixed fortunes as an agricultural enterprise at least in part because the settlers and their London sponsors were incompatible. The colonists, although contracted to do so, bitterly resented having to share the profits of their harvests and were not prepared to contribute their skills or materials to public works which included the island's defences, as required. And, despite their religious scruples, even the 1633 introduction of slaves – who the colonists maintained were being enslaved for being 'heathen' and not African – proved a mixed blessing. Five years later Providence achieved the dubious distinction of having to quell the first slave rebellion in the English colonies.

It was not to be long before the Spanish realised that the insignificant little island occupied by the English represented a serious threat and decided to take steps to remove that threat. The first warning of a likely Spanish attack came when the colonists learnt that their sister colony on Tortuga had been invaded. Then on July 2, 1635 a force under the personal command of the governor of Cartagena, Don Nicolas de Judice, approached from the southeast. It consisted of three ships and four smaller support vessels carrying 400 soldiers. For five days they probed for a way through the coral reefs that encircled the island. The heavy ordnance at Warwick Fort held them at bay and when the Spanish attempted to land on the beach the settlers drove them back with their muskets.

In an audacious ploy the Spanish commander under a flag of truce demanded that the colonists, deemed pirates, depart the island as reinforcements were on their way from Cartagena. This bluff failed and after seven days Don Nicolas withdrew by cover of night. The Providence Company's directors met on January 29, 1636 in London to hear a full account of the previous July's events. It was announced that King Charles I had responded to their accusations of Spanish infamy by granting the company the right of reprisal. An era of privateering by the Puritans in Providence was about to be legitimised. This was seen by the gentlemen adventurers as fortuitous since their investment in the colony had proved unprofitable despite having extended their colonising activities to the Miskito Coast. A year later they even contemplated an offer by the Dutch to buy Providence for 70,000 pounds. By this time the Captain Axe and his Dutch counterpart, Abraham Blauvelt, had established settlements on the Central American mainland.

The company was soon to decide that Providence would be the storehouse for the privateers' rich pickings and a source of supply of their shipboard requirements. The directors looked on this turn of events as the appropriate time to change the governor of the island. Philip Bell, whose unpopularity stemmed from the discontent of the different factions – the zealous religious-minded and the openly piratical – was replaced by Captain Robert Hunt. Hunt's governorship was short-lived and by 1639 Captain Nathaniel Butler was in charge.

Butler's enthusiasm was not for the mundane duties of governing but rather the search for opportunities for reprisal. Within six months of his appointment, he put together a fleet of English and Dutch ships and attacked Trujillo on the coast of Honduras. Because Captain William Jackson, who had also sailed under a commission from the Providence Island Company earlier, had extracted from the town's citizens '8,000 weight of indigo, 2,000 pieces of eight and two chain of gold,' there was little left by way of spoils for Butler.

On his return to Providence he found himself caught up in the disputes of the disgruntled and warring factions. Discouraged by a sense of powerlessness to resolve the conflicts and lead the island into more promising times, he left his post sailing to England on February 23, 1640, with non other than Captain Samuel Axe. His one unintended accomplishment had been to convince the Spanish once again that they should not tolerate Providence being in English's hands. Don Melchor de Aguilera, Captain-General of Cartagena, seized the opportunity to employ naval reinforcements recently arrived from Brazil and put together a fleet of six frigates and a galleon under Don Antonio Maldonado de Texeda. Ironically the Earl of Warwick's captured ship *Robert*, now called *Black Robin*, was amongst the flotilla leaving Cartagena that May morning in 1640 with 700 soldiers and seamen on board.

On May 30, two days after Don Antonio Maldonado had arrived at Providence, he managed to put a force ashore but it was repelled with heavy losses. A gale began blowing shortly after and with no secure anchorage available to them the Spanish departed with over a hundred men dead or captured. In the engagement that followed, the man left in charge by former governor Butler, Andrew Carter, displayed abject cowardice and astonishing incompetence. Ultimately, after he had executed his Spanish prisoners (despite having promised them safe passage), he was recalled to England in disgrace. Carter and his cronies failed to distribute powder and shot, spiked the guns of Black Rock Fort even before it was assaulted, and loaded the fort's food supplies on to a vessel on which he intended to escape.

If this humiliating defeat was not enough to prompt another attack, the news that another 300 Puritans from New England were immigrating to Providence hardened Spanish resolve. With direct orders from King Philip IV, General Francisco Diaz Pimienta organised a substantial fleet to regain Providence once and for all. It consisted of seven large ships, four pinnaces and a number of smaller vessels, manned by 600 seamen transporting 1,400 soldiers. Pimienta took his time developing a strategy, drawing near to the island on May 17, 1641. He did not land for another seven days but waited until his captains had reconnoitred the possible landing sites and for the persistent poor weather to dissipate.

At dawn on May 24, Pimienta made his move taking the Puritan defenders by surprise by launching an attack on the supposedly impenetrable harbour and New Westminster. His ships' artillery answered the bombardment from Warwick Fort whilst his soldiers landed on shore and quickly captured the town and the governor's residence. When the Spanish flag was seen flying over the residence the forts surrendered and the Spanish invaders formally took possession of the island, renaming it Santa Catalina, with a Roman Catholic Te Deum in the Puritan church. Unlike Governor Carter, General Pimienta showed remarkable restraint under the circumstances sparing the lives of his prisoners. A census revealed that there were 350 Europeans and 178 slaves. He sent most of the men to Spain into captivity and 60 women and children he mercifully put on a boat to England, others scattered to the Mosquito Coast and some to Caribbean islands. General Pimienta inherited a well-armed, well-provisioned island and left behind an occupying force of 150 men. For his feat he was awarded a knighthood of the Order of Santiago. It was to be another 25 years before the island was to become a target for the buccaneers again.

Despite the loss of the island, the Puritan 'buccaneers' continued to operate in the Caribbean using commissions issued by the Providence Company for another four years. William Jackson was a prime example. Sailing from the island of St Kitts in July 1642 with Captain Samuel Axe, one of the survivors of the expulsion from Providence, as his vice-admiral and Captain William Rous, another former Providence islander who had previously led an abortive attack on Santa Marta, Captain Jackson with seven ships and over a thousand men rampaged across the Caribbean for three years. During this time he attacked several towns on the coast of Venezuela including Maracaibo. Before returning to England Captain Jackson carried out a series of raids on coastal towns in Honduras, Costa Rica, Panama, Colombia, Guatemala and Mexico. The seeming ease with which Captain Jackson carried out his pillaging and the relative lack of resistance that he met was eventually a critical factor in persuading Oliver Cromwell to send an invading force to the West Indies.

Meanwhile the victorious Spanish admiral, Don Francisco Diaz de Pimienta argued that the island should be held as a Spanish outpost and had chosen one of his officers, Don Geronimo de Ojeda, to be governor. Warwick Fort was renamed Santa Teresa. The soldiers found the island well supplied with cannons, muskets and ammunition abandoned by the Puritans. But morale began to decline very quickly when requests for supplies and colonists (including a plea for 'lewd women') were ignored. Ojeda at one point discovered a mutiny amongst his Portuguese soldiers who were plotting to murder him and others under his command. The mutineers ironically were intent on becoming buccaneers.

The English still planned to retake Providence and the capture of Jamaica in 1655 was seen as a step in that direction. In the same year Cromwell wrote to Major-General Fortescue then in command of English forces in Jamaica:

'We think, and it desired amongst us to strive with the Spaniards for the mastery of all those seas; and therefore we could hastily wish that the Island of Providence were in our hands again, believing that it lies so advantageously in reference to the Main, and especially for the hindrance of the Peru trade and Cartagena, that you might not only have great advantage thereby of intelligence and surprise, but even block up the same.'

The man who did the job for England was Edward Mansfield although he disobeyed orders to achieve the Lord Protector's objective. His past remains shrouded in mystery which apparently was his wish and he was advanced in age by the time his exploits were first recorded. Referred to sometimes as 'Mansvelt' which may have come about as he appeared in Port Royal from the Dutch island of Curaçao with his own vessel, he is generally believed to be of English descent.

In the journal of Colonel Edward D'Oyley, governor of Jamaica, there is a 1660 entry noting that Mansfield had been issued with the ubiquitous 'let pass,' which he no doubt intended to use to attack the Spanish. He offered his services to Christopher Myngs and more than likely participated in the attack on Santiago de Cuba in 1662, accompanying him also on his 1663 Campeche expedition. When the news reached Jamaica in 1665 that the English and the Dutch were at war again in Europe the new governor, Sir Thomas Modyford, unable to muster a regular naval force, invited the Tortuga buccaneers to rendezvous in Bluefields Bay, the spacious

'We think, and it desired amongst us to strive with the Spaniards for the mastery of all those seas;'

anchorage in western Jamaica. Clearly Modyford calculated that the buccaneers would have reservations about entering Port Royal as England was supposedly at peace with Spain and any actions against the Spanish might lead to their detention. In all over 600 men and 13 vessels responded to Modyford's call by November and, with Mansfield as their chosen leader, they agreed to his invitation to seize the Dutch colony of Curaçao. It is quite possible that from the outset they were only paying lip-service to Modyford's wishes.

Mansfield's first action was to sail to Cuba, as was their custom, to scavenge provisions for the expedition. They seized a small Spanish vessel offshore and slaughtered its crew of 22 before attacking a small settlement of Cayo and marching 42 miles inland to the town of Sancti Spiritus. Here, the governor of Havana reported, they cruelly dealt with the inhabitants taking some prisoner to their ships. The marauders destroyed the dwellings, desecrated the church by inhabiting it and seized 300 cattle as ransom. The buccaneers later claimed they were acting on

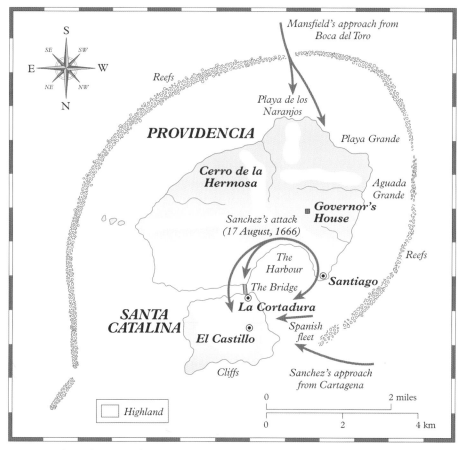

Santa Catalina, the peninsula on Providencia, was successfully fortified by both the Spanish and the English but it was the reefs surrounding the island that made the island difficult to invade. Edward Mansfield recaptured Providence Island for Cromwell from the Spanish in 1666 with an unexpected pre-dawn landing.

Portuguese commissions issued by the governor of Tortuga to give their atrocities legitimacy.

Modyford heard of these diversions and actually sent Colonel William Beeston to ensure that they would return to carrying out their original mission. After six weeks of searching, Beeston failed to find them. Despite otherwise reassuring the governor of his 'zeal to His Majesty's service and a firm resolution to attack Curaçao', with a personal commitment never to show Modyford his face until he had suitably served his country in the matter, Mansfield soon changed his mind. Mansfield's men refused to continue because the rewards were less than the risks justified. The Spanish colonies offered greater promise.

But the buccaneer admiral's fortunes were beginning to falter. Eight of his flotilla left him to independently descend on the town of Nata in the Panamanian province of Veragua. With the remaining force he decided to surprise the provincial Costa Rican capital of Cartago with an overland march. Unfortunately word was carried to the governor of his intentions and several hundred militiamen gathered at Turrialba to await his approach. Even before the Spanish fully engaged the buccaneers and were driving them back to the coast, hunger and exhaustion were taking their toll. Just as Mansfield abandoned this venture, four more ships left him

His reputation fading rapidly, Mansfield decided to at least give Modyford the satisfaction of seeing Providence back under English control. With his two remaining frigates, three sloops and 200 men – English, French, Dutch and Portuguese – and assisted by two prisoners who knew the island intimately, Mansfield brought all his cunning and daring into play to achieve this end.

Approaching Providence on May 25, 1666 from its southern end where he anchored his vessels, his men paddled across the reef in pinnaces in the moonlight. Moving swiftly along the island's narrow paths, they were able to surround the house of Governor Don Estevan de Ocampo as dawn rose. A detachment then moved down the island to the bridge connecting the Santa Catalina peninsula where the Spanish had built a small fort, La Cortadura. The few men who manned this defence were unprepared. Gunpowder, cannonballs and grapeshot were unavailable or in very limited supply; guns were not ready to be fired. By the time the buccaneers were confronting the defenders, there was nothing to do but surrender. When they seized the fort it is said that 27 outdated pieces of armament could be traced back to the English Queen Elizabeth who had reigned in the previous century.

Although the island's population only numbered 200, the 230 men who accompanied Mansfield probably shared booty of 70,000 pesos. Jamaica's governor, Sir Thomas Modyford, reported that little plunder was gained and comprised mainly slaves. The French buccaneers also wanted to take back to Tortuga some of the religious artefacts from the church and for once the English were prevented from indulging in their usual acts of desecration. Leaving Captain Charles Hadsell and 35 men in command of the island, Mansfield sailed for the coast of Panama where he dropped off the Spanish governor Ocampo and 170 Spanish inhabitants at Punta de Brujas.

A wooden bridge today connects Santa Catalina with the mainland.

England officially, some say cynically, disclaimed responsibility for the attack blaming '… some pirates who navigated in those seas and who had not yet subjected themselves to the King after he had regained his crown'. Governor Modyford maintained Mansfield was justified. He did no more than gently reprove him for acting without orders. Afterwards Modyford sent Major Samuel Smith, who had accompanied Mansfield, with a small body of soldiers to reinforce Hadsell and appointed his brother James to be lieutenant-governor.

This was to be Edward Mansfield's last exploit. He died shortly after, with there being two versions of his demise. Spanish historians claim he returned to Tortuga where in 1667 he is said to have been poisoned. But a deposition found amongst English records state that his ship was captured by the Spanish after which he was taken to Havana, jailed and later executed. Twenty years of warnings that Santa Catalina was at the mercy of buccaneers such as Mansfield had been ignored and now, once more, the island became the focus of concern amongst the Spanish colonial authorities.

Its recapture was even seen as a stepping-stone to regaining Jamaica. The feeling in Madrid was that the plague that had swept through London in 1665 and the disastrous fire which had devastated the city a year later had weakened the English. Whilst the English in the Caribbean did not suffer the same anxiety, a man like Sir Thomas Modyford knew that he could not defend Jamaica unless he could turn to the buccaneers for assistance. A council of war was called at Cartagena. The president of Panama himself, Don Juan Perez de Guzman, was put in charge of the recovery of Santa Catalina. His first act was to seize an English ship of 400 tons, *Concord*, with 30 guns, captained by Henry Wasey and approved by the Spanish to trade in slaves as it lay in the harbour at Portobelo. Wasey was put in irons accused of being a spy and his ship manned by 350 Spaniards including many who had been deported from Providence. It was a report from Wasey that confirmed that Mansfield had died in a Havana prison.

With a small contingent of reinforcements from Cartagena, Jose Sanchez Ximenes reached Providence on August 12, 1667. After scouting the island he found that the English were occupying the peninsula and flying their flag over what had originally been Warwick Fort. Ximenez was also reliably informed by three escaped slaves that although the fort was quite well armed there were no more than 60 or 70 buccaneers on the island. Major Smith refused to surrender but after a siege the English sent two men under a flag of truce to offer to do so if the garrison could keep their arms. Ximenez denied the request saying that unless they surrendered unconditionally everyone would be put to the sword. The English eventually laid down their arms and, despite protesting that they were promised a ship on which to depart free men, the Spanish sent them into captivity at Portobelo.

In later depositions to Governor Modyford in Port Royal, the captives painted a horrifying picture of the conditions they had to endure. Thirty-three of them were chained to the ground in a dungeon measuring 12 feet by 10 feet. They were forced to work from five in the morning to seven at night in water. When they weakened from hunger or exhaustion they were beaten with cudgels from which several died. One deposition read: 'Having no clothes, their backs were blistered with the sun, their heads scorched, their necks, shoulders and hands raw with carrying stones and mortar, their feet chopped and their legs bruised and battered with the irons and their corpses were noisome to one another'. This was probably typical of a conventional Spanish prison experience in the tropics. On this occasion Governor Samuel Smith, Sir Thomas Whetstone who had sailed with both Myngs and Mansfield, and a Captain Stanley spent 17 months imprisoned in Panama where Whetstone probably died. Smith was later moved to Havana but returned to Port Royal in 1668.

When the Spanish examined the papers left behind by the English governor of Providence, as well as blank letters of marque or commissions which the Englishman was using to authorise reprisals, they also found instructions requiring Governor Smith to send all prisoners to Port Royal '… so that they might be treated in the same manner that English captives had been treated by the enemy'. The buccaneers themselves, however, seldom took captives and would have been unlikely to transport them to Port Royal. Once again the authorities in Cartagena neglected their newly-reclaimed island. A request for a curate went unfilled as did another for women to lessen the discontent of the garrison of soldiers. According to Exquemelin, the Spanish were to use the island as a penal colony for male criminals.

The reality of the potential threat that Providence held for the Spanish in the Caribbean became a fact in 1670 when Mansfield's acknowledged successor, Henry Morgan, captured it in order to use it as a base springboard for his historic attack on the city of Panama. Morgan's successes at Portobelo, Maracaibo and Gibraltar, amongst other feats of seamanship and generalship were already creating a substantial reputation for him. To his flagship at Isle à Vache near the northwestern tip of Hispaniola he was able to draw his forces from as far afield as Bermuda and the Bahamas, from the remnants of General Venables army in Jamaica and the ranks of the boucaniers in Tortuga and Hispaniola who were at the time rebelling against Governor d'Ogeron and the French West India Company. His company also included mulattoes, Negroes and Indians who served as pilots and guides.

On December 6, 1670, Morgan wrote to Modyford that he had assembled an armada of 1,800 men and 36 ships. At Cape Tiburon he laid on stocks of boucanned meat, fresh fruit and other supplies. Earlier Morgan and his captains had favoured attacking Santiago de Cuba but it was considered too well fortified. Cartagena was an alternative but they finally decided on Panama as it was the source of many commissions, issued by the governor, against the English and 'that it stands most for the good of Jamaica and the safety of us all'. It undoubtedly offered the prospect of the greatest plunder.

On the morning of December 14, Morgan's fleet sighted the island. Captain Joseph Bradley, who had been with Edward Mansfield in 1666, guided the landing party of 1,000 men through the channels and across the reef at Manchineel Bay

The shoreline around Providencia is ringed by reefs, making a landing difficult.

on the south coast. As had been the case in the past when being invaded, the inhabitants withdrew from the larger island and took shelter in the forts on the island peninsula. At this time there was a drawbridge connecting the main island and the Santa Catalina peninsula which was pulled up. Heavy cannon fire prevented the buccaneers from advancing as night fell.

At midnight a torrential tropical downpour drenched the men and their arms, leaving them wet, cold and increasingly disaffected with the undertaking. Morgan sent a canoe under a white flag of truce to demand that the Spaniards surrender or he would give no quarter. The governor requested two hours to deliberate with his council. When the answer came back in the affirmative it came with an unexpected request.

In order to save the honour of his reputation and that of his fellow officers, the governor asked Henry Morgan to take part in a face-saving charade. The Spanish were to seemingly put up resistance before conceding defeat. Surprisingly Morgan agreed, but on the condition that not one of his men would suffer injury or lose his life, to which the Spanish gave their assurance. The mock battle was to take place as follows: The buccaneers would cross the bridge that night and storm Fort San Jeronimo (formerly Cortadura) overlooking it. Three ships were to sail around the island and enter the main harbour as if to take the main fortress Santa Teresa which had four massive stone bastions and was armed with 20 guns. The governor proposed that he could be intercepted and taken prisoner crossing from San Jeronimo to Santa Theresa following which he would be obliged to surrender the latter.

By nightfall the staged conquest began with many explosions and small arms being fired into the air. Soon all the defences were occupied and the population herded into the church safely. Not a life was lost, not an injury received, not a reputation tainted. According to Exquemelin, the principal damage was to the inhabitants' hens, pigs and sheep because of the buccaneers' ravenous appetites. When they ran short of firewood a few houses were torn down and used for fuel. Morgan gave safe passage to his Spanish captives who had been unmolested and set about loading on to his ships all the gunpowder and other munitions he needed before proceeding to Panama. His men dismantled all the smaller batteries on the two islands keeping only Santa Teresa and San Jeronimo which were to be retained and manned by a contingent of men he would leave behind.

His most useful discovery was three criminals who were willing to be guides for his crossing of the Isthmus of Panama. In preparation for this he sent Captain Bradley to take Fort San Lorenzo at the mouth of the Chagres River. When this was accomplished, he left the former Puritan colony of Providence intending to return and establish a permanent settlement later. This was aborted after the arrival of a new governor in Jamaica with orders to prevent attacks on Spanish outposts. Providence as the Puritans knew it, Santa Catalina to the Spanish and today the Colombian island of Providencia, never again played a strategic part in the plans of the buccaneers or the Spanish after Morgan's departure and remained a virtually forgotten island for well over a century afterwards.

Chapter 9

PORTOBELO

THE FAMOUS FAIR

~

Christopher Columbus called the place Puerto Bello but like many place names it has been abbreviated over time to Portobelo. As beautiful as it is, the engineer Bautista Antonelli in 1586 recognised in it the possibilities for creating a well-defended bay and harbour.

Portobelo, unlike many other Caribbean towns, has a number of fortifications remaining from its colourful past but what is there certainly needs restoration if it is to capture the imagination of the curious visitor. Entering from the west, Fort Santiago, built after Admiral Edward Vernon's 1739 attack, is the first of the fortifications to come into view. These ruins include barracks, batteries, officers' quarter, a sentry box and artillery shed. Adjacent to them is a small watchtower built at the same time. It has a dry moat, a well in the centre and its battlements provide a panoramic view of the entrance to the bay.

Little remains of the 'Iron Fort', San Fernando, across the bay, as the Americans dismantled its walls in the last century to create the breakwater at the northern end of the Panama Canal. Fort San Jeronimo on the harbour in the town itself is quite expansive but in a similar condition to Santiago. An 18-gun embrasure faces menacingly out towards the sea. Some walls of the officers quarters, a barracks and guardroom and an impressive façade face the Real Aduana, or royal treasure house, in the centre of the town.

The Real Aduana, an elegant two-storey building, has been restored in what is a continuing programme in the town. One wing is devoted to a small museum with a simple exhibition of historical artefacts, maps, illustrations and photos. The other has a unique display of ornate robes honouring the Black Christ, celebrated in a festival every October. Upstairs is a collection of photos and drawings of colonial Spain's Caribbean fortresses and in the entrance hall a 1617 bronze cannon takes place of pride.

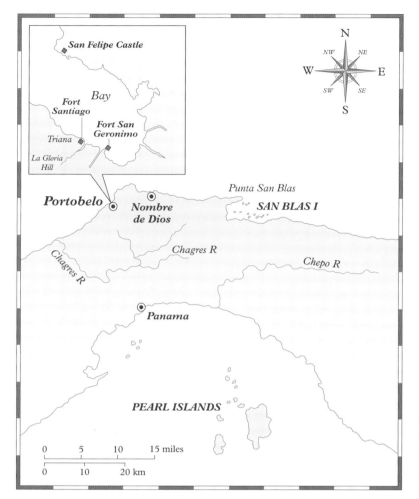

The bay and harbour of Portobelo, aptly named by Christopher Columbus, became a focal point for Central American trade.

After William Parker's attack, Santiago de la Gloria was built to protect the eastern approach to Portobelo.

Henry Morgan, during his 1668 capture of Portobelo, threatened to incarcerate the defenders of San Jeronimo and blow it up.

The Royal Treasure House – Real Aduana – was the objective of the treasure seekers when they invaded Portobelo.

Ry the time the English privateer Francis Drake had sacked Nombre de Dios, the port to the east, three times – in 1572, 1573 and 1596 – it was not that difficult for Juan Bautista Antonelli to persuade the King of Spain to adopt Portobelo as an alternative Caribbean transhipment port for Spanish trade in the Panamanian isthmus. Antonelli simply put it, 'If it might please our Majesty, it would be a good idea that the city of Nombre de Dios be brought and built in this harbour'. At the time Portobelo consisted of only ten houses.

Portobelo was so named by Christopher Columbus on his fourth and last voyage to the Caribbean in 1502. The spacious sheltered bay surrounded by lush vegetation was his anchorage for a week while a patch of stormy November weather passed. It might have been Spain's first choice for a stronghold but the next man to arrive was Diego de Nicuesa, the newly-appointed governor for the province of Castillo de Oro, as the region was known. On landing, 20 of his men were massacred by the Indians forcing him to beat a hasty retreat.

Sailing east the governor entered a spacious bay where the land appeared fertile, a site for a fort was identified and hostile natives were not in evidence. With his men exhausted, weak and their numbers reduced, Nicuesa declared: 'Paremos aqui, en el nombre de Dios'. (Here let us stop in the name of God.) His good fortune was not to last and after a disastrous attempt to oust two of his rivals, Vasco Nunez de Balboa and Martin Zamudio, he was put on board an unseaworthy vessel and ordered by them to return directly to Spain. Nicuesa was never heard from again and his fledgling Nombre de Dios settlement abandoned, not to be reoccupied until 1519.

The following year the Camino Real road which crossed the isthmus to the city of Panama was built to carry the precious metals of Spain's South American possessions to the awaiting galleons for transporting to Seville. Its first Caribbean terminus was Nombre de Dios. For the next 30 years some 15 vessels each year carried merchandise from Spain and on the return trip, silver and gold. By 1552 they began sailing in convoys for protection against pirates both in the Atlantic as well as the Caribbean. As the wealth of Spain's Americas grew so did the ambition of England's Queen Elizabeth and her privateering sea dogs. The saga of Sir Francis Drake, his treasure hunting in the Caribbean and spectacular feat in circumnavigating the globe has been told elsewhere. His association with Portobelo, however, deserves our attention.

On May 24, 1572, Francis Drake in the 70-ton *Pascha* and his brother John in a second vessel set out from Plymouth bound for Nombre de Dios. The uneventful voyage took them between the islands of Dominica and Guadeloupe and across the Caribbean until they sighted Santa Marta on the coast of Venezuela. The admiral's first stop was a safe harbour he called Port Pheasant lying between Tolu and Nombre de Dios. He had been here before and gave it this name not only because of the abundance of what he described as pheasants but also because it provided fruit, fish and fresh water which the expedition desperately needed after the seven-week crossing. In the week he spent at Port Pheasant Drake had his men assemble three pinnaces that he had carried prefabricated from England. These were vital for landing men ashore as they could navigate safely through the reefs and sandbars. Drake was joined by another English privateer, Captain Rance, and his 30 men.

In the pinnaces and Captain Rance's small shallops, 73 heavily armed men attempted to paddle into Nombre de Dios harbour without raising an alarm. Unfortunately, although it was 3 a.m., a merchant vessel carrying wine and other commodities had not long arrived from Spain. Soon the townspeople were woken by the sound of gunshots. As it happened Nombre de Dios had frequently experienced incursions by runaway slaves, known as cimmarones, as well as native Indians whose hatred of the Spanish was to prove extremely valuable to the buccaneers in the next century. The town, although it had no walled defence, possessed a more than adequate contingent of soldiers.

With trumpeters and drummers employed to give an impression of a much larger invading force than really existed, Drake's men engaged in a long and bloody battle for the king's treasure house which had been their sole objective since they had sailed from Plymouth. A contingent of 150 Spanish troops had recently arrived from Panama to provide protection against the cimmarones and counter-attacked with increasing success. Although the English reached the treasure house and claimed to have seen enormous stacks of silver bars, this has been disputed as the annual treasure fleet had sailed some weeks before and nothing was normally kept in the warehouse between sailings. During what was at best a strategic withdrawal, Drake received a bullet in the leg whilst many others were wounded. Their consolation prize was the merchant vessel and its welcome cargo of wine.

On his next attempt Drake's timing much improved. This venture actually began badly. He and his cimmarones allies were about to seize the treasure on a mule train headed from Panama along the Camino Real when one of his men, a Robert Pike, described in an contemporary account as '… having drunken too much aqua vitae without water …' gave away the ambush. Luckily in the following April, again with the assistance of the cimmarones and in an alliance with a French Huguenot corsair, Guillame Le Testu, Drake surprised the treasure mule train as it was approaching Nombre de Dios. Drake and Le Testu successfully plundered the rescua – as the Spanish described the mule train – despite the fact that it was heavily guarded. They departed with what they could carry of the heavy metal. In a report to the King of Spain the loot was listed as 100,000 pesos all in gold. They buried about 15 tons of silver intending to retrieve it later. However, it was the Spanish who recovered it after torturing a Frenchman who had been separated from his companions. Le Testu was wounded, captured and later beheaded by the Spanish. Fortunately for posterity he had already distinguished himself as a hydrographer and several years earlier had produced seven remarkable maps of the world.

Queen Elizabeth knighted Drake in 1581 and four years later authorised a powerful fleet comprising six of her own warships, 21 well-armed merchant ships, 1,500 seamen and over 1,000 soldiers to sail for the West Indies in pursuit of

Sir Francis Drake, painted in the year he was knighted, was the scourge of Nombre de Dios but, when he died of wounds, was buried at sea in Portobelo Bay.

even greater riches for her treasury. The venture was a disaster from the start. Her two most successful sea dogs, who had previously sailed together, were now at odds with each other. Sir John Hawkins, now 63, was to die as the fleet approached Puerto Rico where it was defeated after a debilitating encounter. Drake sacked Riohacha and Santa Marta, contemplated Cartagena but estimated that it was too well defended and carried on to Nombre de Dios where he found nothing worth looting. He struck out once again for Panama but 700 of his men were caught in an ambush after they had sailed up the Chagres River towards the capital and were trapped in a narrow pass where the Spanish were waiting. He had no choice but to retreat. An officer of the fleet, Thomas Maynarde, wrote: 'Since our return from Panama (Francis Drake) never carried mirth nor joy in his face'.

Once on board again Drake began searching the coast of Nicaragua for a consolation prize but, having turned eastwards, not only did bad weather hamper his progress but a fever epidemic also broke out. The fleet anchored at Portobelo. The population fled in a state of high anxiety which was prudent as their town was soon to be reduced to rubble by the English. Drake, now deliriously ill, rose from his bed and asked his servant to dress him in his armour in order that he could die as a fighting man but his strength had deserted him. On January 28, 1596, Sir Francis Drake died and, encased in a lead coffin, his body slipped overboard in the bay of Portobelo off the island of Buena Ventura after a short burial ceremony.

The Elizabethan seadog, Sir Francis Drake, died after his last Caribbean campaign in 1596 and was buried in a lead coffin in Portobelo Bay.

Portobelo (its original official name was San Felipe de Portobelo) takes as its date of founding March 20, 1597, when the settlement was put under the charge of Francisco de Valverde y Mercado by order of the king. It absorbed most of the residents of Nombre de Dios along with the latter's title of city and coat of arms which declared 'Tierra Firme, brenãs de oro'. Planning for the defence of Portobelo had begun when King Philip II had sent Bautista Antonelli on his classic tour of Spanish fortifications in the Caribbean following Drake's final voyage. Antonelli proposed building a substantial fortress on the northern side of the entrance to the harbour with a watchtower, or lookout, at the highest point above it and a smaller fort on the southern side. By the end of the century these fortifications were under construction.

The larger fort was named San Felipe de Sotomayor, better known as San Felipe de Todo Fiero ('Iron Castle') in recognition of its unique construction. Coral, mined under water, and cut easily into blocks while still wet, was bound by a mixture of lime and red clay which itself became extremely strong when it hardened. The walls, nine feet thick, were able to absorb cannonballs without cracking, causing little damage. In fact, when Admiral Vernon in 1739 attempted to destroy the Iron Castle he claimed it took him all of 18 days. The smaller Fortaleza de Santiago on the southern side of the bay contained a battery of five or six guns and was supported by an emplacement above where musketeers could cover the gunners below.

The site for Portobelo was well chosen and frequently described as the best harbour in the Caribbean. In the seventeenth century it could hold as many as 300 galleons and 1,000 small vessels under the watch of the forts, with room for another 2,000 outside. The town itself was built in a half-moon running east and west on the southern side of the harbour, extending back to the edge of the mountains. Two plazas dominated the criss-cross of streets with a bridge over a river joining the two. The centre of Portobelo was to contain 50 houses, a modest cathedral, the Convent of Mercy, a hospital and the king's houses on the main plaza and the administrative buildings on the second plaza. Most structures, some of two storeys, were constructed of wood and set on stone foundations. Four suburbs surrounded the town: Merced where the middle and upper class lived; Triana, home to the indigent Spanish and the king's slaves; Guinea, the housing occupied by the free slaves; and a shanty town of straw-roofed shacks made of cane next to the abattoir.

As superior as the topography was at Portobelo, the climate was as insalubrious as it had been in Nombre de Dios. Because it rained almost every day it was humid and damp with temperatures consistently over 30 degrees centigrade. For a while after January southwest winds kept it drier but its residents frequently fell ill. Despite the initial efforts to protect itself against intruders, the seventeenth century began badly for Portobelo.

The English privateer William Parker had his baptism of fire with Sir Francis Drake at Cadiz in 1587 and cruised the Caribbean in the 1590s, first raiding Puerto Caballos and Campeche. In November, 1601, he set out from his home town of Plymouth with 200 men in two large and three small vessels. He lost one of the smaller vessels, a pinnace, on the stormy voyage to the Cape Verde Islands where he remained long enough to sack the town of San Vincente. Reaching the Caribbean, he held the Cubagua pearl fisheries to ransom then proceeded towards the isthmus, capturing a Portuguese slave trader bound for Cartagena.

Early on the morning of February 7, 1602, his flotilla approached Portobelo harbour. Seen by moonlight and being able to use his Spanish-speaking captives to reply to the challenge from the Iron Castle, Parker in his words initially anchored at '… the Place where my shippers roade beinge the rock where Sir Francis Drake his coffin was throwne overboard'. His prudence was justified. San Felipe was a substantial fortification boasting at the time 35 cannons and a garrison of 50 men.

When Spanish vigilance seemed relaxed, he embarked with 30 of his men and two cannons in a shallop and, passing Portobelo's other defence, the smaller Santiago, he landed at Triana which he immediately torched. With almost no resistance offered them on the outskirts, Parker's men marched into Portobelo towards the treasure house where the governor, Don Pedro Melendez, was waiting with 60 soldiers and civilian militia.

According to Parker's account, the ensuing conflict went badly for the English until Melendez and one of his officers was wounded and retreated into the building. By daybreak the remainder of Parker's soldiers had arrived and after a five-hour siege the Spanish surrendered. The treasure house held little in the way of the silver of Peru as two frigates bound for Cartagena had emptied it only recently. However, a search of the town uncovered enough plunder to satisfy Parker. Governor Melendez was magnanimously treated for his wounds and released without ransom. Loading their booty on to two vessels seized in the harbour, the Englishmen sailed towards San Felipe and the anchorage where their ships waited. As one of the confiscated Spanish ships was mounted with cannons they were able to exchange fire with the Iron Fort and escape relatively unscathed.

Among the wounded was William Parker himself who suffered a musket-ball shot through his elbow. Parker's Caribbean exploits only lasted another year. He

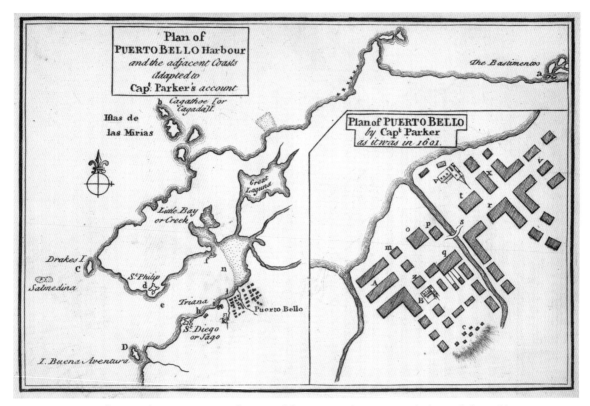

William Parker, a privateer at the turn of the seventeenth century, sacked Portobelo and later went on to become Mayor of Plymouth in England.

became mayor of Plymouth in England for a short while and went on to become a founding member of the Virginia Company. In 1617 he sailed on an expedition to the East Indies where he died. After Parker's attack the Fortaleza de Santiago was abandoned in favour of a more imposing fortification known as Santiago de la Gloria built at the eastern approach to Portobelo. This new Santiago and the Iron Castle on the opposite shore proved an effective deterrent to the buccaneers for the next six decades.

The annual fair, or feria, held when the galleons came for the bullion, had been moved to Portobelo in 1597 in anticipation of finding a healthier environment. But the difference was only relative because of the appalling lack of hygiene which meant that disease thrived and spread like wildfire. From a few hundred, the population grew dramatically with the arrival from Spain, Panama and Peru of merchants and their servants, Crown officials, artisans and 4,000 or 5,000 seamen and soldiers on board the galleons. They stayed for the fair from two to four weeks or longer. As early as the start of the seventeenth century, the French explorer Samuel Champlain described the town as 'the most evil and pitiful residence in the world'. When he passed through in 1637, Thomas Gage called it '… an open grave …' maintaining that 500 lives were lost during the fair and suggested that it should be called 'Puerto Malo' rather than Portobelo for the grief that it brought.

Accommodating the transient residents was another problem. The permanent residents moved into one or two rooms and rented out their remaining space. Others evacuated entirely and moved for the duration to the poorer areas including the slave district of the town. Temporary structures were erected, while west of the town on open land barracks were put up for the duration of the fair for the sailors and soldiers.

Gage complained bitterly at the cost of accommodation and the conditions he had to endure. He described his space as a mouse hole:

'It was no bigger than would contain a bed, table, and a stool or two with room enough besides to open and shut the door, and they demanded of me for it during the aforesaid time of the fleet, six score crowns …' A prosperous merchant might pay 40 times that for a large house. Equally disconcerting was the cost of food and drink. Said the English priest: 'Then began the price of all things to rise, a fowl to be worth 12 reals, which in the mainland I had often bought for one; a pound of

Equally disconcerting was the cost of food and drink.

beef then was worth two reals, whereas in other places £13 for half a real, and so of all other food and provision, which was so excessive dear that I knew not how to live but by fish and tortoises (turtles) …'

The business of the fair was highly formalised. On entering the harbour the ships from Spain would first have to be examined by royal officials sent from Panama. Cargoes were inspected to see that they had been correctly manifested and that no unauthorised goods were on board before unloading could begin. Tents created from the ships' sails were erected in the main plaza and cargo from each ship was piled up to be inspected by its owners. Buyers, sellers and officials met to set the price of the various types and classes of merchandise which had to be adhered to.

The largest single category of imports from Spain was fabrics, ranging from damask and other linens to canvas and sailcloth. Foodstuffs such as flour, nuts, oil, herbs and dried fruits were displayed alongside wines, beer, cider and alcoholic spirits. Building materials, weapons, furniture, books, agricultural implements, glassware, paper, clocks – all finished goods needed for living in the colonies – went on sale. Precious metals from the mines of the Americas were the most valuable cargo exported back to Spain. Sugar, tobacco, cacao, quinine and vicuna wool, as well as a wide variety of tropical commodities, were also regularly traded at the Portobelo fair. Once purchases were made the merchants of Peru and Panama began the long journey homewards. The first leg would take them to Panama on the Pacific Coast where vessels waited to carry the goods south and into the hinterland.

There were two routes to Panama. One was by small coastal vessel carrying up to 30 tons which sailed west to the Chagres River following it to Venta la Cruces where mules completed the journey into the city. The more popular route was by mule overland in pack trains of up to 200 mules carrying 200 pounds each through the rugged interior on the Camino Real. In the same way silver and gold reached the Portobelo fair through jungle, swamps, across rivers and over mountains. When all the transactions were completed and the goods loaded for dispatch, the temporary structures were dismantled and the town returned to normal. From its earliest days in 1575 when the fair was first established in Nombre de Dios, until the last of the Spanish galleons reached Portobelo in 1737, it was the most important of the Spanish Caribbean fairs – including Vera Cruz and Cartagena – in terms of the volume and value of the cargoes passing through it.

Technically the expedition against Portobelo that Henry Morgan led in 1668 was conceived not to ransack and destroy the town but rather to ascertain whether the Spanish were preparing to attempt to retake their former colony of Jamaica. The authorities in Jamaica issued a special commission to Colonel Henry Morgan, as he was referred to on this occasion, commanding him to '… draw together the English privateers and take prisoners of the Spanish nation, whereby you may gain information

of that enemy to attack Jamaica, of which I have had frequent and strong advice'. The original copy of this commission cannot be traced but it is believed to have been intended to restrict hostility to Spain's ships at sea, not its possessions on land.

Regardless of the formalities, Morgan was very quickly able to raise ten ships and nearly 500 men, French and English. The flotilla sailed to the Isle of Pines, one of the buccaneers' popular rendezvous off the coast of Cuba. Here another two ships and 200 men joined up. It has been claimed that Morgan intended mounting an attack on Havana by approaching from the countryside and not by sea. The Spanish had expected it and the town was well fortified and garrisoned. However, his objective was Puerto Principe, not a port at all but an inland town grown wealthy through its trade in cattle and hides.

In a typically terse report to Governor Modyford five months later, Morgan wrote: 'We were driven to the south keys of Cuba where, being like to starve, and finding French in like condition, we put our men ashore, and finding all the cattle driven up country and the inhabitants fled, we marched 20 leagues to Porto Principe on the north of the island, and with little resistance possessed ourselves of same.' He also reported that 70 Spaniards had volunteered to serve against Jamaica thus fulfilling his obligation to gather intelligence. Guided by a reluctant prisoner, Morgan led his men on the 30-mile march over hilly terrain in only 24 hours leaving them tired but eager to proceed. As they approached the unsuspecting town their guide escaped and raised the alarm.

A glamourised interpretation of Henry Morgan confronting his captives at Portobelo.

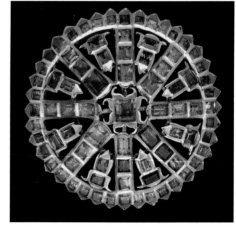

Spanish galleons carried the great wealth of the Americas. Clockwise from the top: Gold bullion from the Nuestra Senora de las Maravillas; *Spanish Colonial emerald and gold seventeenth-century necklace; Gold jewellery from the* Nuestra Senora de las Maravillas *circa l650; Spanish Colonial emerald and gold brooch from the same galleon; Seventeenth-century gold and emerald orb.*

The authorities managed to muster 700 soldiers and militia accompanied by another hundred men on horses and mules to confront the buccaneers. Exquemelin recounts that the ferocity of the buccaneers' fighting coupled with an unlikely adherence to military discipline contributed to the fact that they '... marched in very good rank and file, at the sound of their drums and with flying colours ...' which quickly disheartened the Spanish troops. The townspeople fought gallantly but to no avail and before long the populace was being herded into several churches and a ransom demanded. After sending all the valuables he could find back to the ships, Henry Morgan got his ransom in the form of a thousand head of cattle, with sufficient salt to cure the slaughtered beef which was then stored in casks for the voyage to Portobelo. Although the buccaneers' provisions were vital, the booty of only 50,000 pesos worth of coins and other goods did not satisfy Morgan's men.

The French who had thrown their lot in with Morgan were not encouraged by the prospects of a Central American campaign which he was contemplating and were disillusioned by the poor returns from Puerto Principe. They opted to return to Tortuga and join the notorious Nau L'Ollonais to improve their fortunes. After the long Caribbean crossing, Henry Morgan's much-reduced fleet anchored at Naos Bay to plan a strategy. He was able to persuade his captains that, despite its formidable fortifications and military contingent numbering several hundred, Portobelo could be captured by the skilful use of the element of surprise.

Creeping up the coast, Morgan soon transferred the main body of his men into 23 pirogues and rowed the balance of the way arriving at 3 a.m. on June 27 at Buena Ventura Cove. Travelling on foot, the buccaneers captured a sentry at the entrance to the town. He led them silently to Fort San Jeronimo where he was instructed to demand its surrender or no quarter would be given. In Exquemelin's words: 'Despite this threat the defenders proved stubborn and bravely fired on their attackers, so that at least they could give warning to the people in the city.' Resistance was futile and more than half the 130 men of the garrison died. As expected, in the dungeon they found 11 Englishmen, survivors of the retaking of Providence Island by Don Jose Sanchez Ximenez who now was the governor of Portobelo. The myth that Prince Maurice, uncle of England's King Charles II, was languishing there was put to rest. The unfortunate royal mariner had probably been lost at sea with his ship off Puerto Rico five years earlier.

True to their word, according to Exquemelin, Morgan's men incarcerated the remaining defenders in the castle and detonated its gunpowder magazine to blow it up. Awake and terrified, the townspeople desperately attempted to hide their valuable possessions. Morgan next turned his attention to Santiago de la Gloria, the fort on the southern side of the harbour that, with San Felipe, 'the Iron Castle' on the northern side, was preventing his vessels from entering. The governor had taken over command of Santiago and successfully repelled the raiders with unrelenting musket fire and by dumping huge stones and explosives on top of them. The only advantage that the marksmen amongst the buccaneers had was that they could pick off the Spanish on the ramparts, shooting from the hillside above the fort. The battle continued through the morning with no resolution.

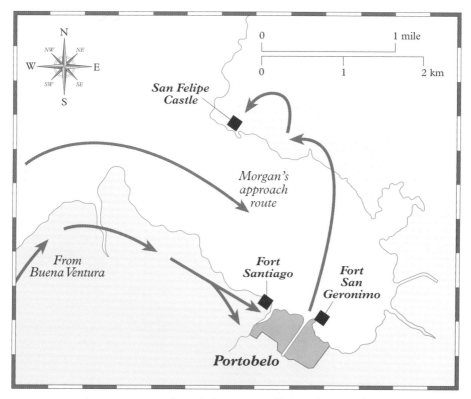

Henry Morgan's 1668 capture of Portobelo was typically launched from land to flank its substantial fortifications.

What happened next is a matter for controversy but this is how Exquemelin recorded it: 'Morgan had a dozen ladders made, broad enough for four men to climb at the same time. He fetched all the monks and nuns, and the governor was informed that unless he surrendered the fort these people would be made to set the scaling ladders against its walls. The contemptuous answer Morgan received was that he should never have the fort so long as the governor lived.' According to Exquemelin all the pleading and begging of the clerics was to no avail and many were wounded or injured putting up the ladders. Despite their efforts, the defenders were soon overwhelmed by the buccaneers. Later Morgan successfully sued Exquemelin's publishers who had to issue a denial of the account.

Tragically, the governor refused to surrender himself despite the entreaties of his wife and daughter. In one final demonstration of his courage, he not only slew a number of buccaneers but also a number of his own men who had shown cowardice in the face of defeat. He refused to be taken prisoner, reputedly declaring, 'I had rather die as a valiant soldier than be hanged as a coward' before he was killed. Witnessing the fall of the town and its forts, the commander of San Felipe meekly gave in and Henry Morgan's flotilla sailed into the harbour unmolested. By the end of the day it was time to enjoy the spoils of victory. Says Exquemelin: 'Having put everything in order, they began making merry, lording it with wine and women. If

50 stout-hearted men had been at hand that night they could have wiped out all the buccaneers.'

The next day the buccaneers began the task for which they had signed on: looting the town, uttering dire threats and promising hideous torture on the rack. Exquemelin maintained that many innocent citizens 'died like Martyrs' because, although they had nothing of worth to conceal, they were not believed. A letter from John Style to the Secretary of State complaining about the depravity seems to confirm the buccaneers' reputation for cruelty: 'It is a common thing among the privateers, besides burning with matches and such like slight torments, to cut a man to pieces, first some flesh, then a hand, an arm, a leg, sometime tying a cord about his head and with a stick twisting it until the eyes shot out.'

Exquemelin's Boucaniers of America *shows Portobelo under siege by Henry Morgan and his buccaneers in an imaginative woodcut.*

John Taylor's manuscript includes an illustration of Portobelo about the time of Morgan's attack.

By the fifth day the viceroy of Panama, Don Juan Perez de Guzman, had assembled 3,000 men and sent them to recover Portobelo from the clutches of the buccaneers. Henry Morgan, probably tipped off by the Indians, sent a hundred of his best men to a narrow pass in the mountains through which the viceroy's men had to travel. The ambush succeeded, and in fact, the outcome persuaded Don Juan Perez de Guzman that Morgan's demand for 100,000 pieces of eight was worth paying to rid the town of the Corsarios.

The viceroy was astonished that a force of little more than 400 could have overwhelmed the defences of Portobelo. He is reputed to have sent a message to Morgan seeking to know by what means he was able to achieve such a feat. Exquemelin explained: 'Morgan received (the viceroy's) envoy with great civility and gave him a French (boucanier's) musket with a barrel four and a half feet long, firing a one ounce bullet … He charged the messenger to tell his master that Morgan presented him with this musket, and that within a year or two he could come to

Panama to fetch it back again.' It was an eerie prediction. In return the viceroy sent Morgan a gold ring set with a rosette of emeralds and begged him not to call on him in the manner he had visited Portobelo, for in that case he might not get such a good reception.

In his official report, Henry Morgan claimed that he lost only 18 men with 32 wounded and had occupied Portobelo for little over four weeks. When he arrived back in Port Royal he declared spoils worth 2,500 pieces of eight which at the time were worth £62,500. Each seaman drew £60 while the king was to receive £600 which was to be kept to help repair Port Royal's fortifications. Morgan had carried off considerable loot as well as cannons from Portobelo's forts and when he was not able to remove a cannon it was spiked and rendered useless. Exquemelin described their return to Jamaica where '… they passed here some time in all sorts of vices and debauchery, according to their common manner of doing, spending with huge prodigality what others had gained with no small labour and toil'.

Portobelo was to get another ten years respite from the ravages of the buccaneers but at no time was the city far from their minds. The last of the buccaneers ambitious enough to write himself into the history of Portobelo was Captain John Coxon, probably one of the least notorious of his generation yet a man who managed to bob and weave within and without the law for 20 years with remarkable skill and a great deal of luck. He first came to light in the logwood trade in the early 1670s when he and others provided a deposition to Sir Thomas Lynch, governor of Jamaica, outlining the logwood cutters' activities on the coast of the Yucatan peninsula in Mexico. The trade was being threatened by Captain Yallahs, a Dutch captain turned Spanish mercenary, who was paid to intercept English logwood cutters' ships contrary to Governor Lynch's understanding of the spirit of the 1670 Anglo-Spanish peace accord.

Despite the fact that England and Spain were supposedly no longer enemies, the merchants of Port Royal saw no reason to discontinue profiting from the buccaneers' enterprise. John Coxon found himself in Port Royal owning a ship in partnership with Colonel Robert Byndloss who was Henry Morgan's brother-in-law, later to become Chief Justice, and Robert Pemberton, a Port Royal merchant. As a result of the ending of hostilities, Coxon was sailing legally with a French commission in partnership with a French buccaneer, Captain La Garde.

In June 1677 La Garde and Coxon seized Santa Marta by surprise, meeting the Spanish fleet carrying with them a number of prominent citizens including a governor and bishop. Coxon on his arrival in Port Royal gallantly escorted the bishop into the presence of the newly-installed governor of Jamaica, Lord Vaughn, where the cleric was given all the courtesies due his position. The governor suffered a less dignified fate. When English officers from the Port Royal garrison went on board La Garde's ship to remove the governor, they were rebuffed by a drunken crew unwilling to release their captive, in all likelihood because each man had earned a mere £20 from the raid on Santa Marta. The French departed in a rage. Vaughn warned Coxon for his future information that it was unlawful to serve under foreign (French) colours.

But the more things changed, the more they stayed the same. The next year Coxon, presumably still in partnership with his Port Royal associates, captured a Spanish merchantman in the Bay of Honduras with a valuable cargo of indigo, cacao, cochineal, turtle shell and silver. By now Lord Carlisle was governor and Sir Henry Morgan, his deputy. When Coxon requested permission to bring his prize into Port Royal, he was instructed by the governor to offload his plunder on to small sloops which would then enter port and pay the conventional customs duty. Not only would this contribute to the island's revenue, including paying the governor's salary, but it would also be interpreted as complying with the law as the goods entered on vessels operating legally. Even Henry Morgan remarked that orders should never be so inflexible as to miss an opportunity for a profit.

However, the incident did backfire to some degree: the dumping of a large amount of Spanish indigo in Jamaica dramatically drove down the price for the local commodity and for a time replaced native indigo and sugar as a medium of exchange. An anonymous account of John Coxon's Portobelo expedition began by recording that in 1679 he called together a group of five buccaneer captains at Port Morant on the northeastern tip of Jamaica. They possessed let passes 'to goe into the bay of Hondurus, to cutt logwood, from his Maj'ties Reall Subject the Earle of Carlisle'. During the events that transpired not a tree of logwood was cut and when they eventually approached Panama and were asked by the governor under whose commission they sailed, the reply was '… we … bring our commission on the muzzles of our guns'.

The original five captains were Coxon, Cornelius Essex, Bartholomew Sharpe (who became their leader and later terrorised the Pacific coast), Robert Allison and Thomas Magott. On January 7, 1680, they sailed eastward from Jamaica and soon ran into a storm which scattered them, but not before they had added a French flibustier, Jean Rose, to their flotilla who luckily still possessed a French commission to attack the Spanish. En route, Coxon raided the San Bernardo islands southwest of Cartagena close to Isla Fuerte where they had intended to rendezvous. Here he stole ten small vessels to navigate the shallow offshore waters near Portobelo. Bad weather continued to dog them but gradually they reassembled being joined by English captains Edmond Cooke and Lynch and another French buccaneer, Lessone, who could add 80 men to their ranks. Fearing that the Spanish would get word of his approach, Coxon and his men allied themselves with the Cuna Indians who the Spanish had been unable to subjugate. The anonymous diarist recorded that '… thay would shew us wheir was Spanish townes plenty of Silver and Gold'.

The Cuna Indians allied themselves with buccaneers like John Coxon and Bartholomew Sharpe to take their revenge on the Spanish.

Before proceeding with this account, mention should be made of two men on the expedition who were to publish memorable accounts of their adventures sailing with these and other buccaneers. The first was William Dampier whose 1697 book *A New Voyage Round the World* was an instant popular success. The son of a Devonshire farmer, he led a colourful life as a seaman, a soldier, the manager of a Jamaican plantation and a logwood cutter before setting out with a Mr Hobby, on a trading voyage to the Mosquito Coast. By chance Mr Hobby's vessel put into Negril Bay on the west end of Jamaica where John Coxon and his captains were en route to Portobelo. After some hesitation, like the rest of Hobby's crew, Dampier deserted to the buccaneers.

With him on one vessel or another for the several years that followed was Lionel Wafer. In 1698 Wafer published *A New Voyage and Description of the Isthmus of America*, which for many years was considered the most authoritative body of information on the Cuna Indians of southeast Panama. It also provided a fascinating insight into his life as a surgeon-buccaneer. Wafer first went to sea when he was probably only 17 as a 'loblolly-boy', someone who serves loblolly, a watery gruel given to the patients of the ship's surgeon. He was employed as an assistant surgeon by the time he was 20 and in 1679 he had come ashore to visit his brother in Jamaica who set him up as a surgeon in Port Royal. It was here that he met Edmund Cooke and accompanied him on his buccaneering excursion. Wafer, like Dampier, began his narrative in detail following the events of the Portobelo attack.

To avoid detection, Coxon disembarked his force of nearly 400 men some distance from the city at Puerto del Escribano, a narrow harbour where Christopher Columbus had taken shelter in 1502. They had to endure a three day march which left them weak from hunger and lacerated by the terrain over which they had walked. Just three miles from their objective on February 17 they were seen by Indians who shouted 'ladrones! ladrones!' (thieves) and ran with a warning to Portobelo. These cries gave the citizens only an extra 30 minutes warning which proved insufficient. The leading party under Robert Allison met little resistance as the townspeople hurried into the fort of Santiago de la Gloria. Two hundred Spanish made an attempt to repulse the buccaneers next day but had to retreat back to their fortress. For two days the buccaneers ransacked the city at will, but fearful of the appearance of a relief column from Panama they transported their booty and prisoners to a cay at Bastimentos near the abandoned town of Nombre de Dios for loading into their ships. Their anticipation was timely: 700 Spanish troops arrived the day after they departed.

Coxon did not sail immediately but lingered in the vicinity looking for unsuspecting shipping destined for the recently ravaged city. His strategy paid off when the buccaneers captured not only a small supply vessel carrying corn and salt but also a new 90-ton Spanish merchantman with eight guns and a wine jar filled with 500 pieces of gold which the anonymous diarist tells us Captain Coxon kept for himself. Spanish sources maintained that the Portobelo attack cost the city 100,000 pieces of eight, half of which was carried away by the buccaneers. Each buccaneer was paid 100 pieces of eight according to English accounts. One report bemoaned the loss of a canoe loaded with 'the best plunder' that the men 'being so covittous to lode deep,' had to watch helplessly as it capsized and sank out of reach.

The illegality of the venture resulted in Governor Carlisle issuing a general warrant for the arrest of Coxon and his companions in May, 1680. This was underlined soon after with another proclamation by Morgan in his new role of scourge of the buccaneers against anyone having 'correspondence' with the outlawed crews. However, friends of Coxon's including most of the members of the island's governing council, offered to put up a 200-pound security bond if he was allowed to return to Port Royal and undertake to sail only on a commission from the King of England!

Coxon, unlike his predecessors, had not effectively damaged Portobelo's fortifications but after his departure the viceroy in Panama revived a proposal by Bautista Antonelli to build a city wall. For ten years the work limped along but was never completed. Although left unscathed for the reminder of the seventeenth century, Portobelo almost became the target of the DuCasse expedition in 1697 that eventually made its focus Cartagena.

By 1682 Captain John Coxon in his newly-acquired Spanish ship, now joined by English captains Peter Harris and Richard Sawkins, anchored at Golden Island off

Panama to renew their relationship with the Cuna Indians who had promised to guide them to greater riches. This resulted in a ten-day march overland to Santa Maria, a modest military post, which they overran before continuing on towards Panama. It was some time later after a successful confrontation with a Spanish naval flotilla in the Pacific that Coxon was accused of not being fully committed, his actions said to have bordered on cowardice. It was then that he parted company with the others and returned to the Caribbean. Despite his Port Royal friends' gesture of loyalty – or perhaps he was unaware of it – Coxon stayed clear of the Jamaican authorities and frequented the Bay Islands off Honduras and the San Blas Islands off Panama in an effort to launch yet another assault on the Central American coast.

In 1682 he arrived back in Port Royal and showed Governor Lynch a commission against the Spanish that he had been granted by Robert Clarke, governor of New Providence Island in the present-day Bahamas, with which he had attacked the Spanish settlement of St Augustine in Florida. Lynch blamed Clarke (who was soon sent back to England under arrest) not Coxon. Coxon was recruited to extract the English logwood cutters from Honduras before the Spanish drove them out. He remained in Lynch's service for a second year, this time employed to capture the notorious French pirate, Jean Hamlin, on the *Trompeuse*, an assignment in which he failed.

The incorrigible buccaneer turned renegade again for a period but in January, 1686, he surrendered at Port Royal to Lieutenant-Governor Hender Molesworth. Arrested and tried in Spanish Town, he managed to avoid being convicted once again because he was next heard of harvesting logwood in the Bay of Campeche. In September, 1688, he again surrendered to the governor of Jamaica, now the Duke of Albemarle, who in turn handed him over to Stephen Lynch. Lynch was the agent of Sir Robert Holmes, the man appointed by England's James II to enforce the outlawing of buccaneers, privateers and pirates. Holmes's agent met such hostility from the various elements in Port Royal that Coxon appears to have got off the hook and some of his counterparts, who had been shackled and thrown in goal, sued Lynch for damages. As spectacular as his career had been, Captain Coxon was eventually heard of trading legitimately on the Mosquito Coast, dying there among the Indians in 1688.

Portobelo, for its past, settled down to a relatively peaceful existence as Spain's principal colonial trading port on the Panamanian isthmus although it never again achieved the prominence that it had with its fabled seventeenth-century fairs.

Chapter 10

PANAMA

HENRY MORGAN'S TRIUMPH

~

Panama City is unique in that it is the only city that the buccaneers plundered that was burnt to the ground not by them but by the order of the Spanish governor. And it is the only city that was not rebuilt on its original site after they had left. Perhaps it was divine retribution that Port Royal, a little over 20 years later, also suffered a major catastrophe. Panama La Vieja on the eastern end of the city contains the ruins of Governor Don Juan Guzman's beloved city. At the time it fell to Henry Morgan, it possessed a magnificent cathedral, eight convents and a number of churches. There were perhaps a thousand buildings ranging from warehouses and business establishments to government offices, a hospital and houses of varying quality.

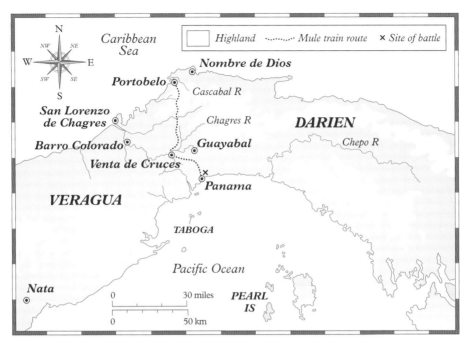

Panama in the seventeenth century was known by the buccaneers to be the funnel for the riches of Spain's Pacific colonies.

Today there are still standing only a scattering of stone skeletons of structures that survived the fire and the ravages of people and time. Scattered walls remain of the Casas Reales or Royal Houses where affairs of state were managed. Best preserved of all are the ruins is the Cathedral de Nuestra Señora de la Asuncion, built between 1619 and 1626. It is shaped like a cross with chapels on either side of the main structure and has a bell tower at the back. Only the walls still stand; even the front façade facing the plaza mayor has crumbled. The Cabildo de la Ciudad and the residence of the city's wealthiest citizen, Francisco Terrin, also faced the plaza. To the north of the cathedral are Casa Alarcon, the remains of the largest and best preserved private residence, and the Iglesia y Convento de Santo Domingo, also better preserved than most structures, which dates back to the late sixteenth century. A number of other sites of convents and churches are located at Panama La Vieja.

To the west is the stone bridge, Puerte del Matadero, which took its name from a nearby slaughterhouse and was the start of the Camino Real. More impressive is the Puerto de Rey, built in 1617, by the northern edge of town, which is believed to be the oldest bridge in the Americas. The Museo de Sitio Panama Viejo, beside the ruins, contains a scale model of the old city before Morgan. A taped commentary carries the history of the city as you view the many colonial artefacts from the period.

Casco Viejo, the Panama that succeeded Panama La Vieja, is today a district in the southwestern corner of the modern city and contains numerous buildings of

The only remains of Old Panama that have survived are the foundations and some walls like that of the Cathedral de Nuestra Señora de la Asuncion.

colonial, post-Morgan character including the Museo de Historia de Panama and the Iglesia de San Jose with its Altar de Oro. Legend has it that as the buccaneers were approaching, a priest painted this altar, then in the old city, black. When the clergyman explained to Morgan that another of his men had earlier stolen the cross, Morgan is said to have declared: 'I think you are more of a pirate than I am' and left. The baroque-style altar made of mahogany painted and veneered with gold found its way safely into the new Panama.

The massive Fort of San Lorenzo is about eight miles from Colon and has a panoramic view of the Caribbean Sea and the mouth of the Chagres River. After Henry Morgan's 1671 attack, a new fort was constructed on the top of the cliff but this was destroyed in 1740 by Admiral Vernon. The imposing fortress a visitor sees today was constructed between 1761 and 1768. It consists of a series of dry moats, cannon platforms dominating all sides, warehouses, barracks, a prison, powder

The Iglesia de San Jose with its Altar de Oro is situated in the Casco Viejo.

magazine and a deep fresh water well. The entrance is approached over a moat which takes the visitor into an imposing guardhouse, a fixed bridge with two arches and a drawbridge. Fortunately restoration on this attractive historical monument is on the drawing boards.

The most remarkable military undertaking carried out in the era of the buccaneers was the sack of Panama City by Henry Morgan in 1670. How he rallied nearly 2,000 French and English buccaneers, organised them into a disciplined fighting force, led them from the Caribbean overland to the Pacific, and captured one of Spain's most important New World cities has baffled historians for centuries. It has been said that he was, in his own right, a military genius.

His rise to fame, or infamy if you were Spanish, from the son of a farming family of modest fortune in Monmouthshire, Wales, to a buccaneer admiral and later lieutenant-governor of Jamaica, knighted for his services to his king, is as fascinating a tale as you will find anywhere in the annals of Caribbean history.

155

Generations of Morgans of Llanrumney and environs had been commanders of English forces on the battlefields of Europe. Henry Morgan, who was born about 1635, in later life commenting on his limited education wrote: 'I … have been more used to the pike than the book' which suggests that he was no more than carrying on in the family tradition. With no other evidence of his upbringing, it is likely that he took part in the invasion of Jamaica and remained afterwards like the rest of General Venables's army. Under Governor Lord Windsor, the survivors of this army were permanently disbanded and self-defence militias formed. By 1662 Henry Morgan is listed as a captain in the Port Royal Regiment and later he was to play a major role erecting the defences of the town of Port Royal. Although Morgan's name is not recorded in the official reports, it is probable that he took part in Christopher Myngs's 1659 raids on Coro and Cumana, then Santiago de Cuba and finally Campeche. The eighteenth-century English historian Charles Leslie wrote of Morgan during this period that his participation in several attacks on Spanish towns enabled him to purchase a small sloop with which to continue fortune-hunting.

In August 1665 three captains arrived in Port Royal after several months raiding the Central American coast, including an ambitious ascent of the San Juan River into Lake Nicaragua and across to the city of Granada. In the official report they were identified as Jackman, Morris and Morgan. It was in Governor Thomas Modyford's report to his patron the Duke of Albemarle in England that Morgan is named as one of these English buccaneers for the first time. The capture of Villahermosa in Mexico, Trujillo in Honduras and the remarkable journey up the San Juan River to sack Granada provided alarming proof of the buccaneers' capacity for warfare.

SIR HENRY MORGAN

Henry Morgan was born in Wales and in all probability accompanied General Venables's army to Jamaica.

156

It was on his return from Central America that Henry Morgan took the hand in marriage of his cousin Mary Elizabeth Morgan, daughter of the unfortunate leader of the capture of St Eustatius. The precise date of the wedding, most likely in Port Royal, is not known but it was probably some time in late 1665. In February of the next year he was promoted to colonel in the Port Royal militia and took the first steps towards strengthening the town's defences. For the two years that followed he appears to have remained on shore. But in 1668 Governor Modyford, alarmed by reports he was receiving that suggested a renewed effort by the Spanish to retake Jamaica, issued a special commission to Colonel Morgan to draw together an expeditionary force to '… take prisoners of the Spanish nation, whereby you may gain information of that enemy to attack Jamaica, of which I have had frequent and strong advice'.

Sir Henry Morgan, a man of many legends, and the most famous buccaneer of all time.

His exploits which followed in Puerto Principe and Portobelo have already been recorded but his audacious capture of the latter showed his organisational and tactical genius at its most effective and confirmed his rightful inheritance of the title of admiral of the buccaneers from his mentor Edward Mansfield. Ironically, a peace treaty between England and Spain had been signed on May 23, 1667. It did not recognise England's authority over Jamaica and although it did, at length, promise safe passage of the subjects of both nations, this was soon to prove inapplicable in the Caribbean. At any rate, the treaty of 1667 was never proclaimed in Jamaica and Morgan got off with a mild rebuke for pillaging Portobelo, a venture which the merchants and fleshpots of Port Royal celebrated with unrestrained joy on his return.

Morgan attacked Puerto Principe in Cuba, en route to Portobelo.

In October, 1668, Henry Morgan rounded up his captains and set sail for the Isle à Vache to prepare for his next expedition. Early in January of the following year when the assembly of men, vessels and supplies appeared sufficient to undertake a new enterprise, a catastrophe took place which nearly claimed Morgan's life.

On January 2 a council of war was called on board *HMS Oxford*, a 34-gun frigate of the Royal Navy and the first to be assigned to Jamaica in nearly nine years. Although sent by the Duke of York to put down piracy and defend the island, she was soon in the command of Edward Collier, one of Morgan's most trusted buccaneer captains. Exquemelin records that after the captains had reached a decision to make Cartagena their target, they set about carousing with a rowdy dinner and many boisterous toasts. As the night grew long and the drinking continued, somehow a spark or careless match found its way into the ship's gunpowder magazine. Surgeon Browne, the medical officer on the *Oxford*, survived to describe the horrific explosion from which only six men and four boys of a crew of 200 survived. As luck would have it, Henry Morgan and those captains who sat on the same side of the table as him were thrown into the sea and rescued. Those on the opposite side to him were amongst the dead.

The tragedy was assumed to have been an accident but the English diarist William Dampier tells a different story: the citizens of Cartagena maintained that on the night *HMS Oxford* blew up, their patron saint, Nuestra Senora de Popa, was seen returning home wet and tired after a long journey abroad. The loss of the naval frigate and the departure of Edward Collier, who had taken command of a captured French 14-gun ship and returned to Port Royal, persuaded Morgan to abandon the Cartagena venture. Moving on to the island rendezvous of Saona on the eastern end of Hispaniola, Morgan encountered a French buccaneer who had accompanied Jean-David Nau L'Ollonais when he plundered Maracaibo and Gibraltar. The Frenchman described their defences as weak and the rewards abundant. The two Spanish towns lay on the shores of Lake Maracaibo, a 5,100-square mile body of water connected to the Gulf of Venezuela by a 34-mile strait. The entrance was hazardous, with a narrow channel twisting and turning between a series of sandbars with three small islands, San Carlos, Pajaros and Zapara to negotiate.

Since L'Ollonais had passed this way a small fort, Fuerte de la Barra, had been built. Commissioned for the purpose of deterring foreign attacks and grandly named Castillo de San Carlos de Madureira, it was added to over the years and eventually restored in the twentieth century as a national monument. Although it possessed 11 cannons which adequately covered the entrance to the lake, its garrison consisted of only eight soldiers and the commander. They held out against Morgan's assault by land but at night set a slow fuse to an ammunition supply and escaped by boat. Once again the admiral's good fortune held out and, according to Spanish sources, the burning fuse was disarmed in the nick of time after the buccaneers entered the fort.

Short of men as he was, Morgan decided to dismantle the fort, spike the guns, remove the gunpowder and ammunition and sail on to Maracaibo. Crossing the Bay of Tablazo, the shallow waters claimed some of his fleet on its treacherous shoals but his men simply crowded on to the remaining vessels. The distance of 20 miles from the fort to Maracaibo meant the authorities had sufficient time to rally the militia and advise the citizens to depart. Having witnessed the atrocities of L'Ollonais only two years earlier the citizens, including most of the men who should have answered the rallying cry, fled seeking refuge in the mountains. Morgan split his men into two bodies, one contingent of a hundred to scour the countryside for loot as well as prisoners to ransom and a second to search the town. It was from Maracaibo that the controversy began as to whether or not Morgan's use of torture did or did not exceed the cruelty level of that which was conventional during such acts of war. However, there is no doubt that torture was applied to reveal the whereabouts of the inhabitants' hidden possessions.

After a week in complete command of the town and having rounded up sufficient booty, slaves, cattle and fresh provisions, the buccaneers headed for the far end of the lake and the town at Gibraltar. Once again they experienced little resistance and were able to increase their wealth with the same modus operandi as before. By the time they set out to recross the fresh water lake, they had added to their eight original flotillas a Cuban merchant ship and several small vessels used for trading in the lake.

Returning to the deserted town of Maracaibo, Henry Morgan was informed by one of its few remaining occupants that three Spanish naval vessels had arrived at the entrance to the lake. Not that he should have been surprised because, since his earlier exploits at Portobelo, Spanish anxiety about their possessions in the Caribbean was mounting. Many sources reported that the buccaneers were planning to attack a major target on the Spanish Main. The congregations at Isle à Vache and Saona did not go unnoticed and the Armada de Barlovento, which was formed to protect the coasts and islands, was alerted. Don Alonzo del Campos y Espinosa, vice-admiral of the fleet, had skilfully traced Morgan's progress from information he received along the coast of Hispaniola and finally from a Dutch captain in Curaçao. Sailing into the Gulf of Venezuela he received confirmation of the buccaneers' whereabouts and, having sent to La Guaira, the port of Caracas, for additional ships, anchored his powerful fleet in the entrance to the lagoon bottling up the intruders.

His flotilla included his flagship *Magdalena*, a galleon of 412 tons; the 218-ton *San Luis* and a converted French merchantman renamed *Nuestra de la Soledad* of 50 tons, the three boasting a total of 72 cannons. When Don Alonzo realised that the fort on San Carlos was not occupied by the buccaneers he set about restoring it. The spiked cannons, buried in the sand, were dug up and the nails drilled out of their touchholes and six successfully recommissioned. Forty musketeers positioned themselves on the battlements in readiness for the approach of Henry Morgan. Don Alonzo, with justification, felt that he was about to deal a damaging blow to the scourge of Spain's Caribbean dominions.

Henry Morgan launched his escape strategy by issuing a demand for safe passages and a large ransom in exchange for not burning Maracaibo to the ground. In his response, Don Alonzo pointed out the hopelessness of Morgan's position: 'if you be contented to surrender with humanity all that you have taken, together with the slaves and all other prisoners … upon condition that you retire home to your own country'. Exquemelin, with his usual flair for the dramatic, described Morgan assembling his officers and men in the central plaza in Maracaibo. Reading Don Alonzo's somewhat lengthy and foreboding reply, he asked them whether they preferred to give up their 'purchase' and take a chance on the Spaniard's offer or whether to fight their way out. 'Fight' was the message which was defiantly conveyed to Don Alonzo. But the odds were overwhelmingly in favour of the Spanish in terms of firepower until Henry Morgan conjured up a cunning ruse designed to even up the buccaneers' odds.

For the next week he had his men disguise the Cuban ship as his flagship by appearing to strengthen its capacity for engaging enemies. Extra portholes were added and drums filled with gunpowder were put in place to simulate cannons. The entire vessel was stuffed with pitch, tar, sulphur and anything else that would burn. Even the decks and rigging were coated with an inflammable substance. To enhance the effect of a fully complemented warship, pieces of wood shaped and painted like men bearing arms and wearing caps were propped up on deck. Just 12 men remained on board, ready to put a flame to this flagship turned fireship at the appropriate moment after grappling her to the enemy's hull.

On the morning of April 27, with winds favourable to the buccaneer fleet, the Cuban ship and two others set a course directly for the *Magdalena*, much to the astonishment of its commander. With 40 guns and a well-armed crew of 280 men, the Spanish were hardly disconcerted at the prospect of combat. Despite the bombardment they received in the unequal duel as they approached the Spanish, the Morgan's three pressed relentlessly forward until the Cuban ship collided amidships with the *Magdalena*. It looked as if the buccaneer admiral's flagship would be captured with sublime ease particularly when a Spanish boarding party found the ship abandoned. Momentarily all was calm but suddenly the sound of explosions filled the air and flames, whipped by the breeze, spread from the captured Cuban ship across to the *Magdalena*. The speed and violence of the conflagration took Don Alonzo and his men completely unaware and within minutes the *Magdalena* was burning out of control. The vice-admiral, like most of his surviving crew, jumped into the sea and sought the shore in the ship's longboat. Of the other two, the *San Luis* was beached by its captain who saw no point in coming to the *Magdalena*'s assistance, its supplies and weapons transferred to the fort, then deliberately set on fire to avoid its capture. The *Nuestra Senora de la Soledad* attempted to sail away but after a mishap with its rigging it drifted helplessly towards land pursued by the buccaneers anxious to add a rich prize.

The problem for Henry Morgan was still how to get past the Fuerte de la Barra, now further reinforced by those who had reached shore. With ships expected from La Guaira and no other way of leaving the lake, he once again attempted to bargain with Don Alonzo who had eventually found his way to the fort. While the negotiations took place, the buccaneers carried out a salvaging operation on the *Magdalena* retrieving over 20,000 pesos of silver, some of it melted by the heat of the fire into large lumps. Morgan also returned to Maracaibo to extort a ransom by way of silver and cattle before returning to the problem of escape.

Morgan's fireship caught the Magdalena *by surprise causing panic.*

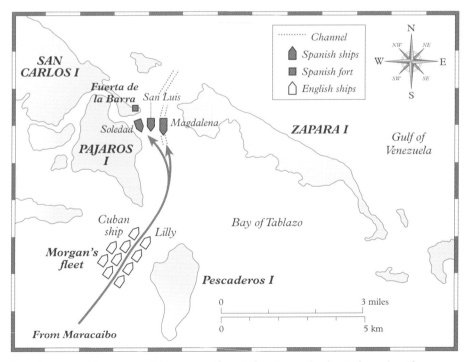

By using guile, Morgan was able to escape from Lake Maracaibo despite being heavily outgunned.

Once more Morgan devised a ploy to mislead the defenders and reduce the considerable risk of running the gauntlet of the fort's cannons. When the buccaneers were seen being ferried into canoes to the shore, the Spanish surmised that a night attack on land with a substantial force of men could be expected. To deal with this Don Alonzo moved some of his guns to cover the possible landside approaches to the fort. This is exactly what Morgan had guessed would transpire. In actual fact the men seemingly put on the beach had returned to their ships lying flat on the bottom of the canoes. Back on board the buccaneers prepared to pass under the fort in the dark of night. With reduced firepower the garrison was able to inflict only limited damage to the buccaneers' vessels as they made their way into the Gulf of Venezuela.

Henry Morgan was soon back in Port Royal, now sailing in the former *Nuestra Senora de la Soledad* having inflicted severe damage on the Spanish royal navy, humiliated Don Alonzo del Campos y Espinosa and further enhanced his growing reputation as England's best hope for the defence of its West Indian territories. It was estimated that his booty was half that of Portobelo but as usual it provided a much appreciated infusion of wealth into the town.

The Caribbean coast of Panama was explored in the first decade of the sixteenth century by Christopher Columbus on his fourth voyage, accompanied by Rodrigo de Bastidas, a wealthy notary public from Seville, in search of gold. It was a member of his crew, Vasco Nunez de Balboa, who escaped his creditors later, stowed away on a ship to the Isthmus and established its first settlement, Antigua del Darien. Balboa rose to become a successful administrator of the region, attempting to be conciliatory to the conquered Indians and taking one as his lifelong mistress. On September 1, 1513, he set out on his historic journey to the Pacific Coast with 1,000 Indian slaves, 190 Spaniards and a pack of dogs.

After 25 days hacking his way through the jungle and traversing the rugged terrain, Balboa waded into the sea, fully clad in his armour, to claim the sea and the land it washed upon for God and his king. Despite the fact he returned unscathed with 40,000 pesos in gold, he had been denounced at court in Spain by his enemies and a new governor, Pedro Arias de Avila, charged him with treason. In 1517 Balboa was arrested and executed.

Two years later Pedrarias the Cruel, as he was to be known, abandoned the Darien region with its unhealthy climate and increasingly hostile Indians and established his headquarters in a fishing village about five miles northeast of the present city of Panama. Although it too had a debilitating climate, Panama became the principal base for the exploration and conquest of South America from the Pacific. Situated as it was at the narrowest point on the isthmus, Panama served as the southernmost point on the Camino Real which was to convey the valuable metals to Nombre de Dios and later Portobelo. The early years were disastrous, with the townspeople dying in droves from diseases to which they had little resistance. The Indians were mercilessly enslaved and massacred by the thousands, forcing them to flee into the interior branded as cimmarones.

By 1529 Panama was described as a town of 600 householders but its progress was retarded by the prevalence of smallpox, yellow fever, dysentery and other maladies. At times it was almost depopulated and, in what can only be described as an act of desperation, some contemporary physicians even blamed the consumption of Peruvian wine! Despite the environment, Panama thrived with the development of Spain's Pacific possessions. As early as 1517, Charles V of Spain had granted a concession for exporting 4,000 African slaves to the Caribbean and Panama became a major distribution point in the Americas. Although little gold was discovered locally, soon the mines of Peru were shipping silver destined for Spain from Callao to Panama to cross the isthmus. As a trading port Panama began to prosper with the inflow of sugar, cotton, cacao, indigo, vanilla, cinchona and a steadily increasing number of other tropical products. Its wealth inevitably attracted the Elizabethan seadogs, most notably Sir Francis Drake. Over a 25-year period from 1572 to 1597, he and his contemporaries were to approach Panama overland from the Caribbean and by sea on the Pacific.

Both the Dutch and the French, who were known to have worked together on occasion with the English, were present in the vicinity. The bishop of Panama in 1570 complained: 'This land is wearied of the cimmarones and the French; and certainly it is a great pity, for those who are doing business both by sea and river are readily despoiled.' Most of the damage was being done on the road to Nombre de Dios and along the Chagres River where coastal vessels were transporting goods to and from the capital. As we have seen already, Drake in 1572 almost succeeded in ambushing a treasure-laden mule convoy at Ventre de Cruces en route to Nombre de Dios and a year later was finally successful in capturing a rich mule train carrying gold and silver but losing two brothers and his French ally Guillame le Testu in the process. In 1577 John Oxenham, who had accompanied Drake in the West Indies on an earlier voyage, crossed the isthmus leading 50 men and on reaching the sea built a 45-foot pinnace from native cedar with which to enter the Bay of Panama. He invaded the Pearl Islands and terrorised the inhabitants before waylaying northbound merchant vessels carrying gold, gunpowder and other supplies. His good fortune was short-lived and on attempting to recross the isthmus Oxenham and 18 of his men were captured. Oxenham was later taken to Lima and hanged.

Panama, like Portobelo, was to enjoy a respite from European depredation for nearly three-quarters of a century. By 1610 it was a thriving city of over 1,000 Spanish men, women and children and just over 3,500 African slaves, mulattoes and free Negroes. It had a small plaza on the seafront from which seven streets ran south to north encompassing a central plaza with its cathedral, five convents, administrative offices, courtrooms and jail. Nearly all the buildings were constructed of wood except eight major structures made from stone. Situated between two rivers, Panama in 1610 had a wooden bridge to the east and a single span stone bridge at the start of the Camino Real. The port catered to ships of up to 60 tons if not fully laden, as the harbour was relatively shallow.

The seasonal rains were conducive to the planting and harvesting of corn, rice and beans. Many temperate climate fruits and vegetables could be grown but the Spanish soon took to tropical alternatives. There were adequate supplies of beef cattle and the sea provided a wide variety of fish and crustaceans. The defence of the city of Panama was not given serious attention until after Morgan. Its defences in the early seventeenth century needed to begin at the mouth of the Chagres River on the Caribbean. Drake's final expeditions resulted in the military engineer Antonelli being instructed to build a fortification to be known as San Lorenzo el Real del Chagres in 1595 to deter vessels from entering.

Don Juan Perez de Guzman, president of the Audencia of Panama, was fully aware of the vulnerability of Portobelo and the city of Panama. Whilst the former was in the process of being reinforced after Henry Morgan's attack, Panama depended on a small contingent of regular soldiers, the militia and volunteers from amongst its citizens. Don Juan's endless requests for assistance from Madrid went unfilled. In June, 1670, Guzman reported to his queen that the English intended to invade with 1500 men via the Chagres and seize the capital. With no hope of getting additional reinforcements in time, he strengthened the defences of San Lorenzo as best he could. He built a new gun platform at sea level and integrated it with the castle on the top of the cliff overlooking the mouth of the river. However, despite its appearance of impregnability as it was situated on a steep bluff, its construction was largely wood with straw and palm leaves for roofing, dictated by a lack of money and of more substantial building materials.

A digression from the main narrative at this point is required to focus on a number of incidents of Spanish insurgency that not only prompted the attack on Panama but also included a defiant challenge to Henry Morgan himself. The peace treaty signed in 1667 between England and Spain had been broken so frequently in the Caribbean that the Queen Regent of Spain ordered her governors in the region to issue commissions against the English which they did. Nothing was known of this by Jamaica's Governor Modyford for several months. Manuel Rivero Pardal, a brash and somewhat eccentric Portuguese (he wrote an epic poem about his exploits ravaging fishermen's rude dwellings in the Cayman Islands), took up the challenge from the governor of Cartagena. He outfought an old buccaneer off the south coast of Cuba by the name of Captain Bernard Claesen Speidyke who ironically was carrying messages of peace and goodwill from Modyford.

Acclaimed a hero in Cartagena, Pardal set out in two more vessels and harried the coast of Jamaica, creating havoc both onshore and off. Finally, arriving at Negril at the westernmost tip of Jamaica, he put up a lengthy and flamboyant challenge on a tree which included '… I am come to seek Admiral Morgan, with two ships of war of 20 guns, and having seen this, I have he would come upon the coast and seek me, that he might see the valour of the Spaniards.' It was only three days after news of Pardal's challenge arrived in Port Royal that the Council of Jamaica set in motion the series of events that would reach their climax with the taking of Panama.

Appointed admiral and commander-in-chief, Henry Morgan received Governor Modyford's commission dated July 22, 1670, accompanied by 11 instructions. His objective was to be the capture of Santiago de Cuba 'and God blessing you with victory (remain) until you have received my further orders …' It was spelt out that the traditional condition of 'no purchase, no pay' would prevail, meaning that all who took part would divide the booty according to the usual rules. He was given the power to grant commissions to others who wished to join him. Modyford was clearly concerned that his actions might not be well received in London because on August 1 Henry Morgan was given additional instructions which required him

When a brash enemy captain, Manuel Rivero Pardal, posted a challenge to Henry Morgan on a tree in Western Jamaica, the island's council was more than ever persuaded Spain was an imminent threat.

to take action against '… the old lawless custom of the captains of privateers going from the fleet when they pleased' and engage in activities prejudicial to the best interests of the English king.

Morgan chose for his flagship the 120-ton, 22-gun *Satisfaction* that Edward Collier had commandeered after the *Oxford* had blown up and sunk. The *Satisfaction* was actually *Le Cert Volant*, a French ship that Collier had earlier arrested for seizing an English merchantman off Virginia. By the time Morgan left Port Royal on August 24, he had engaged 11 ships and 600 men, emptying the town's taverns and brothels, and ultimately recruited his old comrades-in-arms Collier, John Morris, Lawrence Prince, Joseph Bradley and Richard Ludbury amongst others. After a stop at Bluefields Bay in western Jamaica, the English buccaneers sailed for the familiar rendezvous of Isle à Vache. Over a period of four months and despite a number of setbacks caused by seasonally unstable weather, Morgan was able to accumulate sufficient men and vessels needed for the mission ahead.

Edward Collier was dispatched to the coast of Venezuela to collect supplies which he did by ransacking Riohacha, collecting a ransom of meat and maize as well as *La Gallardina*, a Spanish ship that had sailed with Rivero Pardal. The latter himself had the misfortune of encountering John Morris whose assignment was to scout the south coast of Cuba, presumably in the vicinity of Santiago de Cuba. Despite having the smaller ship, Morris engaged and boarded Rivero Pardal's *San Pedro y la Fama* and personally shot the Spaniard through the neck, killing him and causing the Spanish crew to leap overboard.

The word spread of Morgan's venture with French arriving from Tortuga and mainland Hispaniola and even disaffected Bermudians who had suffered when one of their ships was captured by the Spanish. By November Morgan had over 2,000 men under his command and was evaluating evidence from some of Pardal's crew and English prisoners who had escaped from Santiago de Cuba. They informed him both the weather at the time of year and the strength of the fortifications made the Cuban town a risky proposition. Morgan might well have estimated that the likelihood of a good return for his efforts was also in doubt.

But the information he gleaned from the master pilot on board *La Gallardina* as well as from a seaman, Lucas Perez, gave him the evidence he needed to justify attacking either Panama or Cartagena. They confirmed that the governors in both cities were issuing commissions against the island of Jamaica. The buccaneer captains, 37 in all, met on December 2 and out of this conference a committee of the most experienced buccaneers decided on Panama as 'it stands most for the good of Jamaica and the safety of us all to take Panama, the President thereof having granted several Commissions against the English, to the great annoyance of Jamaica and our merchantmen'. None of the buccaneers had ever seen Panama but it would be true to speculate that the city had grown in legend as an entrepôt enormously rich in gold, silver and merchandise.

Another meeting was held and it was agreed to first seize Providencia 'the King's ancient property' to obtain guides, both willing and unwilling, before crossing to the mainland. Before sailing, the administrative details had to be settled, that is the articles of association or *chasse-partie* as it was known. This included the standard conventions for the division of booty, compensation for injury, incentives and rewards for acts of significance such as striking the enemy's colours on a fort. The rules of the English admiralty, under which Morgan was sailing, dictated that the king was entitled to one-fifteenth and the Lord High Admiral who was the Duke of York, one-tenth of the plunder. Morgan was to receive one per cent and each captain eight shares for distribution on his ship with premium pay going to indispensable individuals such as the surgeon and carpenter. To compensate for physical losses, a man could claim 18 slaves or 18,000 pieces of eight for the loss of both arms and one slave or 100 pieces of eight for the loss of an eye.

By the middle of December, Morgan was ready. His 30 ships comprised the largest buccaneer fleet ever assembled in the Caribbean. However, the biggest ship was the admiral's *Satisfaction* with 22 guns, another dozen ships had ten or more and the rest none. What the fleet lacked in firepower it made up for in manpower. It is estimated that over 2,000 men comprised the contingent, representing about 80 per cent of all buccaneers in the English and French islands. Juan de Lao, an Indian cook who had been captured on Rivero Pardal's ship, later told the Spanish authorities that there was also an old English woman who was a witch taken along to prophesy the future and use 'her diabolical arts to advise then what they should do'. There is no other evidence that she actually existed.

The circumstances of Morgan's capture of Providencia have been recorded earlier. His next move was to approach the Chagres River. He and his captains knew that Fort San Lorenzo had to be put out of commission before the Chagres River could be entered. The only other route to Panama was along the Camino Real from Portobelo but the defences of that town had been substantially improved since its earlier capture by Morgan.

Fort San Lorenzo had to be taken as it overlooked the entrance to the Chagres River.

Colonel Joseph Bradley, with three ships and 470 men, was assigned the task of taking San Lorenzo. The governor of Chagres, Don Pedro de Elizalde, maintained that even if 6,000 men were to assault the fort he could destroy them. His logic seemed sound: it stood on a cliff facing the entrance to the river, protected by a sheer precipice on the southern side and a deep, wide river to the north. At the foot of the hill was a strong walled redoubt armed with six heavy cannons with two more batteries, each with six guns on terraces above. The fort itself consisted of six bastions, four facing inland and two out to sea, each a double row of wooden palisades packed with earth, sand and stone to withstand assault. A ravine 30 feet deep requiring a drawbridge separated the hill on which the fort stood from the rest of the headland. The garrison comprised 314 regular soldiers and a number of Indians employed to fight as bowmen.

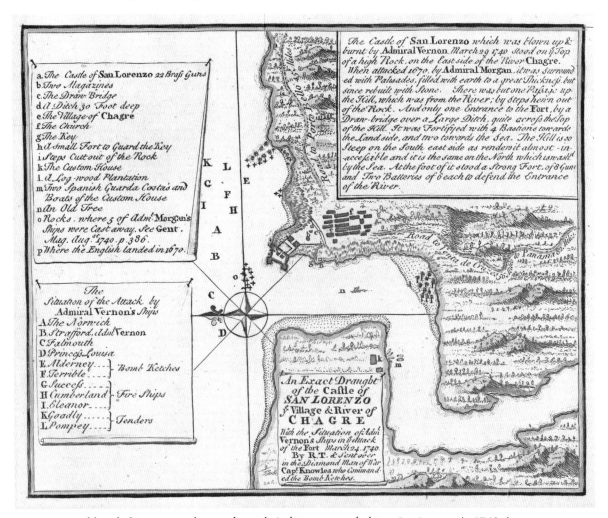

Although this map was drawn when Admiral Vernon attacked Fort San Lorenzo in 1740, it shows why Henry Morgan had to capture it in order to sail up the Chagres River (shown on the right).

Bradley's only hope was to approach the fort from the mainland side which he did, landing most of his men four miles away and marching them rapidly along the beach to arrive two hours later before San Lorenzo. The drawbridge, naturally, had been removed in expectation of their appearance. The buccaneers had no heavy guns but were armed as always with muskets, pistols and cutlasses. Those known as grenadiers carried firebombs and hand-grenades which were to prove effective when they were close enough to be lobbed on to the vulnerable thatched roofs. Despite their exposure to gunfire from the fort which initially caused heavy losses, the English and the French eventually began crossing the ravine in a continuous wave of attacks. As dusk fell they grew close enough to start using fire to cause confusion and to distract the garrison.

Exquemelin cites an incident that signalled the beginning of the end for the Spanish. He claims that one buccaneer, pierced by an Indian arrow, bravely '… pulled it out of his breast, and wrapping some cotton about it, shot it back into the Fort, the cotton kindling in the Discharge, and the Arrow falling upon a House thatched with palm leaves, set them on fire, which meeting with a heap of gunpowder before it was perceived, blew it up …' Soon walls, roofs, palisades, storehouses and even the quarters of the governor were on fire.

By early evening another catastrophe had taken place. A massive bronze cannon that had caused many casualties amongst the invaders suddenly exploded, shattering the outer wall and creating a breach through which the buccaneers poured. The Spanish put up a brave defence but when at first light Morgan's men took up the attack again now engaging the Spanish in hand-to-hand combat with cutlass and machete, the buccaneers began to prevail. Not a Spanish officer survived, including Don Pedro who Exquemelin claims gave Bradley's men no choice but to shoot him dead. More than a quarter of the buccaneers died in action or from wounds, including Colonel Bradley who had both his legs mangled by a cannon ball and lived in agony for another few days.

Five days after the fort was captured, Henry Morgan sailed into sight from Providencia. Meanwhile San Lorenzo had been restored to working order as best possible and equipped with a garrison of 300 men under Major Richard Norman. His men included those least likely to endure the journey that lay ahead.

The expedition up the Chagres River began badly. Morgan's flagship *Satisfaction* and four other ships ran aground on reefs at the mouth of the river and had to be abandoned. However, the task at hand primarily required shallow draft riverboats. On January 19, seven of Morgan's smaller ships along with 36 boats and canoes set off carrying over 1,400 men, arms and ammunition as well as provisions. The destination for the vessels was to be Venta de Cruces, only a day's march from the city of Panama and, despite the rapids and sandbanks, the passage should have taken six days.

Unfortunately conditions were not favourable as it was the dry season and the boats kept running aground. This problem finally became unmanageable. At Barro Colorado, one of the defensive stockades abandoned by the Spanish who were now

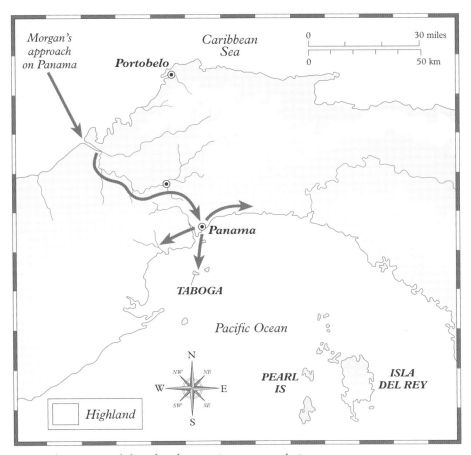

Morgan's men proceeded up the Chagres River to Venta de Cruces.

aware of the fall of San Lorenzo and the magnitude of Morgan's army, they left their ships. The canoes continued up the river whilst most of the men hacked their way through the jungle, harassed by mosquitoes and other pests. The withdrawing Spanish and local populace left behind a trail of destruction, taking with them or slaughtering the animals and destroying foodstuff the invaders were relying on. Hunger, disease and exhaustion was the silent enemy on the journey to Venta de Cruces.

When this important town on the Camino Real was reached the buccaneers expected a fight but once again the Spanish decided the time was not ripe. Once again a scorched earth tactic had been applied. The only supplies untouched were 16 jars of Peruvian wine which were eagerly consumed with the not-unexpected result that most of the buccaneers fell violently ill. The men had now travelled for four days without food but at least the countryside through which they were now passing was more generous. From time to time they had to deal with minor ambushes set when the road narrowed or took them through deep ravines. Don Juan Perez de Guzman used 400 Indian archers and a contingent of musketeers for the purpose but only a handful of the advancing buccaneers died or were wounded.

On January 27 they began crossing the large savanna that would lead them to the city. To their delight they came upon cattle and horses which they killed and ate, half-cooked so starved they were. Having seen the sea from a hillside earlier that day and by the early evening having eaten and rested in the shade out of the broiling afternoon sun, they marched resolutely on towards their goal. Exquemelin records that after nine days under the most exhausting of conditions and upon seeing the spires of Panama's cathedral: 'They gave three cheers and threw their caps into the air for joy, as if they had already gained victory.'

Guzman had been a sick man for some time and had a large and painful tumour on his chest. But he was a man of courage and dedicated to duty. Barely able to sit upright on a horse, he mustered every man who could bear arms and rode out to Guayabal, 16 miles from Panama and ten from Venta de Cruces, four days before the buccaneers appeared on the savanna. Here, he believed, he could confront the enemy from an advantageous position on a hillside. The final decision was to be made by him and his lieutenants in the morning of January 24. Don Juan woke up next day to discover that two-thirds of his 800 men had returned to Panama, fearful of loss of life and property and prepared only to face the buccaneers on the streets of the city if at all. Two days later the evacuation of Panama was under way with women, children and clerics boarding ships with as much of their portable wealth as they could carry.

The president once again rallied his remaining soldiers, the best of whom he had previously sent to Portobelo and Fort San Lorenzo, and volunteers and set up camp on the road to Venta de Cruces at Mata Asnillos. The president thought he held two trump cards: he had 400 Spanish cavalryman whilst few if any of the buccaneers were mounted, and he had two large herds of cattle which 50 Negro cowboys were instructed to drive into the rear of the enemy once they had engaged in combat with his infantry, expecting the beasts to cause confusion and considerable injury. Not counting the cowboys he had an army of 1,600. Against this he faced three disadvantages: very few of his volunteers had suitable guns, they were untested against the experienced buccaneers and, most importantly, he underestimated Morgan's military genius.

The Spanish troops were drawn up to meet a frontal assault in a formation 200 yards long and six men deep. The cavalry would stand by at the flanks ready to charge as the buccaneers advanced. Henry Morgan, on the other hand, organised his 1,200 men into four squadrons of 300. His four field commanders included his most reliable comrades Lawrence Prince and John Morris leading the vanguard, Edward Collier on the left flank; Bledry Morgan (a newcomer and apparently no relation) was in charge of the rearguard while Morgan was in command of the right flank.

After assessing the Spanish formation and anticipating Don Juan's tactics, Morgan dispensed with a frontal attack and ordered Prince and Morris to seize a small hill on Guzman's right flank. From here they could not only fight the enemy on a narrow front for which the Spanish were not prepared but also engage in combat with the

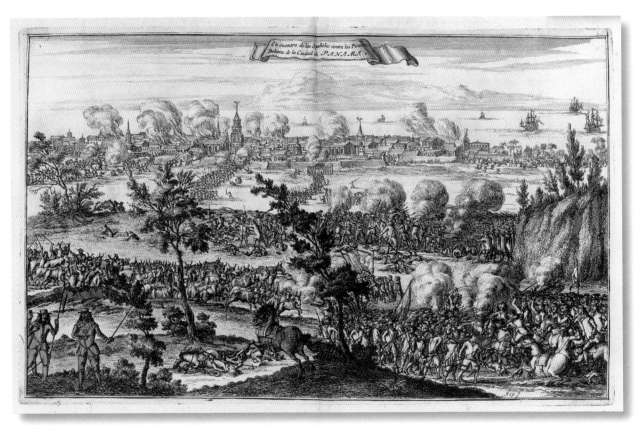

An imaginative composition of the battle for Panama including the stampeding cattle that hampered the Spanish not the buccaneers in the end.

morning sun behind them and in their enemy's eyes. Morgan's vanguard, followed by the main squadrons, ascended the hill finding little resistance; the Spanish cavalry charged, believing that it was cut off from the main buccaneer force. This tactic was nullified by the accurate marksmanship of the French who sent them into retreat by picking off the leading horses. Although this encounter started and ended very abruptly, it seems to have persuaded the Spanish infantry to break rank and rush in the direction of the horsemen, thinking that the buccaneers were in flight.

In disarray, lacking leadership and poorly armed, the Spanish troops were routed in little or no time, a hundred alone were reported to have been killed by the first volley of gunfire. Even the cattle proved to be a liability. Stampeded under Guzman's orders by the cowboys, they were soon turned around by the buccaneers to impede the flight of the Spanish. In the two hours it took to grasp victory it was said that Morgan had lost only 15 men to 400-500 of Guzman's forces. More Spaniards fell when they tried to resist the buccaneers as they entered the city.

The city's captain of artillery had been instructed to spike the few guns he possessed and destroy his gunpowder magazines rather than let them fall into Morgan's hands. As one of the first to flee the battlefield, he knew it was time to do his duty. Two hundred barrels of gunpowder had been distributed throughout the city for the captain to ignite. The noise and the flames were accompanied by the fleeing inhabitants' cries of 'Burn, burn, that is the order of Don Juan' and soon the whole city was ablaze. Realising that the legendary wealth of Panama was going up in flames, the buccaneers attempted to put out the fires but by midnight abandoned the cause. In the morning the proud wooden city lay in ashes and only a handful of stone buildings still stood. Guzman's justification for the conflagration was to deny Henry Morgan the kind of supplies he would need to continue onwards and, in the mind of the governor, try to capture Peru.

The looting began the next day. Treasure was found hidden in walls or down wells dried out by the heat of these fires. Silver melted into lumps in churches and what could not be carried off was smashed. The president's house was vandalised as was his priceless collection of 500 books. Those who did not have the time or resources to take one of the ships that sailed to Ecuador when the buccaneers' approach was reported tried to seek refuge on the islands in the bay of Panama.

Although it was Morgan's buccaneers who sacked Panama, it was the Spanish governor who gave the order for it to be put to the torch.

Although the citizens, again on Guzman's instruction, were to burn all the vessels in the harbour, the veteran buccaneer Robert Searle saved a barque from destruction and with it successfully searched the off-shore islands for booty and citizens to ransom. Once again Exquemelin adds an anecdote that may or may not have been true. It seems that a richly laden galleon, *La Santissima Trinidad*, lay off Taboga unaware that Searle and his men were on the island. When a boat was sent ashore it was seized, its crew captured and the existence of the galleon's valuable cargo revealed. Said Exquemelin, Searle '… had been more inclined to sit drinking and sporting with a group of Spanish women he had taken prisoner, than go at once in pursuit of the treasure ship'.

Morgan sent his men several miles out into the countryside surrounding Panama in search of prisoners and articles of value. He claimed that he eventually accumulated over 3,000 men, women and children in order, in the first instance, to interrogate them. Exquemelin vividly described incidents of maltreatment and torture in the book that he was to publish. It is a fact that he had a grudge against Morgan who he ultimately believed had cheated him. But the official report confirmed that prisoners were beaten and subjected to horrifying pain by the buccaneers in order to find hidden treasure. Exquemelin told of a particularly barbarous incident which, if it is to be believed, certainly epitomised the view which Spaniards held when he described the punishment meted out to an old man they discovered in the empty city.

'One of their captives was a poor cripple whom they found in a gentleman's house outside the city. This wretched man had come across a good shirt in the house, and a pair of silk breeches, which he had put on. A silver key was tied to the points of these breeches. The buccaneers asked him about the coffer which this key had been designed to fit. He had no coffer, he told them, but had simply found the key in the house. When it became plain this was all he was going to tell them, they strappado'd him until both his arms were entirely dislocated, then knotted a cord so tight round the forehead that his eyes bulged out, big as eggs. Since he still would not admit where the coffer was, they hung him up by his male parts, while one struck him, another sliced off his nose, yet another an ear, and another scorched him with fire – tortures as barbarous as man can devise. At last, when the wretch could no longer speak and they could think of no new torments, they let a Negro stab him to death with a lance.'

'One of their captives was a poor cripple whom they found in a gentleman's house outside the city. This wretched man had come across a good shirt in the house, and a pair of silk breeches, which he had put on.'

Torture was brutally applied to determine the whereabouts of hidden valuables.

By the end of February Henry Morgan was ready to leave. Exquemelin claims that 175 mules loaded with booty and 500 or 600 prisoners set out for Venta de Cruces. He was demanding 150 pesos a head as a ransom but much of the human baggage was slaves who would be transported back to Jamaica. By now rains had replenished the Chagres River and the return journey was relatively easy. On arrival at San Lorenzo, Morgan made one final effort to improve his fortunes. He demanded of Portobelo that it pay a sum of money not to destroy San Lorenzo. The threat failed and the Chagres River fort was levelled and its guns spiked.

The time had come to share the spoils. In his report to the authorities, Henry Morgan stated that there was £30,000 to be split up, less than half of what had been taken at Portobelo with as many as five times as many men to share it. After all the deductions, each buccaneer probably got at the most £20. Disappointment was rife to say the least and Henry Morgan was widely accused of hiving off a handsome part for himself which has led to a legion of myths about where Morgan buried his share.

Disturbed by the mood of his men, Morgan apparently left a little too hastily for Port Royal and with only three ships as the others went in search of new opportunities. One such destination was the logwood settlements in Campeche and the Bay of Honduras. Others eventually returned to Jamaica but relations with Spain were changing and Tortuga was more welcoming. Once again the merchants of Port Royal were grateful for the arrival of the ships from Panama and relieved that the Spanish did not, for a time at least, pose a danger to Jamaica.

When Morgan arrived at Port Royal, it had been unequivocally established that a new treaty with Spain had been in force for some time and both Governor Modyford's actions and Henry Morgan's expeditions were contrary to official policy. On May 31, 1671, the Council of Jamaica passed a formal vote of thanks for the execution of his commission and the manner in which he conducted himself. However, both Governor Modyford and Henry Morgan were arrested by royal command and dispatched to England in an effort to placate the Spanish. Henry Morgan spent two years winning back official favour in England, returning to Jamaica knighted and appointed lieutenant-governor of the island.

The sack of Panama inevitably spawned its fair share of legends about Henry Morgan, one of which began with an anecdote by Exquemelin but to which Spanish storytellers added there own twists over time. Amongst the prisoners brought back from Panama's offshore islands was the young and very beautiful wife of a rich merchant, 'no lovelier woman could be found in all Europe,' claimed the author. Morgan set out to woo his captive treating her with respect and kindness even presenting her with fine jewellery. Despite his persistent attempts to gain her favour, she refused

to surrender herself to him. Day after day went by until finally, his gallantry exhausted, he ordered her to be stripped of her clothes and kept in solitary confinement with little to eat. She was amongst the prisoners taken away from the city with ransoms to be paid if they wished to purchase their freedom. Some monks who she had instructed to bring her ransom money attempted to use it for their own release but she was eventually set free. The Spanish historian, Calderon Ramirez, claimed that while in England the Duchess of Portsmouth asked Morgan if he had ever been defeated to which, as the story goes, he replied: 'Yes, Duchess, I was once defeated by a Spanish prisoner back in Panama, a woman who resisted my requests and turned down my sincere affection. That beautiful woman defeated me.'

The next 13 years of Henry Morgan's life were spent in spirited matters of local politics whilst, officially, leading the campaign to stamp out piracy, as the activities of his comrades were now known. His estates kept him wealthy but his dissolute lifestyle took its toll. He died prematurely old at 53 attended by Dr Hans Sloane, the governor's physician. Sloane described Morgan at his deathbed as 'lean, sallow-coloured, his eyes a little yellowish and belly jutting out … I was afraid of the beginning of dropsy.' Searching for a solution to his constant pain and vomiting, Morgan called for a Negro 'doctor' who believed he could cure him with a poultice. Even this failed. He died on August 25, 1688, and is said to have been buried at the cemetery in Port Royal which sank into the sea in the earthquake of 1692. Although his adversary, Don Juan Perez de Guzman, was acquitted of the charges against him at a rigorous trial in 1675, he died in Madrid broken by the experience he had endured.

The city of Panama suffered cruelly. The Audencia of Panama was to lose nearly a quarter of its population either in Morgan's assault or during the epidemic that followed. The old city was abandoned and a site six miles away chosen as it was potentially more defensible and allowed for the development of a port for larger ships. The city was rebuilt in 1673, for the most part with brick or stone and tiled roofs. The houses were reported for the most part to be three storeys high. It had a massive wall to deter intruders and three city gates for access. Panama continued to fear the intentions of the buccaneers, particularly after Coxon and Sharp had proved how profitable it could be to cruise for prizes on the Pacific coast. But there was never again an assault like that perpetrated by Morgan and his buccaneers. It was a triumph, or calamity, depending upon which side you were on and has found its way into the history books of all Caribbean nationalities.

Chapter 11

VERA CRUZ

THE TREASURE GALLEONS

~

Nombre de Dios, then Portobelo in Panama, and La Antigua Veracruz (now just La Antigua), then later Vera Cruz on the Gulf of Mexico, were the four ports from which the wealth of the Americas was dispatched to Spain. This made them a target for the pirates, privateers and buccaneers. Of the four, only Vera Cruz has remained a place of any major economic consequence. A city of enormous importance in Mexico's turbulent history, it is today a major seaport with a Caribbean flavour. As modern as Vera Cruz looks, the early sixteenth-century fortress of San Juan de Ulua across the harbour is an ever-present reminder of the past.

San Juan de Ulua still dominates the harbour of Vera Cruz but, as the port has grown in size and importance, the access to the fort has changed as many as five times in recent years. Today you have to travel north out of the downtown area and circle back behind the port and a park before entering some distance on foot as it is situated within a naval facility.

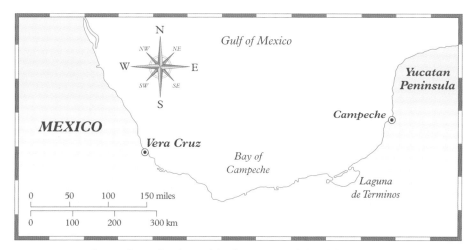

Vera Cruz was the storehouse for the wealth of Mexico and the Philippines to be carried back to Spain.

The massive walls of the fortress of San Juan de Ulua look on to the modern container port of Vera Cruz.

The complex has served for defence, as a port with its customs house and as a prison during the many years of its existence. The massive exterior wall, much of it built of coral, is well preserved and gives a distinct sense of impregnability still. There is a small museum which contains a collection of weapons, a cannon in superb condition and mounted panels tracing the fort's history. Extensions to the fort built later are also open to the public but their history is better told by the guides. The Los Hornos lime kilns where the buccaneer captains assembled their plunder now lie beneath the city's aquarium. The island of Los Sacrificios, where the buccaneers took their prisoners, is off limits because of its sacred Aztec heritage.

The original cathedral where de Graaf first kept the citizens captive was abandoned because of the horror of what took place. When no one would attend services in the cathedral, it was simply allowed over time to disintegrate.

The city's Plaza de Armas is a popular meeting place with its musicians, street vendors and a band shell for concerts. The Palacio Municipal, built in 1627, with its Italian-style tower and Moorish-influenced architecture, the present Cathedral and the Portales de Miranda with its balconied facades dominate the square.

The Polvora Bastion, later renamed Baluarte de Santiago in the middle of the eighteenth century, is the only remaining baluarte, or bulwark, of the nine that enclosed the city and was built after the buccaneers' assault. Although compact it is a substantial seven-sided structure and was known after its name change as the gunpowder storehouse. It has a steep ramp for access and is approached over a deep moat with a drawbridge which would have been raised at night. A large room in its centre is used as an exhibition area for displays of historical interest.

The Baluarte de Santiago, formerly known as the Polvora Bastion, is the only remaining baluarte or bulwark built after the buccaneers' assaults.

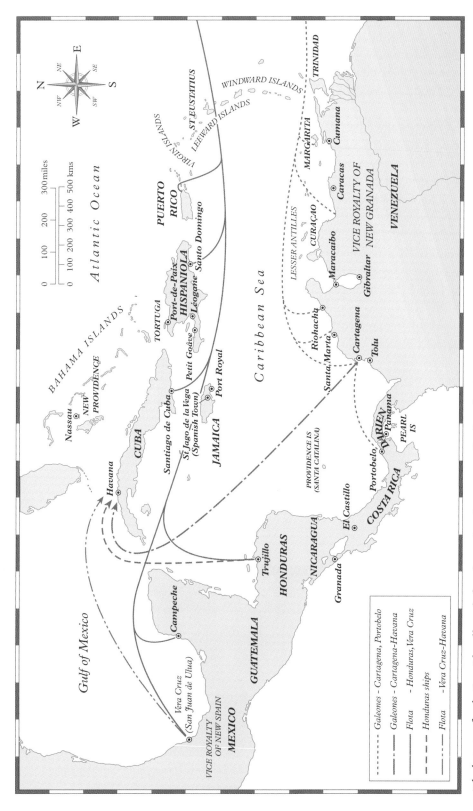

The last stop for the Spanish galleons before they gathered at Havana for the Atlantic crossing was Vera Cruz.

Despite the fact that Vera Cruz has progressively renewed itself over the centuries, one can still find remnants of the city walls in unexpected places such as outside the naval museum.

The last years of the sixteenth century saw Spain reaching the zenith of its wealth and power. In 1580 Philip II of Spain claimed the throne of Portugal on the death of the last legitimate Portuguese heir through his mother and first wife. This gave him the largest commercial fleet in the world on which to convey the riches from his possessions in Africa, Asia and the Americas. The legendary silver mines of Potosi in Peru were producing 250 tons (worth about eight million pesos) annually, as much silver as the rest of the world's mines added together. Half as much again was mined elsewhere in Peru and the same amount in New Spain. Venezuela and Colombia supplied nearly a fifth of the world's gold. It has been estimated that 80 per cent of the cargo carried from the Caribbean to Spain comprised precious metals during Philip II's reign.

Spain's fortunes in the Caribbean were to falter following the intrusion of the English, Dutch and French into the region intent on settling colonies and fostering trade. But to seize a single treasure ship, let alone a whole fleet, was always the highest ambition of the Elizabethan privateers, French pirates, Dutch navy and the Caribbean buccaneers. A variety of strategies were employed in pursuit of this ambition. These ranged from separating a straggler from the main fleet, engaging the treasure ships and cornering them in some remote inlet or bay, or waiting for the Spanish vessels' arrival in one of their regular ports of call. History records that in only a few instances did Spain lose its riches at sea to its enemies whilst the weather, in particular the seasonal hurricanes, or faulty navigation contributed more to Spain's loss of its treasure fleets.

The homeward-bound treasure fleet would have to face the unpredictable hurricane season weather after leaving Havana.

Vera Cruz, Cartagena, Portobelo and Havana, usually the last point of departure on the return to Spain, were the principal ports of call. It was Vera Cruz in 1683, with the sack of the city by Chevalier de Grammont, Laurens de Graaf and Nicholas Van Hoorn, that provided one occasion on which the buccaneers did come face to face with the treasure fleet and with a quite unexpected outcome.

To appreciate why the buccaneers seldom got the chance to confront the Spanish at sea and to get a glimpse of life at sea during the period, documented sources of Spanish maritime history supply a fascinating insight. The voyages of Christopher Columbus took place in caravels rather than the traditional galleys with their contingent of oarsmen, popular for centuries and typically used as warships in the Mediterranean. It was left to Alvaro de Bazan, a Sevillian, who returned to the basic shape of Columbus's caravel, to design a ship capable of long voyages, well-armed and with sufficient space for a large crew and, as time went by, heavy and substantial cargoes.

By the 1550s Bazan had perfected his design for a galleon suitable for transatlantic crossings (earning him the title of Marques of Santa Cruz in the process). Galleons on average were about 30 feet wide and up to 150 feet long, constructed with two or three decks, three or four masts and four or five square and lateen sails. As many

A Spanish galleon could carry up to 400 sailors, soldiers and passengers, 50 cannons as well as several hundred tons of cargo.

as 400 sailors, soldiers and passengers along with armaments and provisions could be taken on board in addition to several hundred tons of cargo. Galleons stood high out of the water which gave them the advantage of being able to fire their cannons down on enemy vessels with withering effect. However, to counterbalance this top-heaviness, ballast stones were often needed to maintain stability.

A galleon might carry up to 50 cannons, typically 12 feet in length, weighing two to three tons and made of cast iron or brass, mounted on a piece of timber or on a carriage supported by a pair of wooden wheels. A conventional cannonball of iron, lead or even brass and stone weighed about 16 pounds. However, the Spanish used a number of different projectiles including an incendiary shot which was an iron ball with a serrated spike wrapped in tar-soaked rope sticking out of either side. When in flames and with luck, the ball would fix itself firmly into the woodwork or rigging of the enemy ship and set it on fire. Another was the bar shot consisting of two projectiles joined together which could literally cut a man in half or tear a sail to shreds. The Spanish galleons even boasted a forerunner of shrapnel, a lead ball with bits of iron cast into it which shattered on impact. Cannon fire was slow and inaccurate even at a hundred yards. It took many broadsides to severely damage a ship and flying wood splinters did more harm to sailors on deck than cannonballs. Smaller, more accurate swivel guns mounted on the forecast, poop and quarterdecks were readied for action, as the two ships grew closer in combat.

The senior commander of a Spanish galleon was normally a general whose responsibility was to organise defence and attack. The reality is that, as one historian

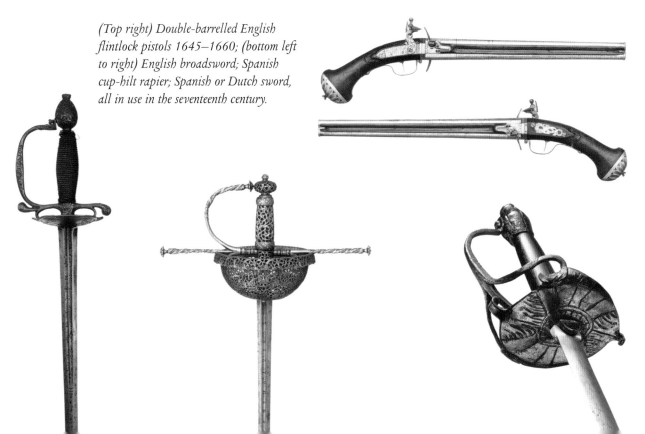

(Top right) Double-barrelled English flintlock pistols 1645–1660; (bottom left to right) English broadsword; Spanish cup-hilt rapier; Spanish or Dutch sword, all in use in the seventeenth century.

put it, Spain was actually a military power at sea and did not recognise naval power in its own right. These military men's background and experience led them to believe that hand-to-hand combat requiring skill, strength and courage was the key to success. After as little as a single bombardment from his cannons, the general would draw his vessel close to the enemy's and board it. The officers and sailors were armed with a mixture of weapons. A bulky musket could blow apart someone at close range and the lighter harquebus and pistol both proved effective but took too long to reload. By the seventeenth century even crude hand-grenades – metal spheres packed with gunpowder and ignited through a wooden tube – began to be employed. The real test of a man's survival skills was when he came face-to-face with his foe armed only with a sword and dagger or perhaps with a pike or axe.

How did you treat a man wounded in battle? Exquemelin speaks of sewing up cuts with animal gut. A comrade in arms who was slashed across the nape of his neck by a sword was bound to a plank to keep him stationery and his severed muscles sewn back together. Anaesthetics were 200 years off so brandy or rum was the most appropriate painkiller in the circumstances.

The commonest surgical procedure was amputation, performed quickly and painfully to limit the loss of blood. This was followed by cauterisation with tar to prevent haemorrhaging and the risk of infection. The most popular prosthetic devices amongst sailors and buccaneers of the period were hooks to replace hands and arms and wooden stumps for legs. Removing musket balls and treating stab wounds were less traumatic injuries for the ship's surgeon. Loss of life or limb was only one aspect of the danger to which a seaman exposed himself and even minor wounds treated with the limited resources available in the era could prove fatal.

Life at sea in a galleon was seldom comfortable and often unpleasant. Space was at a premium and the lower your rank, the less space you were given and the less desirable its location. Even an officer could be assigned a cabin space of less than five square feet with a height of less than six feet. In these cramped, airless conditions everyone from passengers and crew to officers and captain was exposed to vermin. Fleas, lice and bedbugs inhabited clothes and bedding. Cockroaches were commonplace and scorpions could be inadvertently carried on board or bred there. But the worst scourge of all inevitably was the rats. Whilst they were known to bite humans, their chief threat was to provisions and equipment such as ropes and sails through which they gnawed relentlessly.

Carla Rahn Phillips in her book *Six Galleons for the King* tells of one instance where a serious rat infestation actually threatened the lives of everyone on board a ship. The most famous was the disaster-prone Indies fleet returning in 1622, which suffered hurricanes in the Caribbean as well as a rodent plague. More than 1,000 rats were killed on one ship while it was still in Havana harbour. They ate through jars, sacks, boxes, stoppers, and casks. They fell into barrels of fresh water and drowned. They invaded the chicken coops, killing the helpless fowl and eating them. Crew and passengers eventually destroyed more than 3,000 more rats before they got home, some of which were eventually served as food for those more hungry

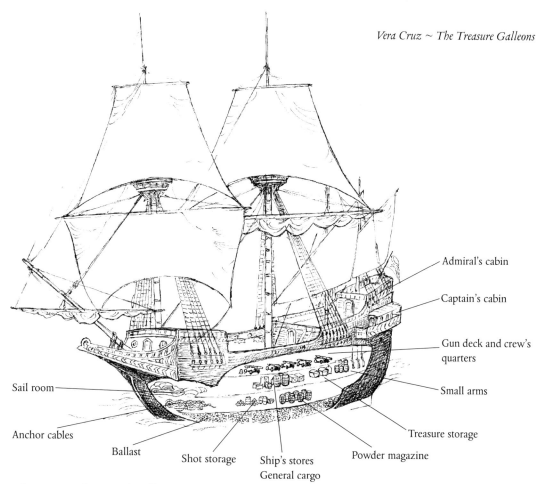

Admiral's cabin

Captain's cabin

Gun deck and crew's
quarters

Small arms

Treasure storage

Sail room

Anchor cables

Ballast

Shot storage

Ship's stores
General cargo

Powder magazine

The interior of a Spanish galleon.

than squeamish. Only a fortuitous rainfall and their arrival in the Azores saved the passengers from dehydration and starvation.

Another contributing factor to the spread of disease was the limited sanitary facilities. Usually seats overhanging the rails at the front and rear of the vessel were provided but often human waste found its way into the bilge, the space at the very bottom of the galleon where all loose liquid in the ship ultimately gathered. A shortage of drinking water and food also provided problems although, as few Atlantic crossings took more than six weeks, conditions seldom deteriorated the way they did for the fleets that sailed from the Philippines to Spain's Pacific colonies which took up to four months. The galleons heading from the Caribbean carried barrels nearly six foot tall containing as much as 4,000 pounds of water. As time passed, bacteria thrived making the water unpleasant to drink. Wine and sometimes cider and beer were available but only the fortified wine from Jerez (sherry) seemed to improve with age. The daily allowance for seamen was about half a gallon of water and two pints of wine while it lasted.

The main staple of a shipboard diet was the ubiquitous ship's biscuit, legendary throughout European navies and merchant fleets. A ship's biscuit was made from whole wheat flour, leavened and permitted to rise before baking. Once baked to its normal consistency it was baked again at a moderate heat. The finished product, known as biscotto or 'twice-cooked' was hard, tasteless and had minimal nutritive value but lasted longer than ordinary bread. Biscuits were packed in sealed boxes and stored to retain their freshness. A ration of a pound and a half a day, downed with something to drink was filling if not particularly nutritious. Galleons' provisions basically included dried fish and meat, cheese, rice and beans, onions, garlic, vinegar and olive oil. Fresh fruit and vegetables were finished early in the voyage. Live chickens, sheep, pigs and even cattle provided fresh meat. Cooking on the main deck was allowed but not below. Small wood-burning metal stoves with three sides protected the embers from the wind and were used by crew and passengers or their servants.

The seamen's worst nightmare, scurvy, which plagued sailors travelling great distances, was rarely a problem when crossing the Atlantic; the standard ailments were seasickness, dysentery, constipation and fevers. The ship's surgeon was probably better prepared to apply his talents to amputations and binding wounds suffered in accidents or warfare than to treating what today are considered everyday medical complaints. Death at sea was honoured with some ceremony if you were a senior rank. However, unless you were near land the dead were normally weighed down with stones or wrapped in a disused sail and dispatched into the ocean with appropriate prayers.

The treasure galleons were based in Seville and Manila. The authorities in Spain decreed that if merchants wanted their vessels to be protected they would have to travel in convoy with the crown's galleons. This did not please the merchants who wanted their merchandise to arrive in the Americas at irregular intervals to keep prices up. A typical fleet might comprise six heavily-armed galleons with several small, fast tenders, as well as a variety of typical merchant ships. The two Caribbean fleets were known as the Flota and the Galeones.

The Mexican Flota set out from Seville in July passing by the Canary Islands and the Azores and sailing for six or more weeks at about four knots until entering the Caribbean at the Leeward Islands, usually stopping at Dominica to take on fresh water. Heading for the Yucatan Channel, the fleet dropped off merchantmen destined for Puerto Rico, Santo Domingo, Cuba, Jamaica, Yucatan and Honduran ports. Its ultimate destination was Vera Cruz on the Caribbean coast of Mexico where it would deposit its domestic cargo for sale in New Spain at a great fair. Here it would be berthed beside the massive fortress of San Juan de Ulua, to be loaded with the silver and gold of Mexico and await the spices, silk, ivory, jade and porcelain of the Orient that had been landed in Acapulco.

The Tierra Firme fleet referred to as the Galeones left Seville between March and May, sailing with the Mexican Flota on its conventional route into the Caribbean. In the early years it entered the Caribbean through Galleon's Passage between Trinidad and Tobago. The accompanying merchantmen would divert to La Guaira, Maracaibo, Cumana, Santa Marta and Margarita whilst the galleons' destination was Cartagena.

Cartagena was the principal town in the rich province of New Granada in the Tierra Firme. The nearby Magdalena River allowed access to the gold mines of the interior as well as to a wide range of agricultural commodities destined for Europe. But the Galeones' main task was to deliver domestic cargo to Nombre de Dios and later Portobelo for distribution to Spain's Pacific colonies like Peru and to carry back the silver from Potosi via Panama. Once again the precious metal was transported overland or transhipped down the Chagres River and sailed up the Caribbean coast to Portobelo. A fair much larger than its Vera Cruz counterpart and lasting often some 40 days was held at this strongly-fortified town.

The two treasure fleets would often try to spend the winter in the harbour in Havana before crossing the Atlantic. It was considered safer than most other Spanish strongholds and had a more comfortable climate than the mainland. There were also large shipyards where repairs and maintenance could be carried out. Once safely out of the Caribbean where prevailing winds made it easier to exit than to enter, the galleons' captains had to contend with unpredictable currents and treacherous shoals as well as changeable weather. Once through the Florida Straits and into the Gulf Stream the voyage became easier. At the best of times, navigational instruments in the seventeenth century gave less than reliable assistance to sailors and it was always best to keep close to the shore, until you had to cross the ocean! Two challenges still had to be met before delivering the king's silver. First, enemies at sea lay in waiting off the coast of Spain so an escort squadron was sent. Finally the galleons had to

Havana was the safest Spanish port in the Caribbean Sea and the place where the treasure fleets combined to return to Spain.

cross the treacherous sandbar at the mouth of the Guadalquivir River to reach the port of Seville.

Geography initially determined where the Spanish chose for collecting, distributing and transporting their valuable cargoes. Of the three main stops on the galleons' Caribbean routes, Portobelo was the least and Cartagena the best endowed with defences although both were relatively easy to reach. Vera Cruz was furthest away from the buccaneers' usual circuit and also reputedly impregnable. Perhaps it was this reputation as much as the promise of vast quantities of plunder that was ultimately too good to pass up for the Dutch buccaneer Laurens de Graaf.

In 1519 the governor of Cuba had appointed Hernan Cortes to lead an army westward in search of mythical riches. Arriving at the Mexican mainland, he founded Vera Cruz and quickly began preparing to travel inland. Shortly after landing, an Aztec chief came to his camp and presented gifts which included gold ornaments. When asked by the chief what the Spaniards purpose was, Cortes made the fateful admission that they 'suffered from a disease of the heart that can only be cured by gold'. It was a disease to which the buccaneers were not immune either.

The first settlement, today known as Antigua, was situated about 22 miles north of the present city. With its open roadstead, shallow draft and dangerous sandbar offshore, the Crown instructed the viceroy, Antonio de Mendoza, to build a fortified wharf in 1535 on the tiny island of San Juan de Ulua, 15 miles south and opposite to present-day Vera Cruz, to provide adequate protection for the treasure fleet. It was not for more than a hundred years that this fortification was much more than two towers and a wooden wall connecting them.

The Elizabethan privateers were a constant menace in the Caribbean from the 1560s but it was John Hawkins whose saga Spanish and English history books most often recall. An Englishman, John Hawkins could have described himself as a businessman because, with a sequence of voyages starting in 1562 to the Caribbean, his intention was to trade in commodities. Of course this was not permitted by the Spanish who claimed a monopoly on trade in the region. He tried various devious ploys both in Spain and Spain's colonies to get acceptance for his cargo which largely consisted of African slaves. The voyage for which he is best remembered was the third under his command. His failure seemed to be foreshadowed even before his departure, as Spain's Philip II was warned that Hawkins was assembling a fleet of six vessels including the *Jesus of Lubeck*, a 700-ton vessel contributed by Queen Elizabeth personally. The 50-ton ship *Judith* was commanded by a young man who would later be knighted for his exploits, Francis Drake. The other vessels included the 300-ton *Minion*, the 150-ton *William and John*, the 100-ton *Swallow*, and the 50-ton barque *Angel*.

John Hawkins described himself as a businessman but when he tried to coerce Vera Cruz into trading, the confrontation that resulted lost the seadog his fleet.

His route took him to the Canary Islands and then to the West African coast where he took on board nearly 300 slaves of whom less than half survived the transatlantic crossing. After pausing at Dominica for water he attempted to trade at his previous ports of call. At Margarita and Burburata in Venezuela he coerced the reluctant colonists into overlooking the crown's restrictions against trading with non-Spanish vessels.

He made a similar attempt at Riohacha and when young Drake was bombarded by Spanish ships the latter destroyed the governor's house with cannon fire, landed men and cannons on shore and forced the local merchants to exchange slaves for pearls and other merchandise. Hawkins approached Santa Marta next but with less violent tactics before sailing to Cartagena in July of 1568. The authorities never even allowed his ships to enter the harbour. With the hurricane season starting, John Hawkins's fleet headed across the Caribbean for the Straits of Florida and England. Off western Cuba it ran into a violent storm which separated the vessels. Losing touch *William and John* continued on to England but the *Jesus of Lubeck* was badly damaged and required repairs.

Drifting into the Gulf of Mexico, Hawkins managed to capture a small ship captained by Augustin de Villanueva who advised him that San Juan de Ulua was where he could repair his flagship. It was September 14 and the lookouts on the fort were expecting the fleet from Spain which was bringing the new viceroy, Don Martin Enriquez de Almansa. Inadvertently Hawkins's vessels entered unchallenged. The English and Spanish accounts vary in some detail as to what happened next but both agree on the final outcome. According to the Spanish, Hawkins, taking advantage of his good luck, took possession of the harbour and demanded to be able to trade, threatening to burn down the town if he was denied. This was refused but now the wily English deduced that the treasure on its return voyage to Spain was soon to arrive. Within a week the fleet from Spain hove into view but remained at a distance after landing some men and arms at San Juan de Ulua in readiness for a confrontation.

John Hawkins's flagship Jesus of Lubeck *was captured during the ill-fated attack on Vera Cruz.*

When it began, the English managed to sink two Spanish ships and disabled another before the viceroy ordered his gun batteries to open fire and brought his galleons forward. The already-damaged *Jesus of Lubeck* was boarded and captured whilst the *Angel* and the *Swallow* foundered. The *Judith* under Francis Drake, and *Minion*, now captained by John Hawkins, managed to escape but soon lost sight of one another. Drake navigated safely back to England to report the disaster. Hawkins's experience was disastrous but it eventually had a curious ending.

Overcrowding and the prospect of death from thirst and hunger persuaded Hawkins after a few days to select a hundred men to land at what is Tampico in Mexico today. He promised to return in a year to rescue them. Unconvinced, the party of men on shore, who were left without weapons as they were too weak to fight, intended throwing themselves on the mercy of the Spanish. They set out for Vera Cruz but in clashes with Indians several lost their lives. Illness and hunger dogged them. Surrendering to the Spanish at Panuca, they were marched as prisoners to Mexico City. Although they were not initially mistreated but put to work as personal servants, workers in mines and on farms, the question of their religion eventually arose. One by one they were arrested and charged with heresy.

As well as those who landed at Tampico, there were the others taken after the battle at San Juan de Ulua, the largest single contingent of English soldiers and sailors ever captured in Mexico in the sixteenth century. Tried by the Inquisition, three or four were finally burnt at the stake in either Mexico or Spain. Most were sentenced to renounce their heresies in public, each man wearing the penitential garment walking barefoot with a candle in hand and then being lashed before being sent to serve six to ten years rowing a Spanish galley.

When Hawkins finally reached England in January, 1569, he began efforts to secure his men's release. He pretended to turn traitor on Queen Elizabeth and offered his loyalty to the Spanish in return for the release of his men. He deceived the Spanish Ambassador in London who wheedled sceptical support out the Spanish crown. The men who survived the ordeal were released. Each man was sent home with money in his pocket and a pardon. A title of Spanish nobility was initially issued to Hawkins to which he responded sarcastically in correspondence 'God deliver us'. Hawkins's misadventure was to be remembered for decades and Vera Cruz for the next century was considered too well-defended a target to be worth contemplating.

The peripatetic English friar, Thomas Gage, had landed at Vera Cruz from Europe in September, 1625 and declared:

'All the strength of this town is first the hard and dangerous entrance into the haven; and secondly, a rock which lieth before the town less than a musket-shot off, upon which is built a castle, and in the castle a slight garrison of soldiers. In the town there is neither fort nor castle, nor scarce and people of warlike minds. The rock and castle are as a wall, defence, and enclosure to the haven, which otherwise lieth wide open to the ocean, and to the northern winds. No ship dares cast anchor within the haven, but only under the rock and castle, and yet not sure enough so with anchors, except with cables also they be bound and fastened to rings of iron for the purpose to the side of the rock.'

Gage strolled through the town noting its wooden buildings, 'the walls of the richest man's house being made but of boards, which with the impetuous winds from the North hath been the cause that many times the town hath been for the most part of it burnt down to the ground'. He estimated it held about 3,000 inhabitants, a good few made wealthy by the goods that flowed over the wharf. The frequency of fires and the unhealthiness of its swampy location Gage reasoned to be why it was not bigger and more populous. His host also warned him against consuming too many unfamiliar fruits and 'drinking after them too greedily of the water' which had afflicted many European immigrants with sickness, even death.

'In the town there is neither fort nor castle, nor scarce and people of warlike minds.'

As the seventeenth century proceeded and other European nations began colonising the West Indian islands, Spanish naval strength in the region declined. The Spanish crown had invested heavily in massive fortresses at the harbour entrances of its Caribbean ports but plans to strengthen San Juan de Ulua were debated, drawn up but usually only partially implemented. Fortunately nature with its blustery north winds made for difficult navigating conditions. The fort and the town opposite was a risky proposition for anyone approaching by sea.

Perhaps the weak link in the chain of defence was the nearby island of Sacrificios, an Aztec burial ground which an astute government official described as having '... a little tongue of very flat, sandy beach where, with three or four launches, (the enemy) could land 150 Musketeers by night without detection and burn the town and rob the entire contents of Your Majesty's treasure ... no help could come from the warden of the fortress of San Juan de Ulua because it is located in part of the sea which lies in a different direction and more than a quarter of league from this town'. His expectations materialised in 1683 although as the result of a different strategy. Another area of weakness was that the new town of Vera Cruz as it had been formally designated in 1615, across from San Juan de Ulua, at the outset had little in the way of fortifications.

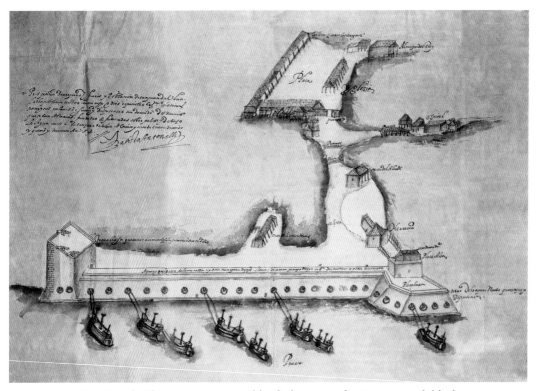

San Juan de Ulua was never stormed by the buccaneers but its presence did little to stop an attack led by de Graaf on Vera Cruz in 1683.

A Flemish engineer, Adrian Boot, in 1621 was directed to make his recommendations. The first bastion, Polvora, was built by 1635 on the southern side to guard the offshore islands, including Sacrificios and the area from the beach to the sandbanks on the land side. A northern bulwark, Caleta, was constructed and two more built with a connecting wall forming a half-moon on the land side of the city. This was considered adequate for the defence of the harbour and city although it was later conceded after the assault of 1683 that the island fortress was not as strong as it had needed to be. Polvora and Caleta bastions had, like the fort across the water, a military contingent but it was usually undermanned and constantly short of arms. The governor could call upon a creole militia in times of emergency and the inhabitants' servants and slaves were recruited to do donkey work such as digging and repairing walls.

A Spanish naval squadron, the Armada de Barolvento, had patrolled the Caribbean from the early sixteenth century to protect Spain's colonies and shipping. It had an added responsibility on occasion to deliver quicksilver required to extract silver in the mines as well as to carry the king's treasure back to Seville. On July 21, 1667, a naval fleet of five vessels under Augustin de Diustegui sailed for the Caribbean to carry out its duties. This particular fleet's success was minimal. In fact it had been destroyed nearly two years later when its commander, Alonso de Campos, mistakenly assumed he had trapped Henry Morgan in Lake Maracaibo.

Subsequent naval squadrons were unable to prevent the rash of attacks on Spanish towns by the buccaneers having as their primary function the protection of the treasure fleet. Spanish governors were reduced to creating their own coastguards to at least be able to detect the approach of intruders. Official approval was given to commissioning Spanish privateers as well as employing English, Irish and Dutch mercenaries whose ships were for hire. However, by 1680 the Armada de Barlovento was given a more vigorous role: it was to be permanently based in the Caribbean to protect Spanish possessions and intercept the poachers. Andres de Ochoa y Zarate had been given the command of the fleet in that year but within 18 months he had been promoted to castellano, or commander, of San Juan de Ulua. Under his leadership the Barlovento squadron enjoyed far greater success than his predecessors, capturing six vessels en route to Vera Cruz, but when he arrived on August 22, 1683, he was to find the city devastated.

Captain William Dampier, in his classic, three-volume work published in 1697, records that Vera Cruz was taken by the privateers, about 'the year 85 (1685), under the conduct of one John Russel an old logwood-cutter who had formerly been seized by the Spaniards and sent to Mexico …' But as no further evidence of this endeavour exists, it leaves Lauren de Graaf's exploits to dominate the era.

When de Graaf eventually entered the service of the French to attack Jamaica, he styled himself 'Laurens-Cornille Baldran, Sieur de Graff, Lieutenant du roi en l'isle de Saint Dominque, capitaine de frégate légère, chevalier de Saint Louis'. However, he was more commonly known by his Dutch name Laurens Cornelius Boudewijn de Graaf.

According to French historians, Laurens de Graaf, or Lourencillo as he was called by the Spanish, was born a Dutchman and served as a gunner or marksman in the Spanish navy. He was married in 1674 to a woman of Tenerife who he divorced to marry again in Tortuga to Marie-Anne Dieu-le-veult 20 years later. There is an apocryphal story that she, hearing that de Graaf had grossly insulted her, went pistol in hand to demand an apology. Impressed by this bold act he proposed marriage.

De Graaf was said to be a tall, blonde-haired, handsome man with a Spanish-style moustache who had sophisticated taste in music and was well-liked amongst his fellow seamen except when his temper flared up. Amongst the Spanish, on the other hand, his name was to strike terror into people's hearts 'and in the public prayers in the churches Heaven was invoked to shield the inhabitants from his fury'. It is said that while sailing with the treasure fleet he was captured by the buccaneers and decided to join them. His experience in the Spanish navy and his fluency in the Spanish language were an obvious asset.

He is first heard of as having made a surprise night-time attack on the ship-building district of San Roman, a suburb of Campeche in Mexico. His men set fire to three vessels under construction and to a large quantity of lumber in storage. The conflagration created panic in the town. Next morning a merchant ship carrying 120,000 pesos in silver sailed unwittingly into the harbour to be seized by de Graaf's men. Apparently during this period of his notorious career he had been sailing as a loner, a pirate acting solely on his own account. By 1682 he even came to the attention of Henry Morgan, by this time acting as governor of Jamaica and committed to quashing piracy. In a letter to the Lords of Trade in England, Morgan reported, 'I have sent the frigate to cruise and have given Capt. Heywood particular charge to look for one Laurence (or Laurent), a great mischievous pirate, who commands a ship of 28 guns and had 200 men on board ...'

De Graaf made his mark in the same year when, sailing in the *Tigre* which he had captured out of the Armada de Barlovento earlier, he caught up with the annual payroll (known as situados) of Peruvian silver on its way to the military garrisons at San Juan and Santo Domingo. The frigate *Francesca* had sailed from Havana captained by Manual Delgado carrying 120,000 pesos in silver and, other goods in July 1682. Off the island of Puerto Rico she was surprised and, after a short battle, 50 of the 250-men crew killed or wounded. Departing in triumph, de Graaf took the *Francesca* for his flagship and returned the remaining Spanish to Cuba. His crew of mostly French buccaneers entered the Bay of Samana and divided up the silver to their satisfaction.

Ironically, when the Spanish colonial authorities learnt of the outrage they retaliated by seizing a shipment of slaves that Nicholas Van Hoorn had been authorised to bring to Santo Domingo. Van Hoorn was astonished when his former ally, Don Francisco de Segura, president of Santo Domingo, advised him to seek payment from de Graaf who had stolen the *Francesca* with the payroll. Van Hoorn managed to escape detention and at Petit Goâve persuaded the French governor, de

Pouancy, to issue a letter of reprisal. His objective now was to seek revenge. It was this incident that led him to de Graaf.

De Graaf had already joined forces with another Dutchman, Michiel Andrieszoon (corrupted to 'Mitchell' in some English narratives). Any likely joining of forces almost dissipated when Van Hoorn had seized two empty Spanish merchantmen lying at anchor in the Bay of Honduras, waiting for goods destined for Spain to cross the isthmus. De Graaf for his part had been craftily biding his time at Roatan in the Bay Islands until the same vessels were loaded with treasure. When Van Hoorn triumphantly arrived with the two empty vessels, de Graaf flew into a rage which subsequently subsided only when he learnt of the former's French commission which would legitimise his actions, transforming him from a pirate to a buccaneer.

History records that on the fateful day of April 7, 1683, a gathering of buccaneers larger than any seen for many years assembled on the beach at Roatan. A flotilla of 13 vessels moved quickly to round the Yucatan peninsula with well over 1,000 men on board including Dutch, French, English, mulattoes and even renegade Spanish. No longer were the buccaneers satisfied with seeking vengeance but they had been persuaded that Vera Cruz would make a lucrative prize.

Vera Cruz was expecting the Flota to arrive from Spain within a matter of days so it was not beyond belief that when two vessels appeared on the skyline they were judged to be merchantmen possibly from La Guaira carrying cacao to tranship to Spain. But as the evening of May 18 drew longer, it appeared that the two were content to stay ten miles offshore for which no one had a convincing argument, least of all 'Don Juan Morfa'. John Murphy was an Irish adventurer whose career began as a buccaneer, then saw him in Spanish service defending Santo Domingo against William Penn and Robert Venables in 1655 and finally settling in Vera Cruz where he became a prosperous merchant. His ominous warning to the governor, 'Sir, those ships cannot be good ones, for they have been able to enter and yet not done so' met with an arrogant brush-off from the governor, Luis Bartolomé de Cordoba y Zuniga.

Despite this the commander of San Juan de Ulua, Don Fernando Sotis y Mendoza, put the fort's complement of nearly 300 men on alert. When a report arrived later from the alcalde mayor of the former capital Antigua of the sighting of more unfamiliar ships, even the governor began taking precautions. Mounted patrols of citizen volunteers were sent out of the city while regular infantrymen were assigned to patrolling the streets. However, his anxiety rose when he was informed that the military had almost no gunpowder.

De Graaf's scouting ships saw that the Flota had yet to arrive in the harbour. This was a critical piece of information because not only would it have dramatically increased the Spaniards' fighting strength but it would also have put several thousand more people in the vicinity who would be present for the trading fair that followed the galleons' arrival. In those circumstances even the nearby pastures would be crowded with as many as 30,000 pack mules.

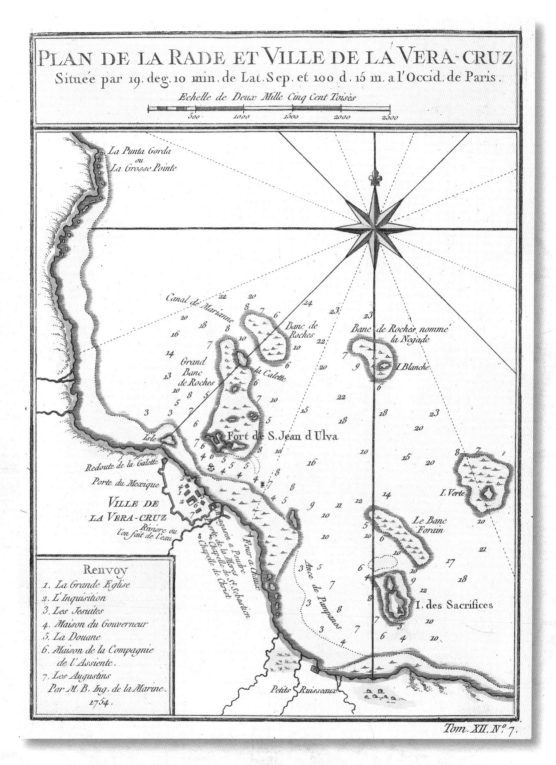

This 1754 French map shows San Juan de Ulua protecting the harbour of Vera Cruz, with nearby Sacrificio Island where de Graaf kept 4,000 hostages waiting for their ransom to arrive.

De Graaf cleverly took his scouting ships out to sea but circled round before the moon had risen to land 200 of his most reliable buccaneers at the mouth of the Vergara River, several miles north of Vera Cruz. Amongst them were English logwood cutters who had been captured and enslaved in the city which gave them invaluable knowledge of the area. They infiltrated the city and, determining that no special precautions appeared to have been taken, signalled the main force to approach. This was a body of another 600 men under Van Hoorn and de Grammont that had come ashore a further three miles north of de Graaf's landing site at Punta Gorda on its broad white sand beach. Although they were detected by one of the mounted patrols, they entered the city before a warning could be spread. In fact, the first indication that something was wrong was when De Graaf had three musket shots fired into the air to launch a coordinated assault on the two bastions and a march to the plaza mayor.

The Polvora Bastion, with only two of its 11 rusty cannons working, fell without any shots being fired. The Spanish at the smaller Caleta Bastion fared little better having two muskets, four swords but no more than three rounds of ammunition. To make matters worse, a windswept sand dune pressing against the bastion wall allowed the buccaneers to virtually walk over the parapet. The Spanish troops rallied and fell back from several positions in the town but the lack of gunpowder, coupled with the element of surprise that favoured the buccaneers so effectively, led to confusion and panic. The plaza mayor was soon in the hands of the invaders and a final stand was made at the governor's place. As dawn broke the sturdy wooden doors were prised off their hinges.

Having taken possession of the city, the buccaneers were herding some 3,000 or 4,000 people into the spacious Merced Church by 7.30 in the morning. They segregated the townspeople, putting the white women, clerics and children on the

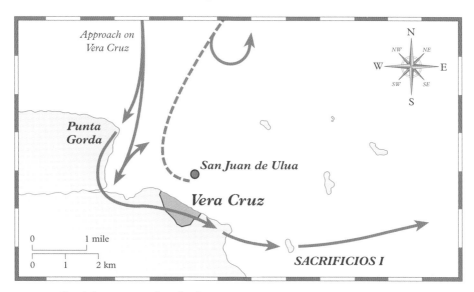

De Graaf and de Grammont's sack of Vera Cruz in 1683.

altar, the free mulattoes, slaves and black women in the front of the church and all the men at the back. One witness afterwards recounted:

'Groups of pirates kept coming to the church constantly to select those whom they fancied from among the women of all classes in the society who were being held prisoner there to satisfy they brutal appetites. The terror was so great that there was not a single case of a man who would have killed his wife, daughter or lover rather than see her exposed to the unbridled desires of those undisciplined troops.'

It was a time to take revenge, too, not only by those trumpeting the Protestant cause but also by those who had suffered at the hands of their Spanish captors. Several logwood cutters who had been seized at Laguna de Terminos, including one who had served in John Murphy's house, sought the Irishman out. Murphy had armed his household retainers and courageously resisted but for fear the buccaneers would slaughter his wife and six children he surrendered. He was taken to the plaza mayor where de Graaf had his hands tied behind his back and hoisted him on a scaffold. Despite the agonising pain, he only angered his tormentors further when he declared he was penniless as all his possessions of any value had already been looted. In a fit of uncontrollable rage, the Dutch buccaneer slashed him in the head with a cutlass, severely wounding him and almost taking his life after mercilessly clubbing him. Cut down, he survived to be thrown in a cell with other prominent citizens after a buccaneer surgeon had patched him up. His fate was not unique as many more were tortured in a determined effort to extract the wealth of Vera Cruz from its inhabitants.

Houses, business places, public buildings, churches and convents were systematically looted and vandalised. On the second day, May 18, Van Hoorn sent four of his men to bring the royal accountant, José de Murueta Otalora, to the governor's palace where he had installed himself. Van Hoorn confronted the accountant with the fact that his men had not even found 50,000 pesos when a city the size of Vera Cruz must have millions. Murueta Otalora explained that they had not had time to hide anything as they had been taken by surprise. He said the buccaneers should go back and search again. This incensed Van Hoorn who returned him to the church with a message: tell him where money was buried or he would put the populace to the sword and burn down the church and town.

Meanwhile, having to stand crushed together, the captives suffered to the point where women and children were suffocating and dying. Two sacks of ship's biscuits and a few bottles of water were all the sustenance they received. On the first day of the occupation it was not long before the commander of San Juan de Ulua across

'Groups of pirates kept coming to the church constantly to select those whom they fancied from among the women of all classes in the society who were being held prisoner there to satisfy they brutal appetites.'

the harbour, Don Fernando Solis, realised that an assault had taken place. Daylight revealed the buccaneers' vessels at anchor near the mouth of the Vergara River and later five of them approached the channel. He sent an urgent message to the viceroy in Mexico City whilst militias from the outlying districts were being formed to counter-attack. Seeing early evidence of this, the buccaneers renewed their efforts to unearth loot from its hiding place and stepped up their intimidation of the populace.

The first appearance of the countryside militia brought an unexpected response from de Grammont. Emptying the royal stables, he put a hundred buccaneers on horseback and opened the gates to mount an unorthodox cavalry charge which sent the astonished Spanish into a hasty retreat. The buccaneers discovered Governor de Cordoba hiding in the royal stables with an injured leg. He was beaten and dragged before de Graaf who incarcerated him in a cell with the unfortunate Murphy amongst others.

The second day, May 19, brought more misery to the prisoners in the church. A witness later recorded the deteriorating conditions:

'Meanwhile in the church the sweat, the smell, the lack of sleep and food, the stinging of mosquitoes which was such a nuisance in the region, the overcrowding and the intolerable company of the corpses which had remained locked up there from the day before filled the first night we spent in captivity with anguish and lamentation. In addition to this there was the discomfort caused by smoke, as the pirates kept lit all night a lot of candles which, along with the heat and smoke, gave the sombre surroundings the most mournful and lamentable glimmer. Besides the lack of sleep and the need for it the pirates engaged in striking those whom the waves of bodies kept trapped at the edges against walls and benches.'

By this time the buccaneer leaders had begun focusing on ransom as the only remaining method of extorting more plunder from the unfortunate citizenry. Many prominent men of the cloth were amongst those intimidated. The aging rector of the Jesuit College was beaten and told he was worth 50,000 pesos. Two more priests, a Franciscan and a Dominican, had their ransoms set at 200,000 pesos. After singling out a few victims, the buccaneers set out to terrorise those in the church by rolling in barrels of gunpowder which they threatened to detonate.

Time was beginning to run out for De Graaf whose original strategy was to carry out a lightning strike and withdraw. The island fortress remained in Spanish hands so no ships could enter the harbour. The viceroy had been informed and garrison from inland towns were preparing to retaliate. De Graaf outwitted the Spanish by beginning the evacuation, transferring his plunder to some unoccupied lime kilns called Los Hornos, a mile south of Vera Cruz, instead of returning to his original landing place. On Friday, May 21, the negotiations such as they were settled on a ransom of 159,000 pesos although he had first demanded a million. This was to be paid by friends and family in the interior. The captives would be held until it was received. His strategy was to use his victims as porters to carry off the spoils as well as provisions for the return voyage. The mulattoes and slaves de Graaf intended to take with him to sell back into slavery. His men spiked any cannons they found and destroyed the small arms in the royal arsenal. At 11 o'clock on the Saturday morning the doors of the Merced Church were opened and the male occupants directed to load on to their backs the bundles of booty readied in the square.

It wasn't long before the buccaneers returned to enrol the black and mulatto women as well and ultimately the clerics in the huge task. Waiting at Los Hornos were boats to ferry the booty and the ransomed captives out to Sacrificios Island, two miles offshore, but not after many had fallen by the wayside of exhaustion, mistreatment and from neglect suffered in the aftermath of the incarceration. Ironically Sacrificios had received its name from the earlier Spanish who found evidence of human sacrifice. Only 300 people were left on the mainland to bury the dead and minister to the dying. For a week 4,000 despairing Spaniards waited on the island for the ransom to arrive and the buccaneers to depart. It was during this period that the animosity that existed between the two Dutchmen, Van Hoorn and de Graaf, ignited. De Graaf had to confront his adversary when the former sent a message back to the city threatening to behead half a dozen captives in a demonstration of his displeasure at the garrison of San Juan Ulua firing on his men.

Tempers flared and Van Hoorn drew his sword only to have his wrist slashed open by the stronger, more skilful de Graaf who promptly clapped him in irons. Only a month later the wounded Dutchman died of gangrene infection off the Isla Mujeres.

It took until May 29 before the ransom arrived in chests on the shore opposite Sacrificios Island. To their dismay, 1,500 mulattoes and slaves were put on board ship by midday and not long after midnight the buccaneer flotilla began departing. Then, as if fate would avenge the inhabitants of Vera Cruz, the hoped-for Flota, under Admiral Don Diego Fernandez de Zaldivar, appeared in the vicinity of the buccaneers with two warships and nine merchantmen all loaded to capacity with cargo and very much unprepared for a pitched battle. The Spanish admiral held a conference on Sunday, May 30, and again the next day, at which the senior pilot of the fleet pointed out that by bearing down on the enemy and scattering them, the Flota would have to beat its way back to port against prevailing winds which would take 10 to 20 days.

With a general sigh of relief from the buccaneers, the captains by default permitted de Graaf to leave unmolested, while on shore the citizens of Vera Cruz contemplated in frustration their loss of over 250 men, women and children, 800,000 pesos in coin, 400,000 pesos-worth of wrought silver, 200,000 pesos-value of jewellery and ornamentation and a huge amount of goods, provisions, armaments and 1,500 hundred mulattoes and slaves. The damage to the city was incalculable and the cruelty inflicted beyond belief.

In a letter appealing for help to the viceroy in Mexico, the citizens of Vera Cruz summarised their pleas as follows:

'In short, Your Excellency, this city is annihilated, its inhabitants naked, without shelter, without the spirit to endure such bitter torment, and totally without human consolation and only because of such great grief do we turn our eyes to your

Excellency, our only protector and source of hope and beseech you to protect our city, fortifying it and defending it from the repeated strikes from these pirates as if we were to fall into the hands of foreign rulers would lead to the total destruction of this kingdom. But this city places its defence at the feet of God, His Majesty and your Excellency, and may God protect it for many years as this kingdom is in need.'

It was after de Graaf's exploits that the Spanish Crown paid serious attention to the protection of Vera Cruz. The fortifications that were subsequently built discouraged the buccaneers from repeating the assault of 1683.

Governor Don Luis de Cordoba, along with his lieutenants, was arrested, court-martialled and sentenced to death. To the outrage of the citizens his sentence was commuted to banishment from the West Indies and a prison term in Africa. De Graaf continued an active career at sea for over 15 years offering first his loyalty to Sir Thomas Lynch, the governor of Jamaica (not accepted) and then aligning himself with the French in Santo Domingo, for whom he took part in the attempted invasion of Jamaica in 1694. At the end of 1698 he joined Pierre le Moyne d'Iberville at Petit Gôave who was recruiting to colonise Louisiana. It is known that in 1700 he was in the new French settlement of Biloxi on the Mississippi River and was to have been one of those to have established a settlement in Mobile, Alamba, but he died in 1704.

The last word on the notorious de Graaf must go to the Spanish historian Juan Juarez who declared his true ambition was not a lust for riches but a thirst for revenge.

'His hands would not be stained with blood, nor would his stockings and his shirt be spotted with dust and wine. His pleasure would lie in reclining, like a grand lord, in the governor's residence and from there listening with satisfaction to the accounts of the excesses committed by his subordinates and impassively treating with scorn the pleas and laments of the rich men of Vera Cruz, the noble ladies, the venerable old men and the priests.'

De Graaf and his confederates in the assault on Vera Cruz had used their commissions solely for personal gain. It was this kind of self-indulgence that contributed to the growing disfavour with which buccaneering was being viewed as the seventeenth century grew to a close.

'His hands would not be stained with blood, nor would his stockings and his shirt be spotted with dust and wine.'

Chapter 12

CAMPECHE

LOGWOOD CUTTERS AND BUCCANEERS

~

Campeche is generally described as a relatively isolated city located on the western side of the Yucatan peninsula in Mexico but the advantage of this is that the old city centre, five blocks by nine blocks, still retains much of its colonial elegance which is the focus of an on-going restoration process. An attractive feature of this process is the use of rich tones of yellow, brown, green, gold and red wall paint on the buildings in the zone.

The ramparts surrounding the town have in some cases been removed to allow freer movement of traffic but sections are still intact. For someone following the trail of the buccaneers, the first baluarte to visit is San Carlos which was first called San Benito but was renamed after Spain's King Carlos II in the mid-seventeenth century. It contains a small museum of the buccaneering era with weapons, maps and other artefacts and traces the events of the period in text and illustrations. Although modest it has been well researched and thoughtfully presented. Baluarte de San Juan and the Puerta de Tierra, the original land gate through which you entered Campeche, provide the setting for a light and sound show. Actors and narrators tell the story of Campeche with a large dose of booming cannon fire and enthusiastic drama on the battlements which include a swordfight between a Spanish soldier and a buccaneer in a courtyard below. A narrated slide show presented on the grassy verge outside the gate takes the hour-long presentation to its colourful climax of sound and fury.

Campeche suffered a series of attacks by the buccaneers who often recruited the nearby logwood cutters.

In the nearby Baluarte de Santiago there is a small botanical garden, whilst in the Baluarte Nuestra Senora de la Soledad there are carved Mayan stelae, some of which are said to be over a thousand years old. Two substantial eighteenth century forts are located outside the city. To the northeast is Fuerte San José intact with cannons, rifle slits and a museum displaying the types of weapons from the buccaneers' era. The other, Fuerte San Miguel, houses a fascinating collection of Mayan artefacts including jade funerary masks.

The Baluarte de San Carlos was one of the original bastions built on the hexagonal city wall.

A second fortification, Fort Miguel, was built to secure the entrance to the city and can be seen today.

One of the oldest cathedrals in Campeche, the Cathedral la Immaculada Concepcion, stands after four centuries on the Central Plaza.

As was the practice in Spanish colonial settlements, Campeche grew around a central plaza and has attractive examples of seventeenth-century colonial architecture in its vicinity. The Cathedral la Immaculada Concepcion was constructed here between 1540 and 1705. Across the square is a single-stored building known as Casa 6, once the home of a wealthy colonial merchant, with 20-foot ceilings and an open courtyard. It has been authentically restored and contains a useful bookshop. Finally, in a small park near the seafront there stands a statue of a young woman who, a legend in poetry has it, is looking out to sea for her buccaneer lover who promised to return.

There were probably very few inhabitants of Campeche who looked forward to the return of the buccaneers. It never was especially wealthy but, like a number of other Spanish coastal towns, it was typical fare for the buccaneers' appetite. Fortunately, for the past 300 years it has led a much more tranquil existence.

Captain William James, who was to have pursued fame and fortune with Christopher Myngs's expedition to Campeche in 1663 but lost his ship in a storm, went on to write himself into the history books. He was the Englishman who stumbled upon the remarkable value of logwood, a fact that turned buccaneers into loggers, nearly started a war on more than one occasion and raised revenue for Charles II to maintain Nell Gwyn, the London actress who was the monarch's best-known mistress.

Capturing a large Spanish merchantman transporting logwood, Captain James sailed for England intending to turn it into an armed vessel with which to continue his buccaneering career. To his astonishment, the seemingly mundane cargo would fetch the enormous price of £100 a ton because of its value for making dye. In fact, so little had he thought of the logwood that he burnt much of it for cooking fuel on the voyage. To appreciate the significance of this stroke of good fortune, it was said that a single load of 50 tons was worth more than a full year's cargo of other merchandise.

On his return to the Caribbean he entered the lucrative trade which led to the settlement of the western Yucatan coast by buccaneers turned loggers, and ultimately resulted in the birth of British Honduras (known today as Belize). Until the beginning of the eighteenth century, the Spanish were to complain repeatedly about the loss of logwood cargoes at sea and the harvesting of this remarkable tree on land on the Yucatan peninsula between Cape Catoche and Laguna de Terminos in the Bay of Campeche, which was 130 miles from the colonial town of San Francisco de Campeche.

It was said that Charles II levied a tax on logwood in order to maintain his mistress, Nell Gwyn.

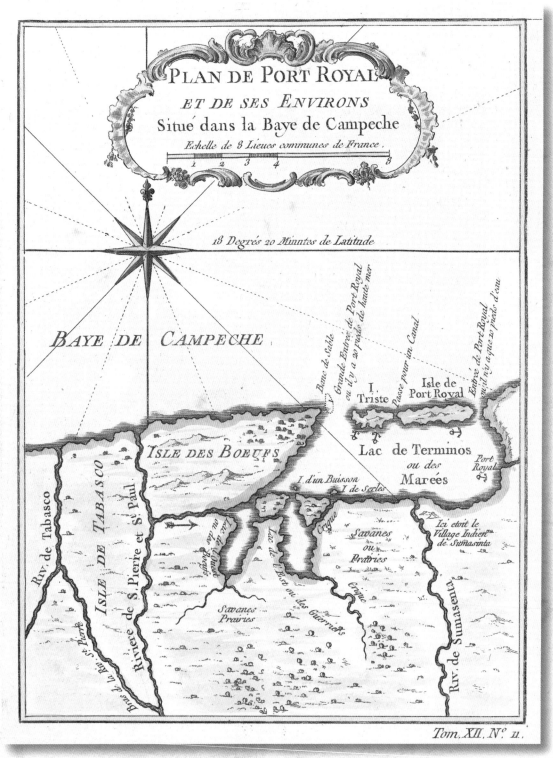

This French map shows the Laguna de Terminos in the Bay of Campeche where the logwood
cutters plied their trade.

If you had lived in the fifteenth century in Europe the choice of coloured fabric for your clothes would have been basically restricted to black, yellowish-brown and grey. There was a limited amount of costly red and purple dyes but these were mostly used for royal and ecclesiastical garments. It was the voyages of discovery to Central and South America that introduced the red dye of Brazil wood from the land called Tierra de Brazil by the Portuguese and from logwood found in the Yucatan.

Known by its botanical name *Hacmatoxylum* (bloodwood) *campechianum*, logwood has a dark red heartwood core which, when crushed and submerged in water, turns the fluid a brilliant red. The wood is dense and extremely hard; as it sinks in the water it has to be supported by more buoyant wood in order to float it down a river. In appearance the logwood is a relatively short, spiny tree with an unusual trunk that resembles a group of stems joined together. Its abundant yellow blossom blooms all year round giving off a pleasant fragrance.

The logwood was later planted on the Caribbean islands in the seventeenth and eighteenth centuries but, like much of the tropical forest, it was cut down and not replaced. By the mid-1500s Spanish merchants were importing substantial cargoes of logwood having been introduced to it by the Mayan Indians. For the next 100 years when the Spanish exclusively controlled the market for this remarkable wood, they were able to obtain up to £100 a ton for it. The value of the dyewood had not gone unnoticed by Spain's enemies in the region. Two early perpetrators of assaults on Campeche made reference to it. William Parker in 1597 referred to its use as a versatile dye and Cornelius Jol, Pie de Palo, regularly called on the coast to extract it, even leaving his name Jol's Hole on the island of Turneffe off Belize.

Even before the capture of Jamaica from the Spanish in 1655, it is said that there were English settlements along the Yucatan coast presumably there for the purpose of cutting logwood. Just ten years later it was a thriving enterprise. The Bay of Campeche stretched along the western side of the Yucatan encompassing Laguna de Terminos which contained a number of islands that had already been ideal for pirates to await their prey, careen vessels for cleaning their hulls and to hunt turtles for their meat.

This coast was swampy and could usually only be approached from the sea which meant that the Spanish found it nearly impossible to drive out the settlers from their interior outposts. With problems enough defending towns like Campeche and Champoton they literally ignored the trespassers for decades. If they did not have their own supply, the buccaneers found it relatively easy to raid Spanish logwood settlements and steal the logwood cut and stripped by Indian labour ready for shipment.

In due course buccaneers turned logwood cutters, usually temporarily, and began harvesting the trees themselves, settling in the area around Laguna de Terminos. This narrow inlet of some 30 miles in length is subject to an unusually high tide that races in rapidly. Logwood grew prolifically on the islands and banks of the streams that flowed into it. The island protecting the lagoon from the open sea, now known as Isla del Carmen, was their base. The eastern end they named Port Royal possibly after its Jamaican counterpart and the western end, Triste, deriving its name appropriately from the word tryst, or meeting place. On the appropriately-named Beef Island there was sufficient wild livestock to feed the men, many of whom had lived on Tortuga.

Stealing logwood was one thing, harvesting was another. Probably the most renowned of buccaneer diarists other than Exquemelin was William Damper who wrote about his experiences in his book *Voyages to Campeche*. He described the hard life these men endured and their inhospitable environment during 1675 and 1676:

'The logwood-cutters inhabit the creeks of the east and west lagoons, in small companies, building their huts close by the creeks' sides for the benefit of the sea-breezes, as near the logwood groves as they can, removing often to be near their business; yet when they are settled in a good open place, they choose rather to go half a mile in their canoes to work, than lose that convenience. Though they build their huts but slightly, yet they take care to thatch them very well with palm or palmetto leaves, to prevent the rains, which are their very violent, from soaking in.

'For their bedding they raised a barbecue, or wood frame three foot and a half above ground on one side of the house; and stick up four stakes, one at each corner, to fasten their pavilions; another frame they raised covered with earth for a hearth to dress their victuals; and a third to sit at when they eat it. During the wet season, the land where the logwood grows is so overflowed, that they step from their bed into the water perhaps two foot deep, and continue standing in the wet all day, till they go to bed again; but nevertheless account it the best season in the year for doing a good day's labour in.

'Some fell the trees, others saw and cut them into convenient logs, and one chips off the sap, and he is commonly a principal man; and when a tree is so thick, that after it is logged, it remains still too great a burthen for one man, we blow it up with gunpowder. The logwood-cutters are generally sturdy strong fellows, and will carry burthens of three or four hundredweight; but every man is left to his choice to carry what he pleases, and commonly they agree very well about it: for they are contented to labour very hard. But when ships come from Jamaica with rum and sugar, they are too apt to misspend both their time and money. If the commanders of these ships are free, and treat all that come the first day with punch, they will be much respected, and every man will pay honestly for what he drinks afterwards; but if he be niggardly, they will pay him with their worse wood, and commonly they have a stock of such laid by for that purpose; nay, they will cheat them with hollow wood filled with dirt in the middle and both ends plugged up with a piece of the same drove in hard, and then sawed off so neatly, that it's hard to find out the deceit; but if any man come to purchase with bills payable at Jamaica, they will be sure to give him the best wood.'

'The logwood-cutters are generally sturdy strong fellows, and will carry burthens of three or four hundredweight;'

The heat, which reached over 90°F for most of the year, and the humidity complemented by endless swarms of mosquitoes, alligators lurking in the mangroves and other variations of discomfort, disease and life-threatening wildlife made a logwood cutter's existence miserable for most of the time. Whilst the buccaneer loggers were constantly threatened by the Spanish, the Mayans who they encountered were fearful of the woodsmen. Dampier recorded their raids on Indian villages where they carried off the women to perform whatever duties they wished in their rude dwellings, enslaving the men to be sold in Jamaica. In addition to having the chance from time to time to join a passing buccaneering expedition, a logwood cutter could expect to earn a £50 profit annually when, in the early mid-seventeenth century, logwood was fetching £25 to £35 a ton in Port Royal.

Curiously the logwood trade flourished despite royal proclamations and acts of parliament in England that forbade the use of logwood in dyeing which had been in force between 1581 and 1662. Dyers maintained that the expensive dyes they traditionally imported were far superior (and certainly made for a more profitable sale). Although imprisonment was the sentence for breaking the law, clearly some intrepid dyers found ways around the prohibition. After 1662 logwood could be freely imported but was subject to a duty of £5 a ton. From 1676 and 1685 the English duty was fixed by the Crown at £500 per annum enabling Charles II to maintain Nell Gwyn, his actress mistress, in the style to which she was becoming accustomed.

Not unexpectedly, the end of the Spanish monopoly on the sale of logwood depressed its price, especially after the peace made with Spain in 1667 and the Treaty of Madrid in 1670 requiring England to suppress buccaneering. The number of buccaneers entering the logwood trade inevitably increased after this date as the result of which the Spanish authorities stepped up their efforts to drive the English out of the Yucatan.

At the time, Governor Modyford of Jamaica noted in his journal that 32 ships carrying a complement of 424 men and armed with 74 guns were employed in the logwood trade to Jamaica. When his successor, Sir Thomas Lynch, came to office he reached the conclusion that the legality or illegality of the English logwood trade had to be settled or the peace would evaporate. He repeatedly requested clarification from London. 'For God's sake give your commands about logwood' the official correspondence records him as having pleaded. This, however, did not prevent him condoning the activity as he simply required all ship's captains to swear that they had not stolen their cargoes from the Spanish or caused them any violence.

The crux of the issue was whether or not the terms of the Treaty of Madrid included the Yucatan in as much as it stated that Spain had withdrawn all claims to Jamaica 'and other islands and countries in the West Indies in the possession of His Majesty or his subjects'. To the Spanish this definitely did not include the Bay of Campeche. One directive issued by the Spanish government ordered the construction of flat-bottomed boats specifically for use in the shallow waters around the coastal reefs and cays, swamps and rivers entering the southern Gulf of Mexico.

They were to be 90 feet long, 16 to 18 feet wide with a draft of about five feet and to be equipped with oars and sails. A large gun would stand on the bow and four small ones in the stern and the boat, known as a pirogue, would hold 120 men.

The English government's unhelpful instructions were that logwood cutting could continue so long as it took place in 'desolate and uninhabited places'. The Spanish for their part continued taking reprisals. Seeing the opportunity to start a new career, former buccaneer Jelles De Lescat, better known as Captain Yellowes or Yallahs, sold his frigate for 7,000 pieces of eight to the authorities in Campeche and entered into the service of the Spanish now that Port Royal was officially arresting buccaneers. His success in capturing over 30 vessels carrying logwood started to drive Spain and England towards war again. Lord Vaughn, now governor of Jamaica, protested without success.

In the ten years between 1672 and 1682, Sir Thomas Lynch estimated that Jamaica's commerce had lost some £25,000 to Spanish seizures of English vessels, mainly engaged in the logwood trade. Previously, in 1671, Lynch had reported that in that year 2,000 tons of dyewood had been cut and transported to Jamaica which at that time was worth four times the value of the emerging sugar industry in the island. But to be caught by the Spanish meant paying a terrible penalty. A Captain Buckenham, who was captured in the Bay of Campeche, was taken to Mexico City where he was seen on the street with a log chained to his leg and a basket on his back, peddling bread for his master.

Although the English occupied the Yucatan well into the eighteenth century, the buccaneers and other logwood cutters were searching for a less dangerous and more profitable location, if not occupation. Many found their way to the Bahamas which, by the next century, became a pirate haven. It is not surprising, as a consequence, that when the Spanish suppressed the logwood trade it led to a rise in piracy in the Caribbean and along the east coast of North America. Others joined the logwood cutters who had gone south to Belize, from where England's primary supply of dyewood originated for the next 200 years. Significantly, the national emblem of independent Belize depicts both a white and black logwood cutter.

In the sixteenth, seventeenth and early eighteenth centuries the northern Central American lowlands bordering on the Caribbean, except for major towns like Campeche and Trujillo, were often largely outside Spanish administrative control. To have established adequately-defended settlements, missions and the other trappings of permanent colonisation would have diverted funds from other more politically and economically viable endeavours. The northwestern corner of the Yucatan peninsula was administered from Merida, an inland town with a farming economy supported by Mayan Indians who provided the labour and paid tribute to their Spanish masters. The further away one went from such a colonial outpost, the less the lives of the Indians and settlers alike were subject to colonial authority. Spain's neglect of its colonists also opened the door for the other Europeans entering the region to carry on a profitable trade in contraband. However, the Spanish conquistadors had originally looked to the western Yucatan for a harbour from which they might ship the silver and gold that Mexico was providing for the royal treasury.

The Mayans, who had occupied the Yucatan for centuries before the arrival of the Spanish, lived a simple life hunting, fishing and farming but they were determined warriors and difficult to subdue. In all it took 30 years from 1517 when the Spanish first arrived until the defeat of the Mayan priest Cilam Anbal to finally overcome their resistance. In the end European weaponry and European diseases claimed the day. It was Francisco de Montejo, appointed Adelantado de Yucatan in 1526 by the King of Spain who, with his son and nephew, spent three decades of their lives fighting battles and forming alliances to get the Mayans under control. However, Francisco Hernandez de Cordoba was to be credited as the founding father of Villa de San Francisco de Campeche as the Mayan settlement of Ah Kim Pech was known after 1540.

As the port and town of Campeche grew in size and wealth, it was soon to become the target of French Atlantic pirates who began making raids into the Caribbean by the second half of the sixteenth century. One report tells of 50 men on a pirate vessel sailing into Campeche harbour, sacking the town and seizing a store ship recently arrived from Spain with its cargo of merchandise and other merchant vessels as well as 'a number of married women, some illustrious persons and other, and (wreaking) great havoc …' The first popularly recorded attempt by an English renegade to take Campeche – the Elizabethan sea dog John Hawkins had passed it by in preference for Vera Cruz – was William Parker of Plymouth who had been the scourge of Portobelo.

Parker managed to take the townsfolk by surprise. His strategy began with a display of strength offshore where his two ships and a barge cruised to and fro showing no intention of entering the harbour. The first wave of panic resulted in some residents hastily hiding their valuables whilst others, more experienced, carried them to safety out of the town. As time passed confidence returned and the town's two mayors let down their guard: Don Francisco Sanchez rode out to his country estate to deal with business matters while Don Pedro de Iterian decided not to put the town on alert.

Parker was not only informed of this complacency but also managed to employ an inhabitant of the town, Juan Venturate, who offered to show him a suitable place to land his force undetected. Parker weighed anchor and gave the impression he was destined for the high seas, landing instead at a pre-arranged place in mangrove swamps where Venturate waited. Parker entered the town at night through the district of San Roman and, taking advantage of the element of surprise, had control of Campeche assisted by the fact that the sun had not yet risen. Unprepared to abandon his town, Mayor Iterian rallied defenders at the convent of San Francisco whilst Mayor Sanchez, on hearing distant gunfire at daylight, gathered a force in the countryside. Wisely Don Sanchez systematically began blocking the exit streets, moving inwards as the contingent at the convent, which was growing in number, counter-attacked.

Finding their retreat cut off, Parker's men at first attempted to fight their way out but after heavy losses suddenly turned about face and returned to the centre of the town, determined to remain. In the two-hour confrontation that took place the fighting was savage. Parker himself was wounded, shot through the chest leaving a bullet lodged in his back. When the opportunity availed itself, his forces broke for the harbour where boats lay waiting. In the retreat wounded men and almost all the booty was abandoned. Juan Venturate was caught trying to swim to one of the buccaneer boats raising suspicion in people's minds that resulted in his imprisonment. When his treachery was revealed he was condemned to death. His sentence was to have his flesh torn away by burning tongs until he died a death, described by Spanish historian Juan Juarez Moreno as 'one of the harshest ever imposed in Campeche on any criminal or enemy of the town'. Not satisfied with driving off the pirates, the Campechenos armed a frigate in preparation for war and manned it with sailors from the town to pursue the corsarios. Assisted by another frigate sent by the authorities in Merida, the pursuers caught up with Parker and captured one of his vessels, the barque *Adventure*.

Parker himself retaliated and sailed back to Campeche, intent on retrieving the boat and his men, but after over two weeks of facing unrelenting artillery resistance he abandoned his plan. He was to return a year later with a larger force but this time he got no further than the beach where he had landed. Although wounded at Campeche, William Parker went on to capture Portobelo in 1601 and after several other successes in the Caribbean he retired eventually to the Thirteen Colonies.

The Dutch, too, were focussing their attention on the riches of Spain's Central American possessions. The Dutch West India Company in 1633 dispatched Jans Janszoon de Hoorn to the Caribbean with Trujillo in Honduras as his objective. He was then to sail south to intercept vessels from Granada passing down the San Juan River into the Caribbean.

Unfortunately Trujillo had not enjoyed the benefit of a visit by the transatlantic galleons for two years so it gave up little by way of booty for the Dutch invaders. The settlers apparently set fire to their own houses and, although Janszoon took the town in two hours, he left with a few cannons, a ransom of 20 pounds of silver, hides, sarsaparilla and indigo. He continued to Campeche, achieving comparable success but again with little plunder. A force of 350 Spaniards and 100 Indians put up determined resistance despite being taken by surprise. Presented with a ransom demand, the governor protested that neither the town nor its citizens had the kind of wealth Janszoon imagined as cattle and logwood were their principal assets. The Dutchmen captured 22 small ships in the harbour, kept nine loaded with cacao and logwood, sold another four back to the Spanish, burning the rest before departing.

A curious combination, Cornelius Jol and a former slave from Havana, Diego el Mulato, were the next to assault Campeche which they did in August, 1663. A Franciscan Friar, Diego Lopez Cogolludo, on a visit to the Convent of San Francisco recounted the sequences of events. Early in the morning of August 11, a flotilla of 11 ships and two barques approached the harbour and anchored. Initially the townspeople believed they were Spanish as a fleet of merchantmen was expected. However, only one appeared to be Hispanic in origin. Nightfall and nothing came to pass. By next morning a contingent of over 500 Dutch, English, French and Portuguese landed to the west of the town and began marching into the San Roman suburb. The first line of defence – three artillery pieces and 50 soldiers commanded by Captain Domingo Galvan Romero – stopped the progress of the pirates until they gave the impression of retreating. When the unsuspecting Captain Galvan and his men left their trenches to follow, the buccaneers turned about and routed them, killing Galvan amongst others. Coincidentally the unfortunate Spanish officer had once been a close acquaintance of Diego el Mulato.

The main resistance came as the invaders approached the mayor plaza where 300 men were to offer a stiff defence. Both sides knowing this was a crucial encounter fought determinedly. Once again Diego el Mulato and Pie de Palo adopted a cunning strategy by withdrawing a body of troops and deploying them to the intersection of the side streets to the plaza which were less rigorously defended. This manoeuvre forced the remaining Spanish to sound the retreat having lost many prominent citizens and military. As in the past, the district and convent of San Francisco were destined to be where the Campechenos made their last stand. But rather than reduce further their shrinking numbers and assuming that relief would soon appear from Merida, the one-legged Dutchman and the ex-slave decided to loot the town (which included a large number of wine-cellars contributing to widespread drunken revelry). After two more days all that remained was to extract a ransom of 40,000 pesos.

The man who had most to lose personally, Captain Domingo Rodriquez Calvo, already wounded in the battle for the plaza, opposed capitulating and refused even to enter into any discussion with his enemy. With the defiance of the townspeople and the news that the Merida reinforcements were on their way, the plundering escalated. Before the sacking ended, Diego el Mulato searched the town for the stubborn Captain Calvo, threatening to cut off his ears and nose but leaving him alive for some unjust action taken against him when the mulatto had lived in Campeche. Two years after the departure from Campeche, Pie de Palo with 14 vessels fought a Spanish fleet of seven galleons under Don Carlos de Ibarra in which the Dutchman and most of his crew perished. The fate of Diego el Mulato was not unexpected. Although overcoming three armed vessels sent out to arrest him and slaughtering every Spanish-born on board, he was captured in 1673 and himself suffered a cruel execution.

The English privateer William Jackson, on his 1644 circuit of the Caribbean, attempted an assault of Campeche. When he was rebuffed he took nearby Champoton, kidnapping two priests who were later released in Florida and later wrote an account of their experiences. However, it was probably the successful assault on Campeche by the English buccaneer Lewis Scott in 1661 that encouraged Christopher Myngs, accompanied by Edward Mansfield and young Henry Morgan, to mount an expedition in 1663. Scott, unlike Diego el Mulato, successfully plundered the town in addition to extracting a ransom. Myngs had already earned a huge reputation for himself by raiding Cumana and Puerto Cabello off the coast of Venezuela, looting the small town of Coro where he had stumbled across the 22 chests of silver and going on to capture the Cuban capital of Santiago de Cuba. Having persuaded the authorities in Jamaica that Campeche was a worthwhile prize, he once again rounded up the buccaneers led by Edward Mansfield. The final numbers included French and Dutch who joined from Tortuga forming a contingent of more than 18 vessels and 1,000 seamen and soldiers.

A ship that had been cruising in the vicinity of Campeche arrived in Port Royal in February before Myngs landed, with news that suggested that sure defeat would have faced the buccaneers. Its commander, Captain Mitchell, maintained that the residents, with advance notice of Myngs's imminent arrival, had sent their women, children and belongings inland to Merida; that 1,500 men set up in batteries armed with guns taken off ships in the harbour awaited the English and that reconnaissance vessels were patrolling offshore to give early warning. Anxiety in Port Royal escalated.

Christopher Myngs was to be disappointed by the returns from sacking Campeche.

Whether the Campechenos were alerted or not, the buccaneers carried out a familiar manoeuvre to achieve their goal. A demand to surrender was turned down by the confident governor. The bulk of the men were landed four miles up the coast at Jamunla at midnight on February 8 whilst the ships anchored offshore to give an impression that an invasion was not taking place. Despite heavy fighting the townspeople were no match for the buccaneers; Campeche was to be in Myngs's hands by the next day.

The fortifications of Santa Cruz to the southeast of the town and San Benito offered little resistance because, according to Spanish sources, 'they were unfit … badly-constructed fortresses'. Spanish history claimed that despite this '… during three hours combat the defenders carried out their duty with great valour until the last reinforcements had been subdued and these fortresses had been occupied. The enemy took control of the town with the death of 54 residents and a large number of wounded and they took prisoner 107 men who were barbarously abused.' After Myngs was injured as the result of cannon fire and had returned to the *Centurion*, Edward Mansfield took command. Initially chaos reigned with widespread looting and indiscriminate destruction as buildings and their contents were set on fire.

Spanish sources tell of the carnage '… they sacked the town from which they got large quantities of gold, silver and merchandise, not sparing the jewellery and ornaments from the temples where they perpetrated hectic outrages, stabling and burning all the statues, profaning their altars and displaying their insatiable greed even in the sepulchres where they assumed there was silver buried among the corpses.' Don Antonio Maldonado de Adana who had command of the Castillo Santa Cruz undertook to negotiate with Mansfield to stop the remorseless destruction. He found the buccaneer leader willing to end the arson in exchange for being allowed to draw a sufficient supply of fresh water from the town's wells. On February 23 the fleet got underway with its spoils, which included 14 vessels of varying sizes captured in the harbour.

The official record of prizes taken at Campeche indicated that nine ships and their cargoes yielded £1,341 which, after expenses including £10 to Edward King whose leg was shot off, totalled only £782.4.0d, and had to be split between 1,500 men and the ships' owners. Clearly dreams of great riches were frustrated. Immediately after the departure of Myngs, Mansfield and Morgan the municipal council of Campeche took what measures it could with its limited resources to improve the town's defences. This was achieved primarily by creating a network of strategically-placed trenches and strengthening the fort of San Benito.

Peace treaties, strengthened defences and increased vigilance did not deter two English buccaneers, George Spurre and Edward Neville, from sailing to Campeche in the summer of 1678 and sacking the hapless Spanish town once again. This time their numbers were augmented by nearly 200 buccaneer logwood cutters recruited at Laguna de Terminos. It was reported by the Spanish that although the majority were French and English, their number even included a Spanish friar. And once again the Campechenos were taken by surprise with a landing at dawn at an isolated spot six miles outside of town. Quickly in control, the buccaneers stayed until a ransom had been extracted and departed with their loot including 250 black, mulatto and Indians to sell as slaves at Laguna de Terminos. Colonel William Beeston, who was to become the lieutenant-governor of Jamaica, noted their return in his journal some weeks later candidly mentioning that the authorities had issued a pardon and given permission for the men to bring ashore their plunder and enjoy their ill-gotten gains in the taverns of Port Royal.

The most renowned of the French flibustiers was to be Sieur or Chevalier de Grammont, a man whose most notable exploits took place on the Gulf of Mexico. Little is known about his birth in France which took place about 1650, or his early years. The Spanish knew him as Agrammont and he was popularly referred to as Chevalier de Grammont, the title he ultimately received from the governor of Tortuga. He is said to have killed a man in a duel at the tender age of 14 and ran away to sea to avoid the consequences. Like many before and after him he joined the outcasts in Tortuga and on the mainland of Hispaniola. He quickly earned a reputation for bravery and as a leader of men but on the dark side it was his cruelty to prisoners for which he was often remembered. By the late 1670s he had gained prominence commanding the French buccaneers and sailed on Admiral d'Estrees's disastrous expedition to Curaçao which had ended when most of the fleet went aground. Although the French admiral abandoned the abortive invasion, de Grammont opted for Maracaibo as a more lucrative objective taking with him 2,000 men on 19 large and small ships.

Using the technique of approaching the principal fortifications guarding the entrance to Lake Maracaibo from the rear by land with half his force, de Grammont used cannons off loaded from his ships to bombard the walls and force the defenders to capitulate. Panic took over in Maracaibo and surrounding areas, even the governor retreated with a body of men inland to Maicao while the buccaneers occupied the central plaza virtually unopposed. After taking what they had come for and maltreating the residents, de Grammont put Maracaibo to the torch before moving across the lake to repeat the assault on Gibraltar. The outrages continued for nearly six months until on December 3 the rapacious buccaneers finally sailed for Petit Goâve arriving on Christmas Eve to a rousing welcome.

De Grammont's reputation grew further when he led a force of less than 50 men into La Guaira, the port for Caracas, and occupied it with ease despite the existence of a garrison of three times that number. On hearing of the audacious attack, the military in Caracas quickly mobilised a counter-attack, fearful that de Grammont's buccaneers would have the wealthy capital city in their sights. Spanish soldiers under Captain Juan de Laya Mujica who had escaped the initial assault regrouped and drove the buccaneers to the water's edge killing several and wounding their leader who received a cutlass slash on the neck. However, the Frenchmen managed to get away with their spoils and most of their lives although many drowned during a hurricane as their ships approached Petit Goâve.

By the summer of 1685, de Grammont's buccaneers began gathering once more on the eastern side of the Yucatan near Cape Catoche. Their activities did not go unnoticed by the Spanish. Leading the defence of Campeche was Felipe de la Barrera y Villegas, a soldier who had already won praise for driving

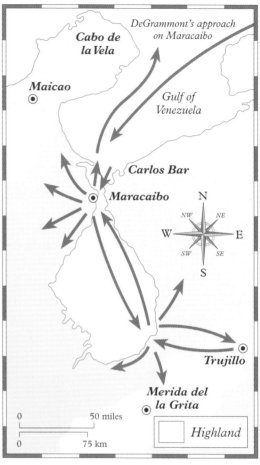

De Grammont's attack on Maracaibo in 1678.

In 1865 the Chevalier de Grammont carried out the most devastating attack that Campeche had ever suffered.

English logwood cutters out of the Laguna de Terminos in 1680 and capturing a 24-gun merchantman there. In expectation of the invasion the residents were dispatched inland and defensive positions taken up.

On July 6, 1685, the biggest invasion ever witnessed in Campeche was launched. From the vessels hovering offshore 700 buccaneers in pirogues headed for the beach but de la Barrera's four companies of militia amounting to 200 men were waiting for them. The buccaneers were not prepared to face them in such unpromising surroundings. Next day the invaders divided into four groups carrying the fight into the town from all sides and encircling it. Their cause was assisted when Captain Cristobal Martinez de Acevedo of the coastguard frigate *Nuestra Senora de la Soledad* had decided to scuttle his vessel to prevent it falling into enemy hands. Although he had planned to sink the ship by boring holes in the hull, time ran out and he was forced to detonate explosives to achieve the same result. The subsequent explosion further terrified an already frightened populace.

Maurice Besson in *The Scourge of the Indies* describes the scene afterwards inside Campeche that is typical of what took place when the buccaneers broached the walls of a Spanish colonial town. 'Panic spread through the town; the citizens ran to arms, crying that the filibusters had brought infernal machines with them, and that the 22 long boats were so many fire-ships. Two battalions hurriedly left the ramparts and ambushed themselves in a sunken road through which the filibusters would have to pass. The advance guard of the assailants came under a tremendous fire, fortunately badly aimed, and there was a moment's indecision. The filibusters, who would have none but hand to hand fighting, dashed forward, and impetuously pushed the Spaniards back. They gave way, and, the filibusters with them, passed again into the town. The townsmen had had time enough to make barricades. Furniture, carts, stones and doors torn from fastenings provided impassable obstacles, and from them was poured a very heavy fire with both artillery and muskets. De Grammont saw the peril, and threw his men into the first houses he came upon. Mounted on the terraced roofs, the filibusters shot down the defenders of the barricades.

In an instant, the corsairs had succeeded in climbing up the roofs, hiding behind the shutters, and opening fire upon the soldiers and the gunners. Under the hail of fire, the defenders of the barricades protecting the main street of Campeche were obliged to give way. De Grammont himself, with a hundred brave fellows behind him, scaled the obstacle, captured the guns and turned them against the Spaniards. The place was then virtually taken; hand-to-hand combat was sufficient to enable the filibusters to gain the mastery of the other strongholds. House doors were smashed open with hatchets, and racing door to door, they massacred the citizens in the narrow alleyways and patios. In three hours, de Grammont had made himself master of the town, and the notables implored him to put a stop to the bloodshed.' It was nearly a week before relief came into view, although the town's main fortification was holding out. On the morning of July 12 two columns of militia appeared from Merida to join a disorganised wave of volunteers who had returned to the town.

De Grammont was to win this battle with sharpshooters picking off the Spanish from the town ramparts while a second contingent circled behind them. The fort gave more trouble to subdue. Besson wrote that '600 filibusters, perched on neighbouring steeples and housetops, never ceased to put straight even the most insignificant Spanish that had appeared at the smallest embrasure'. Having decided next morning to storm the battlements, de Grammont discovered at daybreak that the defenders had melted into the night leaving behind only a young Spanish officer who had refused to retreat and an English artilleryman. De Grammont, who hated the English, had the artilleryman's head chopped off whilst the Spanish officer he released with his sword intact in recognition of his valour.

As he had at Maracaibo, de Grammont was determined to extract a fat ransom. A message was sent to Governor Juan Bruno Tellez de Guzman demanding 400 head

Campeche finally began building a wall with four bastions in 1686 after decades of pillage and destruction by the pirates and buccaneers.

of cattle and 80,000 pesos which was flatly rejected. The governor boasted Spain was wealthy enough to rebuild any town de Grammont destroyed and find new inhabitants. Enraged, de Grammont decided to test the governor's resolve and began firing the buildings. He next informed the governor that he would massacre his hostages, when again denied his ransom, by beginning the executions in the main square. After half a dozen had died, de la Barrera led a delegation to de Grammont's partner, Laurens de Graaf, who he deemed to be a more humane man. De Graaf persuaded the Frenchman to desist, which he did, departing Campeche after spiking any cannons that he found and setting fire to remaining buildings.

After he returned to Petit Goâve, de Grammont was rewarded with the title of Chevalier, or Lieutenant to the King, by Governor de Cussy for his services to the monarch. De Grammont briefly continued his buccaneering career, losing his life and crew in a storm at sea a year later. It was only in 1686 that the Spanish crown finally agreed to build a new walled city in Campeche. On January 3 the cornerstone was laid, well over a hundred years after the pirates and buccaneers had first wreaked havoc. It was from Campeche that the death knell of the buccaneer logwood cutters was sounded when Captain Don Alonso Felipe de Arando routed them decisively in the Bay of Campeche in 1717. But for decades the logwood trade had sustained the buccaneers by providing a temporary income between their other more profitable enterprises.

Chapter 13

CARTAGENA

THE LAST CAMPAIGN

~

The 1697 assault on Cartagena by Jean-Baptiste Du Casse served as an appropriate close to the era of the buccaneers in Caribbean history. It revealed simultaneously their effectiveness in battle at the same time as their depravity in victory. They satisfied their needs in the service of the French crown. But as much destruction as they and de Pointis's regular troops inflicted on the city, its network of walls, bastions and forts, probably the strongest in the Caribbean down the ages, there still remains a remarkable architectural heritage.

Many of the fortifications have been rehabilitated, remodelled or replaced over time, whilst others have deteriorated. The defences of Bocachica have disappeared. The castle of San Luis was finally abandoned after the English Admiral Edward Vernon destroyed the castle of San Fernando which had been completed in 1759.

San Luis was originally built on the Caribbean side of Tierrabomba Island and in recent times erosion by the sea has actually revealed some of its foundations. Its successor, San Fernando, sits virtually at the mouth of the outer bay on the waterline. This castle and the Angel Rafael Battery behind it were designed to confront an invasion from Tierrabomba by land. They have been restored and provide a unique experience for visitors who can walk down a 700-yard tunnel which runs from the centre of the battery down to the sea, in order to allow a besieged garrison to escape at the very last moment. Another battery that the French in 1697 would not have had to contend with is San José on an island opposite San Fernando. It consists of a central courtyard, soldier's quarters, powder storage and a 21-gun battery that extends out into the bay. All three of these fortifications must be reached by boat.

Fuerte de San Sebastian del Pastelillo was built to protect Cartagena and today is a restaurant and yacht club.

The two forts at the entrance to the inner bay, Santa Cruz de Castillo Grande at Punta Judio and on the opposite, eastern side, San Juan de Manzanillo, were no longer considered useful for defence by the middle of the eighteenth century and for a period were retained as warehouses. Today the few remains of the former can be seen from the sea at a private naval club. Similarly what evidence that is left of Manzanillo is situated on the grounds of the president's official guest residence.

San Felipe del Boqueron, the first structure to be built to protect the town of Cartagena and contain artillery for guarding the treasure fleet when it was anchored, has survived the passage of time for decades. It was only replaced by the castle of San Sebastian del Pastelillo when Admiral Vernon's campaign to capture Cartagena exposed its limitations. Built on the same site as the latter, San Sebastian also failed to meet the requirement of the city's defence although it was never truly put to the test. Today it is a popular restaurant and marina. Inside the restored fortifications are the sentry posts, powder magazine, water cistern and a spacious parade ground entered through a portal dated 1743.

The walls surrounding colonial Cartagena were begun in 1602 and were modified and extended for generations. Santo Domingo was the first bastion built to repulse attacks from the Bocagrande peninsula. The bastions of Santa Catalina and San Lucas took the brunt of the 1697 assault from the opposite direction. Despite the pounding sea on the Caribbean side and wartime sieges, the bastions and walls are intact and well-preserved.

To the east of the city, the convent of the La Popa still stands and welcomes visitors to its chapel with its elaborate gold-leafed altar and eclectic museum. After its destruction by the buccaneers under Du Casse, it was rebuilt. The fortification on San Lazaro hill, San Felipe de Barejas, built by Governor Don Pedro Zapata still dominates the city today above the battery of La Redención. The castle of San Felipe is a far cry from the modest fort of Zapata's. It is a massive fortress of staggering dimensions. It was here that Spain savoured her most spectacular success in the Caribbean when Admiral Vernon was soundly defeated in the eighteenth century. Remarkably, there is no museum of the buccaneers' era in the city of Cartagena. With its battlements intact and despite the relentless modernisation, the enduring architectural heritage of the city it is a reminder that the buccaneers did not always have it their own way.

Castillo de San Felipe, set on the San Lazaro hill, still stands today, the strongest fortress ever built by the Spanish in its colonies.

Cartagena, like several other Caribbean cities, had an early history characterised by a renegade turned founding father, Indians who resisted colonisation and the unwelcome attention of predatory pirates. Named on a voyage of exploration by the explorer Juan de la Cosa in 1501 after the city in Spain, the Bay of Cartagena did not attract the attention again of the Spanish for another 30 years. When it did it was as the result of a contract or 'capitulacion' granted to Pedro de Heredia by the queen of Spain who was known as Juana la Loca (or Crazy Joan). Heredia was born of an aristocratic family and while a young man fought six adversaries at once as a result of which he was badly wounded. He subsequently took revenge and killed three of them, obliging him to flee the country. After several years in Santo Domingo and Santa Marta, Heredia obtained the contract to explore, capture and settle the region around the Bay of Cartagena. On January 14, 1533 Pedro de Heredia landed a small force of 150 men and 22 horses on the Bocagrande peninsula and entered the recently-abandoned Indian village of Calamari.

Historical lore has it that he found an old Indian by the name of Corinche left behind in the village on the site of present-day Cartagena, who was persuaded to guide the Spanish to a better site for a settlement offering a supply of fresh water. Wily Corinche led them into an ambush in what is known today as Yurbaco, where the warlike Yurbaco Indians were waiting. In the battle that lasted almost a day, Spanish firearms and mounted soldiers eventually prevailed but not before Pedro de Heredia almost lost his life. He continued his penetration of the hinterland, not only receiving a friendlier welcome from the interior Indians but also finding ample supplies of food and sources of gold. Returning with eight gold ducks weighing a kilo and a half each and a solid gold, 60 kilo porcupine, he quickly realised the advantages of pacifying the Indians around the bay.

San Sebastian de Cartagena, more commonly known as Cartagena de Indias, was founded on June 1, 1533, on the site of the original Indian village. Easily the most obvious reason for choosing it was the protection of the double bay in which to shelter shipping and create a strong system of defence. Within 20 years Cartagena showed increasing signs of prosperity. The discovery of gold provided a vast new source of wealth which added to the trade already passing through the thriving port. The population was expanding steadily through European immigration. News of Cartagena's prosperity spread to Spain's enemies, attracting French then English pirates and privateers seeking to enrich themselves at Spain's expense.

Only ten years after the city's founding, Roberto Baal, more formally known as Jean-Francois de la Roque, a French nobleman, landed 1,000 men in the night from five ships to surprise the inhabitants. Heredia himself led the defence but the populace had to flee, leaving the pirates to loot and rampage until a ransom of 200,000 pieces of eight was handed over. Ironically, only a year later the gallant founder, Pedro de Heredia, was denounced and returned to Spain to defend himself against his colonial enemies. His ship was wrecked approaching Cadiz and in an effort to save himself he leapt overboard only to drown in his attempt to reach the shore.

Martin Coté and Juan de Beautemps, also French pirates, attacked Cartagena in 1559 with seven ships and another thousand men, overcoming determined resistance before sacking the city and collecting a substantial ransom. The first of the English privateers to set his sights on Cartagena was John Hawkins. His initial mission was to exploit the need for African slaves as the indigenous population in the Caribbean was becoming depleted. He approached the governor of Cartagena on his 1568 voyage with a request to be allowed to land slaves and other cargo for trading from his five vessels. When he was refused, he proceeded to bombard the city for eight days until, unable to prevail, he departed threatening to return. Hawkins had expected to be able to trade with the Spanish colonies and the unprofitable outcome of the voyage, as well as the disdain with which he was treated, was bitterly resented in England.

Persuaded that Spain intended to launch a major campaign against England, Queen Elizabeth saw an opportunity to weaken the Spanish crown and replenish the national coffers with a Caribbean expedition on a scale never before attempted. She chose Francis Drake to lead the mission. Twenty-two vessels with 2,300 men sailed for the Caribbean from Plymouth on September 14, 1585. Drake's plan was an ambitious one in which he was to capture Santo Domingo, Cartagena and other fortified Spanish towns, attack the treasure galleon port of Nombre de Dios, then Panama and finally Havana, where he was to install a permanent garrison.

On New Year's Day, 1586, his massive force landed ten miles from the walls of Santo Domingo by cover of night. While the army approached from one side, Drake gave the impression that the landing was on the opposite side. This manoeuvre gained the tactical advantage that was all that was required to capture the city after a remarkably short engagement. By February Drake had ransacked the city, carried off 200 to 300 guns, fully provisioned his fleet and, after seizing the best of the vessels in the harbour, set off for Cartagena encouraged by his success.

By this time Cartagena was undoubtedly Spain's Caribbean centre of commerce, both as the storehouse for its gold, silver and pearls and as the mercantile port for the vast interior. However, as grand as its reputation must have been, in 1586 it badly lacked adequate defences. El Boqueron, known today as the fort of San Sebastian del Pastelillo and then the only significant fortification, was simply a fortified circular tower at the entrance to the inner harbour. The outer harbour could be entered past the redoubt at San Matias and through a channel at Bocagrande between Tierrabomba Island and the Bocagrande peninsula from where Cartagena could be reached by land. In the belief that such an audacious attack was unimaginable, the

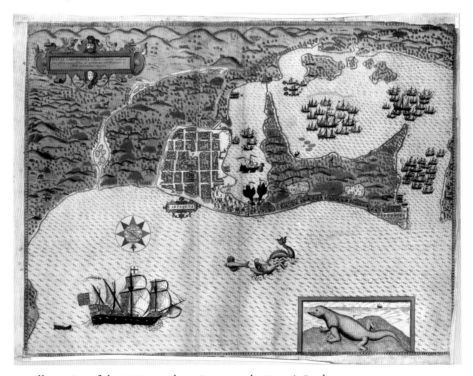

An illustration of the 1586 attack on Cartagena by Francis Drake.

Spanish Crown had consistently ignored pleas for the necessary fortifications and garrison to more effectively defend the city. The governor could assemble no more than 1,200 men, including 400 Indian bowmen, 20 Negro musketeers and 150 soldiers, on two galleys in the bay.

Drake entered Bocagrande without opposition and put ashore the troops on the beach from where they moved forward, coming into contact with a breastwork with six guns behind a stonewall. The galleys anchored near the shoreline provided additional firepower. Once again Francis Drake cleverly faked an assault on El Boqueron as the main objective of the English attack. Meanwhile the land forces had entered the city itself, despite fierce fighting, and seized the central plaza. Having driven the garrison and the populace with their valued possessions out of the city, Drake proceeded to demand a huge ransom. He was able to obtain barely a quarter of what he was expecting, agreeing to accept 112,000 ducats and whatever loot he could gather from the 200 houses and half-completed cathedral they plundered. After six weeks and with yellow fever reducing his force to only 700 or 800 men, Drake withdrew. Weakened as they were, the English bypassed Havana, aborting the grand design, and returned to England with little reward.

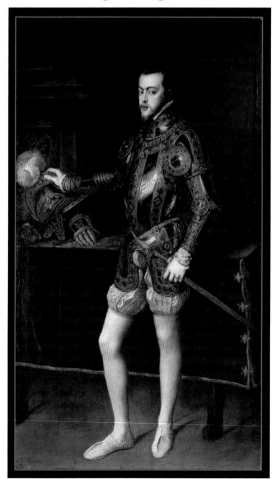

Historian Kenneth Andrews records that there were some 76 English privateering expeditions comprising 183 individual voyages in the Caribbean between 1585 and 1603. Allowing also for the countless incursions of the French corsairs, many of whom were Huguenots with a fanatical religious loathing for the Spanish, it is not surprising that as Cartagena entered the seventeenth century the Spanish authorities came to the realisation that their Caribbean colonies were in jeopardy.

But it was Francis Drake's seizure of Cartagena that convinced King Philip II of Spain of the necessity for fortifying his principal Caribbean cities and maintaining strong and regular naval patrols. So began the costly construction of massive fortresses both on the island colonies and on the mainland.

The same year as Drake's assault, the Italian military engineer, Bautista Antonelli,

On hearing of the cost of fortifying Cartegena, King Philip II swore he could see the battlements from Spain.

made his first visit. But it was not until after 1610 that Cartagena began acquiring extensive stone fortifications that eventually resulted in the walled city and a ring of forts around the inner and outer bays. The cost to the royal treasury was so great that it was said that Philip II, when asked why he was staring morosely out of a window to the west said: 'I am looking for the walls of Cartagena. They cost so much they must be visible from here.'

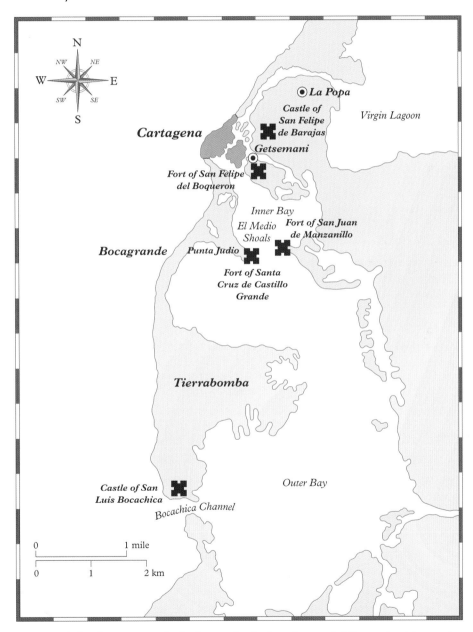

Cartagena's fortifications were built, destroyed, rebuilt and expanded for nearly 200 years in an effort to keep out Spain's enemies.

Before the Bocagrande silted up, the entrance to the Bay of Cartagena was blocked by a massive chain.

The Caribbean coast of Tierra Firme, or New Granada, present-day Colombia and Venezuela, was constantly under threat. Around the pearl islands of Cubagua and Margarita to the coastal towns of La Guaira, Maracaibo, Cumana, Coro, Riohacha, Santa Marta and Cartagena, pirates and privateers plied their trade for 150 years. Not only were these Spanish outposts busy trading centres but in the case of Cartagena it was a conduit for treasure destined for Seville. In the late summer of each year the Tierra Firme fleet, the Galleones, departed from Spain on the six to eight-week voyage from Spain comprising as many as 40 merchantmen protected by five or more warships. The fleet would wait at Cartagena whilst the precious metals were shipped from Arica and Callao on Peru's Pacific coast to Panama, before being transported, as we have seen, by mule-train overland or on riverboats to Nombre de Dios and, later, Portobelo to be loaded.

As the colonies of England, France and Holland became more securely entrenched, weary of being the victims of buccaneers armed with commissions from Port Royal and Tortuga, the Spanish sought to further strengthen their seaborne defences during the last quarter of the seventeenth century. The Council of the Indies in Spain had repeatedly been requested to provide a fleet to patrol the Caribbean Sea. In a 15-page document described as 'a most impressive memorial enumerating damages inflicted by the buccaneers', King Carlos was asked to provide at least one large and three small ships because of the increasing menace. Eventually, confronted by a litany of broken promises, the crown not only provided five frigates ranging in size from 140 to 450 tons but also promised that three more ships being built in Holland would be assigned to the Caribbean. The royal fleet sailed on October 5, 1677 with 192 guns and more than 1,000 men.

Meanwhile Louis XIV of France had made peace largely on his own terms with Spain in Europe but set out to achieve his ambitions in the West Indies. His intention was to force the Spanish into granting France exclusive trading privileges to the detriment of the English and Dutch. In order to effectively plan and execute his strategy, Louis instructed his most successful naval commander, the Comte d'Estrees, to make a reconnaissance of Spain's Caribbean ports which he did. The size and fire power of his naval expedition caused considerable alarm and, when he paid his 'courtesy call' on Cartagena, the governor without objection gave up all his imprisoned French flibustiers, while the Comte coolly made detailed drawings of the city's defences.

Adding to Spain's anxiety was Captain John Coxon's sack of Portobelo, the defence of which was lambasted in official reports as 'shameful if not criminal'. The crown reacted by sending the 1680s treasure fleet with 25 vessels carrying arms, ammunition, building materials and tools, as well as a thousand infantrymen and gunners. By the start of the 1680s the Spanish had a squadron patrolling the Caribbean far larger than the Dutch, French and English in the region and bigger than the usual fleets the buccaneers assembled for a major campaign. The objective of this squadron of ten large vessels totalling 3,000 tons, 380 cannons and nearly 2,200 soldiers and sailors was to rid the region of buccaneers and pirates and patrol Spain's territorial waters.

Spain was to be assisted in her efforts to suppress the buccaneers when the English authorities, pressed by the merchants in Jamaica in particular, decided that the future prosperity of its Caribbean colonies would be better served by trading rather than depending on the buccaneers' booty. Since the mid-1670s the ex-buccaneer, now knighted, Sir Henry Morgan was in pursuit of his former associates in his role as lieutenant-governor. The French continued to hand out commissions to the buccaneers up to the end of the century and as Port Royal emptied, Tortuga, Petit Goâve and Léogane in the Cul-de-Sac attracted buccaneers seeking French commissions.

When war broke out between England and France in 1689 the conflict was soon channelled to the West Indies. After the governor of Tortuga and French Hispaniola, Tarin de Cussy, had taken a force of 1,000 men, many of them buccaneers, to seize and burn St Jago de los Caballeros to the ground, the Spanish supported by the English navy retaliated and killed de Cussy near Cape St Francois on Hispaniola, taking the lives of 300 French in the engagement. Laurens de Graaf, one of the two Dutchmen who captured Vera Cruz in 1683, with commissions granted by de Cussy before his death, led two marauding attacks on the north coast of Jamaica. However, this was just a taste of France's intentions towards the island. The first and only serious but unsuccessful attempt to take Jamaica was made in 1694 and brought to prominence Jean-Baptiste DuCasse, soon to participate in the spectacular attack on Cartagena.

DuCasse, not long appointed governor of French Hispaniola, set out with 22 ships and approximately 1,500 men including 800 buccaneers led by Laurens de Graaf. Two Irish soldiers serving against their will in Port Royal had deserted and found their way to Governor DuCasse. They proposed to him that the disastrous earthquake that had destroyed two-thirds of Port Royal in 1692 had severely weakened the town's defences and left it extremely vulnerable. When DuCasse approached Port Royal, however, he discovered that contrary to reports, considerable progress had been made in rehabilitating the town's remaining fortifications. Sailing west to Carlisle Bay he landed his troops but, after protracted engagements with military and local militia, he surprisingly withdrew with 1,300 slaves amongst his prizes. His most memorable moment in history was still three years away.

Jean-Baptiste DuCasse, now governor of French Hispaniola, called upon the French buccaneers for the assault on Cartagena in 1697.

Like LeVasseur before him, DuCasse was born into a Huguenot family probably in 1646 near Bayonne in the south of France. He rose to prominence as a young officer of the Compagnie de Senegal where he established trading arrangements favourable to the French and entered the slave trade, first sailing to the Caribbean in 1680. He turned his energies to buccaneering and, in an early incident, he captured a large Dutch merchant vessel which brought him to the attention of Louis XIV, who commissioned him a lieutenant in his royal navy on the strength of his feat. He carried out a number of campaigns against France's enemies: the Dutch in Suriname and the English in St Kitts, as well as driving the latter away from Guadeloupe where they had been blockading the island. On de Cussy's death, which took place while DuCasse was in France, he was appointed governor of French Hispaniola. On his return, he took over his responsibilities at Port-de-Paix on the mainland of Hispaniola. He quickly imposed his authority, warning the buccaneers that, whilst they would not be restrained or persecuted, he considered them subjects of their king to whom their loyalty was due.

Between 1695 and 1697, DuCasse devoted himself to trying to tame the frontier society that he had inherited. He brought the remaining settlers from Tortuga to the mainland because he believed it had outlasted its usefulness as its soil was no longer fertile. His correspondence reveals a man frustrated by the problems of shaping a new society. The colony, he said, was 'composed of the refuse of all the Kingdom, men of the sack and cord, without honour and without virtue'. His plain outspokenness retained the loyalty of the buccaneers in the Cul-de-Sac settlements. An anecdote recounted during this period has a flibustier seeking out DuCasse to demand money which he claimed was due to him. Confronted, DuCasse is reputed to have retorted: 'I know well that behind my back you call me a dog, a rogue and a thief. But I do not care. If you are not satisfied with me, take my sword and run it through my body. As for money, I have none and you will not get any.' He was coming to the realisation that in the not-too distant future the buccaneers would prove to be a liability to France and would need to be suppressed.

In September 1696, France's Minister of the Marine Pontchartrain directed DuCasse to provide men to launch an attack on Cartagena. Jean Bernard Desjeans, Baron de Pointis, had obtained the approval of the King to carry out this assault which would not only humiliate the Spanish but reward the enterprise, well supported by private investors, with a potentially handsome profit. DuCasse, for his part, although an enthusiastic supporter of such a plan several years previously, was now rather more anxious to press the case for occupying all of Hispaniola.

Four months later he was formally ordered to gather as many buccaneers as he could and wait for de Pointis, who finally arrived in February, 1697. This was to be an ill-starred joint venture. De Pointis resented DuCasse and considered his buccaneers unworthy of the recognition accorded them. He described them in his account of the event as 'men who moved back and forth like the waves of the sea', who were 'sanguine not valiant' and 'men with whom I found contact horribly disagreeable'. Because the buccaneers were, in effect, subjects of the king they had to be accepted: 'I was content to let them know that they would find in me a leader who would give them orders, but not a companion in their quest for fortune.' Acknowledged as a brilliant commander, de Pointis was said to suffer from two common faults, vanity and avarice, and the latter was ultimately to cause the buccaneers to unleash terror on the citizens of Cartagena. From the outset he was bent on humiliating DuCasse, very obviously making him a junior partner in a campaign led by a military superior.

The entire West Indies went on alert not knowing what the French had in mind. Jamaica's governor, Sir William Beeston, sent a sloop into the Cul-de-Sac on March 11 to gain intelligence but it was chased out by three of the fleet. The news brought back was that already several hundred buccaneers had mutinied against de Pointis's arrogant treatment of them and had returned to Isle à Vache. Beeston's first assumption was that Jamaica was to be the target but when the French fleet rendezvoused at Cape Tiburon and set sail, he decided Portobelo was the prey. How wrong he was.

Cartagena was described as trusting and happy in those closing years of the century, 'more dedicated to the Arts of Mercury than the imitation of Mars' with its focus being on making a profit from commerce rather than on preparing to defend itself. The construction of fortifications to protect Cartagena was carried out over nearly 200 years that ultimately ended in the eighteenth century. Almost every detail of Bautista Antonelli's original 1594 drawings was included in the urban defences

of the city. But the building of these structures depended very much on the generosity of the Spanish Crown, primarily in the form of the annual situado, a grant originating from the Viceroy in Lima. After that the authorities in Spain had to approve a local plan. Exchanges of opinions and resolving issues that arose could take years, and years more were added by shortfalls in funds.

Most of Cartagena's fortifications were built by slaves, prisoners from the gaols and skilled artisans directed by engineers. Over the two centuries a strong tradition of building defences meant that technical skills were often passed from artisan father to son.

Louis XIV appointed Baron de Pointis to lead the attack on Cartagena with over 5,000 men.

Cartagena was also fortunate to have an ample supply of raw materials ranging from stone to quick lime to make mortar, and to bricks and tiles manufactured from fine clay found on the outskirts of the city. It was not to be for a lack of building capability and competence that Cartagena's defences failed to repulse DuCasse and de Pointis.

How far had the authorities reached in terms of fortifying the approaches to the city since Antonelli's survey? Although the Bocagrande entrance through which Hawkins and Drake had entered the bay was the primary concern because of its proximity to the city limits and inner harbour, this problem was to all intents and purposes resolved when three galleons foundered on the sandbar stretching out to Tierrabomba Island. Within a few years the sandbar was only 300 yards wide and covered with mangroves. This changed the bay's topography, with the tides reconfiguring the Bocachica channel at the other end of Tierrabomba, opening it to navigation to even the largest galleons.

As a result there was now only one entrance into the bay of Cartagena and in 1647 the crown issued the order for San Luis de Bocachica to be built. The result was four bulwarks, a ditch and a two-story structure. Where guns and troops had been assigned on other minor fortifications, they were now to be redeployed concentrating on this major new fort completed in 1661. It was inadequate from the start and was situated in a windless, unhealthy location. Earlier in 1631, Santa Cruz de Castillo Grande had been rebuilt at the mouth of the inner harbour and a small artillery battery installed on the opposite side, known as San Juan de Manzanillo. A further fort on the island of Manga was constructed inside the inner harbour to complete the complex of fortifications guarding the principal anchorage.

There was one other key point in the design of Cartagena's defences: the hill of San Lázaro to the east overlooked the Media Luna gate and causeway in the city. For ten years Governor Francisco de Murga pressed the Spanish Crown relentlessly for financing for a battery and only in 1647 was a royal cedula issued requiring a small castle to be built to accommodate four to six pieces of artillery and 30 men. According to one interpreter of Cartagena's history, impetus may have been added to the decision to proceed when a herd of goats climbed the hill in the night causing the nearby inhabitants to sound a general alarm thinking it was an enemy invasion. A small triangular fort was completed in 1657 at the top of the hill and named by Governor Pedro Zapata de Mendoza, San Felipe de Barajas after Spain's King Philip IV. Apprehensive at the time because of England's recent capture of Jamaica, the governor had little trouble raising a 'loan' from the local merchants to finish the construction. The official records for the year 1691 suggest that Cartagena was reasonably well garrisoned with 430 men at various posts. But two years later that deployment was 80 men short and by the time Governor Diego de los Rios y Queseda received the news that de Pointis had sailed from France, there were only 150 men to guard the town of whom 37 were gunners.

The governor ordered the mobilisation of ten militia companies from the towns outside Cartagena to reinforce San Luis, Santa Cruz and San Felipe. In the port at Bocachica he stationed his most heavily armed naval vessel to complement the firepower at San Luis. He also laid down a chain of palm trees to restrict access through the main channel. Deeper in the outer bay on the eastern side he positioned another armed ship in Pasacaballos to prevent intrusion through the narrow channels by canoes. Diego de los Rios also set about recruiting a cavalry company and a volunteer body comprising 28 musketeers, nine harquebusiers and three gunners. He was confident enough to write a letter in which he declared 'the town was never as well defended as it is at present'. Captain Sancho Jimeno, warden of San Luis, must have thought otherwise when, alarmed at having a complement of only 90 men, he requested reinforcements. The measures that the governor took were totally inadequate as he is said to have optimistically believed that the French fleet's real objective was the treasure ships harboured at Portobelo.

The French force that was drawn up outside Cartagena on April 13, 1697, was substantial. The flagship *Sceptre* under Captain Guillotin boasted 84 guns and 650 men; Vice-Admiral Levy commanded 420 men on the 64-gun *St Lewis* and Rear-Admiral Viscount Coetlogon, 450 men and 70 guns on the *Fort*. All together the fleet comprised 28 ships including the naval vessels, the 44-gun *Christ* captured from the Spanish, a bomb-thrower, nine frigates and seven transport ships. On board were over 5,000 men – 110 officers, 55 cadets, 2,100 seamen, 1,750 soldiers and about 1,000 buccaneers, free Negroes and volunteers.

Initially de Pointis planned to land on the Caribbean Sea side of the city but when he attempted to go ashore himself the small boat carrying him capsized in the heavy surf. He soon realised that to successfully carry out his mission he would have to enter by way of the Bocachica entrance to the outer bay, first neutralising the fort at San Luis. Don Sancho Jimeno, by his own account, recorded, 'without losing any time they began to cannonade the castle and by three o'clock in the afternoon the whole fleet was aiming at it'. Before long the inexperienced and undermanned garrison at San Luis began suffering a heavy toll of wounded and dead. The bombardment lasted through the night into the next day.

On April 15, DuCasse and de Pointis put 1,200 men on Tierrabomba intent on attacking San Luis from the rear. Good fortune also favoured the French when they intercepted and captured a coastguard vessel with reinforcements approaching San Luis. De Pointis sent one of his captives, a Franciscan friar, and a soldier, Don Sanco Jimeno, to the fort's commander proposing that he surrender. Despite being badly outgunned and outmanned, the governor later wrote that he found it impossible to surrender his troops or his weapons especially as he believed he could hold out with the ammunition he had.

On hearing his adversary's reply, de Pointis increased the tempo of his attack. The castle was further weakened when the gun carriages for the cannon disintegrated from the reverberation as they had been shoddily constructed. Now San Luis was under severe attack from land and sea. Don Sancho Jimeno recorded that at four in the afternoon scaling ladders were being placed up against the castle's walls. At this point he estimated that over 4,000 cannon shots and 500 bombs were fired

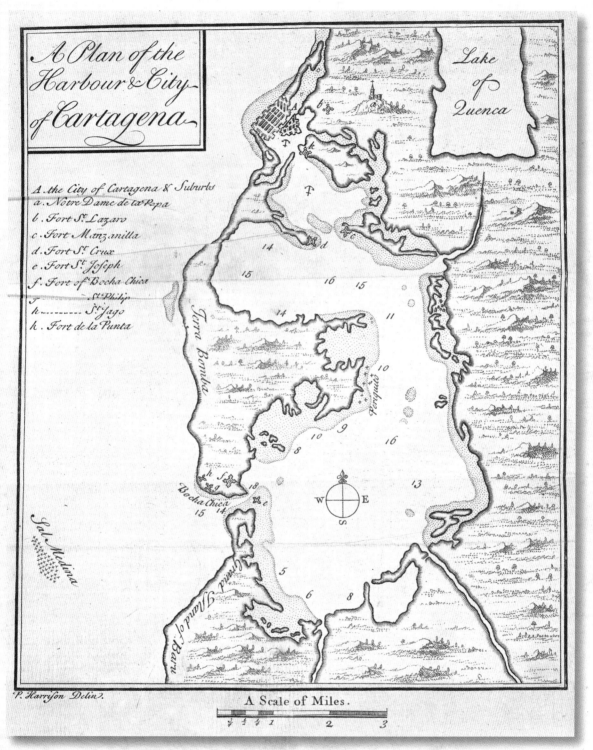

A Plan of the Harbour & City of Cartagena

A . the City of Cartagena & Suburbs
a . Notre Dame de la Popa
b . Fort St. Lazaro
c . Fort Manzanilla
d . Fort St. Cruz
e . Fort St. Joseph
f . Fort of Bocha Chica
J . ‒‒‒‒‒‒‒ St. Philip
h . ‒‒‒‒‒‒‒ St. Jago
h . Fort de la Punta

Lake of Quenca

Terra Bomba

Tenquito

Grand Island of Baru

Bocha Chica

Salt Medina

A Scale of Miles.

P. Harrison Delin.

This map of Cartagena was included in A Genuine and Particular Account of the Taking of Cartagena by the French and Buccaneers in the year 1697 *by Sieur de Pointis.*

and some 400 of the enemy killed. A contrasting report at the end of the battle maintained that the French navy lost only six soldiers, the buccaneers seven and the Spanish 21 men.

Whatever the toll of dead and wounded, the reality was that fear and panic were sweeping over the garrison. Don Sancho Jimeno had earned a reputation for brutality in a previous assignment when his task was to hunt down escaped slaves. As San Luis was garrisoned largely by mestizos and slaves he attracted little loyalty. No more than a dozen men were prepared to fight on whilst the rest pleaded to surrender. It was on this day, April 16, 1697 that Don Sancho Jimeno de Horozco entered the pages of historical legend.

De Pointis suspended the attack and asked his opponent to come to the parapet of the castle whereupon he once more asked him to surrender. Don Sancho Jimeno stood firm, repeating what he had told the friar to convey the day before: 'I will neither surrender nor ask for mercy'. On hearing this, Baron de Pointis cleared a field below the castle walls and called on the terrified inhabitants to throw down their arms which they did. Threatening to kill those who persisted in occupying the fort, de Pointis coerced the garrison into opening the gates. Finally Don Sancho Jimeno emerged, unarmed, still maintaining that he was not surrendering but that 'those who were handing over the castle were infamous men who did not wish to fight'. In a gesture of chivalry, Baron de Pointis took his own sword and handed it to Don Sancho Jimeno saying that it was not right for a man of his distinction to be unarmed. Magnanimously the baron transported his adversary to the nearby island of Baru where his wife had a home.

Before leaving Cartagena, de Pointis was to blow up San Luis leaving the Bocachica entrance undefended. On April 18 the French fleet crossed the outer bay and anchored facing the castle of Santa Cruz de Castillo Grande. The previous day the authorities had dictated that it be abandoned and its garrison and artillery withdrawn to defend the town. While the French personnel took over the unoccupied fort, the buccaneers were dispatched up the hill to the monastery of the Nuestra de la Popa which had already seen the departure of the friars with its irreplaceable image of the Virgin Mary. DuCasse, who had been wounded during the San Luis siege, temporarily gave way to Joseph de Gallifet who found the Spaniards firmly entrenched. If the French were to command the hill of La Popa it would mean that the citizens of Cartagena would find escaping to the interior difficult.

The castle of San Felipe de Baraja on the San Lazaro hill was the next objective for de Pointis. Again this was a tactically important goal as it overlooked the principal approach to Cartagena through the suburbs of Getsemani and the Media Luna. Fierce fighting ensued during which the fort's warden, Don Juan Manuel Vega, died of wounds having fought a desperate battle with only 70 men. From the naval vessels, high calibre cannons and mortars were landed and hauled up to the captured San Felipe to support the bombardment of the town's remaining defences. Baron de Pointis, constantly critical of DuCasse's contribution, wrote:

'… the soldiers worked like lions, sleepless; the sailors disembarked the artillery;

'... the soldiers worked like lions, sleepless; the sailors disembarked the artillery ...'

the Negroes helped the one and the other, and it is now time to say that the Negroes were very good assistants to us, but I can't say the same of the buccaneers: You couldn't get them to cooperate in anything, and it is therefore my opinion that the portion of the booty which they received later was robbed from those who sacrificed so much in the enterprise.'

The fort of San Sebastian de Pastelillo, which had also been abandoned by the town's general council, was now used to bombard the town as well as San Felipe. That fort's warden, Juan de Berrio, had left it to another man, Juan Miguel de la Vega, with a contingent of 70 meztizos and Negroes to defend. Not long after the French attacked they killed him and fled. On April 25 de Pointis prudently stopped the offensive – he himself had been superficially wounded by a grenade – to regroup and strengthen his position. On April 30 he sent DuCasse to the gate of Media Luna apparently to demand the surrender of the city. The true reason was that he wished to ascertain whether a breach in the wall would allow a frontal assault to succeed. DuCasse met Francisco de Santaren who was defending Media Luna with 100 men and 11 cannons and learnt what he needed to know.

The French renewed their attack and broke through into the suburb of Getsemani. Santaren, complaining of a severe attack of gout, dictated from an armchair that the majority of defenders should withdraw inside the town walls. Confusion caused many Spaniards to be brought down by bullets and artillery fire from their own side. Before long, Getsemani was in the hands of the French. Santaren was later accused of capitulating to the enemy to save his own skin. His accuser, Don Sancho Jimeno, hero of San Luis, claimed he saw Santaren buy a sloop from the French and sail away under French protection.

French naval vessels pounded the town from offshore. One bomb penetrated the dome of the church then known as Iglesia de la Compania (today, San Pedro Claver) destroying the high altar. Morale fell to its lowest point and from all quarters the governor was asked to surrender the town. The carnage of the Media Luna gate and in Getsemani left little hope of a counter-attack or even further resistance. As bravely as the militia had fought beside the military garrisons, Cartagena capitulated after the 17-day siege. On May 2 Baron de Pointis saw four white flags waving from the town walls signifying the calling of a truce and the start of negotiations. De Pointis demanded all the contents of the treasury and the silver, gold and jewels of the inhabitants. In exchange he would allow the governor, high officials, the military and militia and those townspeople who wished to leave to do so with full honours, taking with them an amount of money relative to their social status. Those who opted to remain could keep their landed property and half their money so long as they swore allegiance to French King Louis XIV.

Four days later Governor de los Rios, flags unfurled, rode out of Cartagena at the head of a column including the remaining men from the garrisons, infantrymen, government ministers, town officials, priests, men, women and children: in all, it was said, 3,000 Cartagenians. De Pointis entered the town on a sedan chair, still recovering from his injuries, and went straight to the cathedral where he had a celebratory Te Deum Laudamus sung. He proceeded to the counting house where he stayed while the ransom was paid. In his account of the event, de Pointis confessed that they did not receive what they expected from this reputedly fabulously wealthy town and, anyway, on hearing of his approach many had fled with their possessions into the interior. Although he had promised to respect the property of the church, de Pointis proved not averse to using the buccaneers to extract money from the religious orders. 'The buccaneers had a sense of smell of a pointing dog in sniffing out treasure', he wrote. Whilst he protested that he tried to use them as little as possible he said, 'I noticed that only their presence untied the tongues of the friars'.

The buccaneers are recorded as having used intimidation, threats of torture and death to dispossess the churchmen of their ecclesiastical treasures, from chalices and crosses to church bells and even linens, furniture and coaches. Before they had left Hispaniola, the buccaneers had been promised one tenth of the first million and one thirtieth thereafter of every million gold crowns. When de Pointis announced that their share was a mere 40,000 crowns – even by his own reckoning he had

After a seventeen-day siege Cartagena surrendered to avoid further carnage and destruction.

hoarded eight to ten million – DuCasse stepped in to support the buccaneers' claim and inevitably the buccaneers mutinied.

In planning the defence of colonial towns in the Caribbean the authorities could count on the inevitable onslaught of diseases such as yellow fever and dysentery, fuelled by the heat and humidity, on Europeans unaccustomed to the climate. Long sieges were almost guaranteed to turn likely victory into inevitable retreat. In the case of de Pointis's troops and Cartagena, they stayed too long masters of the town. By the third week in May the seasonal rains brought on dysentery and more than 800 men fell ill. Anticipating the wrath of his former mercenaries who were planning to board his ships, and severely weakened by illness amongst his forces, de Pointis, with his treasure loaded and after mining and blowing up numerous fortifications, sailed out of the bay of Cartagena on May 25.

Better acclimatised, the thousand buccaneers, no longer restrained by de Pointis, descended on Cartagena and imposed a reign of terror that lasted for more than a week. There were no exceptions or exemptions as regards from whom and by what method they extorted the silver, gold and precious stones still remaining. To coerce the inhabitants into revealing the whereabouts of their possessions, the buccaneers imprisoned them in the cathedral, installed barrels of gunpowder and threatened to light a fuse unless they submitted. Legend says they removed more than one and a half million crowns in booty. Before they disembarked they pillaged houses, public buildings and churches.

De Pointis, despite a skirmish with English Admiral John Neville and an Anglo-Dutch fleet that had entered the Caribbean to assist the Spanish, returned to France in August of 1697. The buccaneers were not so fortunate. Sailing for their anchorage at Isle à Vache they encountered Neville, having two of their vessels transporting most of their booty captured and two others driven on shore. Spanish accounts suggest that some of those captured were taken back to Cartagena to rebuild what they had destroyed. DuCasse, once again in his governor's post, protested to King Louis that de Pointis had cheated him. To placate him the French king made him Chevalier of St Louis and granted 1,400,000 francs to those from Hispaniola who had taken part. Due to bureaucratic bungling and the passage of time, little of the money ever reached the Caribbean.

Peace between France and Spain was made that same year with the Treaty of Ryswick. However, the French could not resist issuing a commemorative medal. On one side, in Latin, there is a beautiful woman at whose feet are scattered coins with the inscription: 'This was pillaged from the treasure of the Spanish'. In 1700 DuCasse resigned as governor and returned to France where he was promoted to admiral in the French royal navy. As Spain and France were now at peace it was ironic that he returned to Cartagena five years after his exploits there but this time as a Spanish ally. Ill health in 1715 forced him to retire following which he was soon to pass on. In his Memories, the Duc de Saint-Simon described him at court as '… a tall, thin man who, with his corsair's manner and much fire and vivacity, was gentle, polite, respectful, and who was never false to himself'.

It was about the time of DuCasse's return to France that the French crown began pursuing the same policy as the English had, more than a decade earlier, of suppressing the buccaneers. In the final years of the seventeenth century the enmity between the Atlantic European nations that had so consumed them abated and the maintenance of peace, not war, was taking precedence. In the Caribbean their commercial interests saw trade along with growing of tropical crops like sugar as more profitable than waiting for the buccaneers' spoils to enter port. It was the end of an era. Now pirates succeeded the buccaneers but, unlike the latter, they preyed on ships of all flags and were outlaws pursued by all nations.

A commemorative medal was struck by the French depicting a beautiful woman with Spanish treasure scattered at her feet.

Chapter 14

THE END OF
THE ERA

~

A s the 1660s drew to a close there was growing evidence that the buccaneers, as one historian put it, had 'over fished'. Between 1655 and 1661, 18 cities, four towns and countless villages in the Spanish Caribbean and Central America had been ransacked with disappointing returns being more the norm than the exception. And as Spain's political power weakened, she began to accept that it would be preferable to recognise the legitimacy of the new colonies and open negotiations to allow their mother countries of England, France and Holland to trade freely in the region. Furthermore, the growing affluence of Barbados and Martinique, thanks to sugarcane, suggested that Jamaica and Hispaniola would benefit from a less anarchic environment.

The 1670 Treaty of Madrid between Spain and England called for an end to the depredations by the Port Royal buccaneers in exchange for recognition by Spain of England's West Indian possessions. Ironically it was signed in the year Henry Morgan sacked Panama. The Dutch made a similar agreement in 1673 at the Treaty of The Hague. In the case of the French, the winding-down of the use of the buccaneers took almost to the end of the century. For them negotiations began with the Truce of Ratisbon in 1683 and concluded with the Treaty of Ryswick in 1697 in which Spain formally ceded the French-occupied part of Hispaniola to France. The employment of buccaneers as a strategically vital instrument of political policy has been recounted in detail. It became increasingly clear that the mercenaries had served their purpose and were becoming a liability.

An ornate engraving commemorating the signing of the Treaty of Ryswick in 1697 between France, Holland, England and Spain which also marked the end of the buccaneer.

Whilst some of them turned planter, logwood cutter, merchant seaman or even sailor in the navy, many continued to sail in search of plunder. French commissions were issued for over 20 years after the Treaty of Madrid and the English often played a double game supposedly pursuing a policy of suppressing the buccaneers whilst encouraging them to continue plying their trade through the back door. Henry Morgan was amongst the most notorious of double-dealers.

Leniency towards the buccaneers, who still enjoyed the fleshly pleasures of Port Royal, fluctuated as English governors changed. Sir Thomas Lynch twice attempted to carry out his king's directives but was only anything like successful the second time when he was reappointed in 1682 and discovered a more supportive mood amongst the Jamaican merchants and planters. The progress he made was halted in 1687 when a new governor, the second Duke of Albemarle, restored a disgraced Henry Morgan to the lieutenant-governorship but both men died the following year and the damage they had done was repaired. It took some time for the buccaneers to abandon Port Royal which in 1689 was still being described by John Taylor as 'a Sodom filled with all manner of debauchery'.

One of the more serious concerns in the West Indies as the years went by was the loss of manpower in the colonies which began coincidentally with the arrival of Cromwell's expedition in 1655. Whilst the original boucaniers turned to buccaneering their numbers were supplemented from the settler populations of the English and French Antillean colonies. In the three years between 1668 and 1671 it was estimated that nearly 3,000 able-bodied men left their workplaces in Jamaica alone to join ventures led by the likes of Henry Morgan. And a naval sailor who could expect to earn a meagre £20 a year serving His Majesty Charles II was able to make £120 from Morgan's assault on Portobelo. This manpower drain was not conducive to encouraging the development of commerce and in particular, agriculture.

Undermanned and still not yet served by an appropriate naval presence, Jamaica after 1670 became vulnerable to attack particularly from the French whose West Indian ambitions came to the boil during Louis XIV's reign as commissions were readily available to buccaneers in Petit Goâve.

In addition a new breed of pirates, habitués of Spain's own colonies, were now ambushing the growing number of merchant ships off their coastlines. The Spanish government at home encouraged its own breed of buccaneers known as 'Biscayners'. In 1685 the shipowners of Guipuzcoa on the Bay of Biscay offered to act as privateers in the service of their country against the contraband traders and enemy corsarios. The king agreed to a three-year contract in exchange for 20 per cent of the spoils. In August 1686 eight ships carrying 500 men and boasting 104 guns set out for the Caribbean. They were to wreak considerable havoc for the period of their agreement, the terms of which they largely ignored, plundering any ship that came their way.

Until buccaneering began degenerating to a point where it was counter-productive and creating a near-chaotic state of anxiety for seafarers if not for land dwellers, it had provided economic impetus particularly for the new English and French

245

colonies. In Port Royal it sustained the growth of the town as a trading centre and allowed for investment in agriculture, particularly sugar, which was to generate staggering wealth in the next century. Hispaniola, like Jamaica, enjoyed a similar experience. By the time he died, Henry Morgan owned several plantations totalling over 4000 acres.

What tangible heritage did the buccaneers leave behind in the Caribbean? Place names resonate especially: Bluefields in Nicaragua and Bluefields Bay in Jamaica carry the anglicised version of Abraham Blauvelt's name. There is a Coxon's Hole on Roatan but there is some doubt that he was present when it was named; Yallahs in Jamaica is named after Captain Yallahs, or Yellowes, who sold out to the Spanish and bounty-hunted logwood cutters; Morgan's Head on the Colombian island of Providencia takes its name from Henry Morgan. Maps, too, connect us with the buccaneers. Exquemelin's book included charts of Maracaibo and Panama, the latter showing Morgan's sea and land manoeuvres. Of the amateur cartographers who sailed with the buccaneers, the most remarkable was Basil Ringrose whose journal contained maps drawn on the expedition he joined to cross the Isthmus of Panama and rove the Pacific coast.

Buccaneers were by nature itinerant, staying long enough in one place only to careen and provision their ships, exchange their loot for a good time or rendezvous with others in preparation for another venture. They chose Tortuga, Port Royal, Curaçao and, later, Petit Goâve from which to operate on a transient basis. But meeting places often referred to included Isle à Vache and Saona off Hispaniola, Golden Island in the San Blas islands off Panama, Cuba's Isle of Pines and Roatan in the Bay Islands. Even the extensive archipelago coastal territory stretching from present-day Belize to the Bay of Campeche, which the buccaneers occupied to cut logwood, possesses little or no evidence of their presence 400 years later.

The echoes of the past are best heard on the battlements of those places which were the object of their avarice – the castle of San Juan de Ulua at Vera Cruz, the walled cites of Cartagena and Campeche, El Castillo on the San Juan River and the massive fortifications in Havana, Cartagena, San Juan and Santiago de Cuba.

It was the prospect of the spoils that must have motivated the hundreds of Europeans, former slaves and freemen, and even a few Amerindians who sought their fortunes at sea as buccaneers. Their capacity to come together as a brotherhood of sorts in order to carry out their depredations has been demonstrated. What they had in common was the fact that each had gained a degree of liberty not experienced before. It held out the prospect of equality of treatment and made much of a dependence on fraternity. But with this new-found independence came what was ultimately known as 'the Custom of the Coast' or 'the Jamaica discipline', a set of self-imposed regulations and practices by which their brotherhood depended for survival.

The evidence, as we have seen, is that at best when led by skilful and daring men they were a fearsome force to contend with; at worst they were remorselessly cruel and destructive. But even acts of barbarity as judged by our twenty-first-century standards were not as alarming to seventeenth-century Europeans. Men of different religious and warring nationalities were capable of burning people at the stake, tearing them apart between two horses, and slicing off noses, ears and other extremities. In the Caribbean revenge was always a motive in conflicts between the usually Protestant buccaneers and the Spanish Roman Catholics. When captured the Spanish usually treated the buccaneers without mercy; when the Spanish hostages refused to disclose the whereabouts of their wealth the buccaneers showed very little compassion.

If your enemy did not kill you and you survived your wounds there were debilitating diseases that habitually swept through the Caribbean – dysentery, tuberculosis, yellow fever and smallpox to name a few. And then there was 'kill-devil' also called 'rum bullion' or rum which when bottled in lead pipes slowly poisoned the imbiber. Even Sir Henry Morgan succumbed to the ravages of being 'much given to drinking and sitting up late'. Despite this he received a 22-gun salute from the naval vessels in Port Royal harbour leaving to posterity his plantations and a personal estate of £5,000, a considerable amount for 1688, but little by way of souvenirs of his colourful career.

Piracy succeeded buccaneering, flourishing in such disparate places as St Croix, the Bahamas and New England well into the eighteenth century. A generation of outlaws emerged to fill the pages of history books and popular literature – Jack Rackham, Anne Bonny and Mary Read, Edward 'Blackbeard' Teach, Captain Kidd and many others. It was also the beginning of the age of the admirals of European royal navies committed to protecting the young colonies of England, France and Holland. These men were to play a far more conventional role than the buccaneers had during the seventeenth century on the Caribbean frontier.

'*Several filibusters who had been killed in a fight went to knock at the gate of Paradise, where none of them before that time had ever been admitted. But now, Saint Peter having opened the gate without having made too close enquiry as to who might be without, our Adventurers failed not to enter Paradise with great haste, and there remained, despite the command given them to depart, as soon as they were known for what they were.*

Never had Saint Peter been so troubled until he devised an expedient that succeeded. A Ship! Where? Forthwith the filibusters asked ... To leeward, said Saint Peter, pointing to a spot that was without Paradise. After her! Cried the filibusters at once, and dashed forth, imagining that they were giving chase. But as soon as Saint Peter saw them go outside, he quickly shut the gate upon them, and we are told that after that time he was always at great pains to avoid all such surprises.'

Taken from Maurice Besson *The Scourge of the Indies*, in the notes upon the Indies written by the historian Margry.

GLOSSARY

~

almirante the vice-flagship of the Spanish fleet, usually sailed at the rear

Audencia Spanish governing body over large areas of Spain's New World territories

barque/bark fast three to five-masted sailing vessel favoured by the buccaneers

bastion a five-sided structure, part of the main wall or rampart, to allow defenders to subject the attackers to cross-fire

battery a fortification to hold several pieces of artillery, usually built in front of the main fortress

brigantine medium-sized vessel with two masts built for speed

capitana the flagship of the Spanish fleet

careen to beach a ship on its side in order to clean its hull of marine growth and waterproof it with tar

Casa de Contraction Spanish administrative body empowered to regulate colonial seaborne commerce

cay a reef or sandbar

cedula a decree issued by the Spanish crown

chasse-partie articles agreed on to regulate the division of plunder

cimmarones fugitive African slaves in the Spanish Caribbean

cochineal valuable red dye produced by drying and crushing the bodies of female insects that feed on certain cacti

corsario or corsair the Spanish categorisation for a pirate, privateer or buccaneer in the Caribbean

corvette small, fast French frigate

cutlass a heavy sword with a slightly curved blade up to three feet long

flibustier or filibustier a French term for a buccaneer

La Flota the Spanish fleet that carried the treasure of Mexico from Vera Cruz

frigate a three-masted, single-deck vessel, often a warship accompanying larger warships but sometimes a freight carrier galeone or galleon. Two or three-deck Spanish merchant ship or naval vessel with three or more masts; heavily armed usually

Los Galeones used to refer to annual Spanish convoy serving the Spanish Main, Cartagena and Portobelo

galliat small galleon

harquebus an early portable gun needing a fork upon which to rest the barrel

indigo plant that produced blue to purple dyes

letters of marque commissions; authority given to legally pursue an enemy of the state

logwood reddish heartwood used for making dyes

musket an early forerunner of the rifle that fired a single lead ball at a time requiring a flame or spark to ignite gunpowder

pieces of eight or peso Spanish silver coin used to measure the value of plunder

pike a spear up to 16 feet long, not thrown but used to thrust at the enemy

pinnace longboat, a ship's boat used as a tender for a warship or merchantman

pirogue or piragua; large dugout canoe usually rowed but sometimes sailed

plate silver usually cut into bars, also silverware

privateer usually a ship's captain operating under letters of marque to seek reprisals

prize usually a ship seized as booty

purchase euphemism for booty of all kinds

real Spanish silver coin worth one-eighth of a peso

requa/recua mule train; as used to carry goods across the Isthmus of Panama

shallop small rowed boat

situado monies allocated for payment to Spanish soldiers

sloop fast single-masted vessel with a shallow shaft and highly manoeuvrable; could be heavily armed and reach up to 100 tons

yacht or jacht, a small, fast ship used by the Dutch for coastal trading. Similar vessels were known as ketches or pinks

BIBLIOGRAPHY

~

Besson, Maurice, *The Scourge of the Indies: Buccaneers, Corsairs and Filibustiers*, translated by Everard Thornton, London: George Routledge & Sons Ltd., 1929.

Bridenbaugh, Carl and Roberta, *No Peace Beyond the Line: The English in the Caribbean 1624-1690*, New York: Oxford University Press, 1972.

Cordingley, David and John Falconer, *Pirates: Fact and Fiction*, New York: Artabras/ Abbeville Publishing Group, 1992.

Cruickshank, E. A., *The Life of Sir Henry Morgan,* Toronto: The Macmillan Company of Canada Ltd., 1935.

Earle, Peter, *The Sack of Panama*, London: Jill Norman & Hobhouse, 1981.

Exquemelin, Alexandre Olivier, *Bucaniers of America*, Edited by William Stallybrass. New York: Dorset Press, 1987.

Gage, Thomas, *The English American: A New Survey of the West Indies, 1648*, edited by A. P. Newton, London: George Routledge & Sons, Ltd. 1928.

Galvin, Peter R., *Patterns of Pillage*, New York: Peter Lang Publishing Inc., 2000.

Goslinga, Cornelius, *The Dutch in the Caribbean and on the Wild Coast, 1580-1680*, Assen, The Netherlands: Van Gorcum, 1985.

Gosse, Philip, *The History of Piracy*, New York: Tudor Publishing Co., 1946.

Haring, C.H., *The Buccaneers in the West Indies in the XVII*, London: Methuen & Co. Ltd., 1910.

Kemp, Peter, and Christopher Lloyd, *The Brethren of the Coast*, London: William Heinemann Ltd., 1960.

Lane, Kris, *Pillaging the Empire: Piracy in the Americas, 1500-1750*, M. E. Sharpe Inc., 1998.

Marley, David, *Sack of Vera Cruz: The Great Pirate Raid of 1683*, Windsor, Ontario: Netherlandic Press, 1993.

Marley, David, *Pirates and Privateers of the Americas*, Santa Barbara, California: ABC-CLIO Inc., 1994.

Newton, A. P., *The Colonising Activities of the English Puritans: The Last Phase of the Elizabethan Struggle*, New Haven: Yale University Press 1914, also London: Humphrey Milford, Oxford University Press.

Newton, A. P., *The European Nations in the West Indies*, London: A & G Black Ltd., 1933.

Norris, Gerald, ed., *William Dampier: Buccaneer Explorer*, London: The Folio Society, 1994.

Parry, J. H., *The Spanish Seaborne Empire*, London: Hutchinson & Co. (Publishers) Ltd., 1966.

Pawson, Michael, and David Buisseret, *Port Royal: Jamaica*, Kingston, Jamaica: The University of the West Indies Press, 2000.

Phillips, Carla Rahn, *Six Galleons for the King of Spain*, Baltimore, Maryland: The John Hopkins University Press, 1992.

Wood, Peter, *The Spanish Main*, Amsterdam: Time-Life Books Inc., 1979

INDEX